LYIN'
CHEATIN'
BASTARDS

LYIN'
CHEATIN'
BASTARDS

ALLISON ADLER, JENNIFER A. FREEMAN, CLAIRE YOUNG & VICKI ZWART

ANGUS CARROLL, EDITOR

assassin bug
PRESS

Lyin' Cheatin' Bastards
Written by Allison Adler, Jennifer A. Freeman, Claire Young, and Vicki Zwart
Angus Carroll, editor

Design Consultants: Claire Young, Jackie Capozzoli, Patricia Frey, and Ashley
Balcerzak

ISBN 978-0-9859006-0-1

To America. We're sorry.

TABLE OF CONTENTS

★ ★ ★

INTRODUCTION

IT WOULD BE FUNNY WERE IT NOT SAD: It took only five minutes to find enough disgraced politicians to fill a book—even counting only scandals that took place after Jan. 1, 2000 (To cover all the politicians who have ever lied or cheated is too much to contemplate).

Holding public office is a special privilege. We invest our public officials not only with power, but also with trust. We cannot expect them to be perfect, but we can expect them to be decent. Many fall short of the mark.

If only a handful of public officials failed to meet our expectations, that would be one thing. A bad streak, perhaps. But today we see so many politicians, judges, and other public officials being arrested for criminal activity, or confessing to yet another inappropriate relationship, it may be time to ask if there is a deeper problem. Indeed, when Eliot Spitzer (LCB #11), the governor of New York and the state's former attorney general is forced to resign in disgrace for hiring prostitutes, but ends up on television as a host of a news program, it may be time to reevaluate our standards, not just theirs.

Seventy-seven *Lyin' Cheatin' Bastards* have been identified from 2000 to 2012. If that doesn't sound like many, remember these are just the ones who got caught.

RANKING THE BASTARDS

There are many ways to get on the *Lyin' Cheatin' Bastards* list: Resign in disgrace; get impeached or imprisoned; be recalled or censured; or demonstrate an exceptional level of hypocrisy or dishonesty. Whatever the specifics, it all boils down to the same thing: *Lyin' Cheatin' Bastards* have all done something that calls into question their character or integrity—qualities that bear directly on their fitness to hold public office.

The entire scoring system is faulty, but it has been applied evenly to everyone, so in that sense it is perfectly fair (detailed analysis of each Bastard is given in the scoring section, on page 227).

Table 1: The Scoring

	Description	Score
1	Prison sentence	10 points for each year
2	Convictions	1 point for each
3	Impeached	25 points
4	Removed or terminates	25 points
5	Resigned in disgrace	50 points
6	Cheated on spouse	25 points
7	Money stolen	1 point of each million
8	Ethics violations	1 point or each
9	Censure	10 points
10	Recalled	25 points
11	Hookers	10 points
12	Special Awards	25 points
13	Stupidity Adjustment	25 points
14	Drugs or alcohol	10 points
15	Molesting minors	1,000 points

Many items are yes/no. If, for example, the official was impeached (3), 25 points are awarded. Straight forward. A few are more complicated, like Money Stolen (7). Here the subject gets 1 point for every million dollars he or she managed to steal, but the amount must be a calculated figure, not a guess, and must be over $100,000. (These are the big leagues. No points for petty theft.)

Several of the Special Awards (12) and the Stupidity Adjustment (13) are admittedly subjective—though, in most cases, obviously deserved. Subjects receive 25 points for each. Special Awards include Tackiness, Hypocrisy, Tax Evasion, Audacity, Caught on Tape, and GAGL (Gay Anti-Gay Legislator). Subjects can—and often do—win more than one Special Award.

Two officials' crimes were so heinous they needed their own scoring category: child molestation (15). If not for the extra 1,000 points, these Bastards might have hidden somewhere in the middle of the list. One official was convicted and is in prison; the other confessed but escaped jail because the statute of limitations had expired by the time the truth came out. They are the number #1 and #2 Bastards, respectively.

ANALYZING THE BASTARDS

The Bastards fall into five major categories: Congress (21), mayors (15), state legislators (14), governors (12), and "other" (15). Of the 21 Bastards in Congress, 17 are in the House and 4 are in the Senate.

Not surprisingly, Sex (40) is the most frequent scandal, followed by Money (27). The Other category includes Power, Cover Up, Drugs & Alcohol, and other miscellaneous offenses, but accounts for only 10 of the 77 Bastards. Sex accounts for more than half the scandals involving members of Congress, state legislators, and governors, but not for mayors. No one knows what this means.

What can be said with certainty is Republicans are far more focused on Sex than Democrats (who seem to be more interested in Money). In fact, the Republicans had almost twice as many sex scandals as the Democrats (they also edged out the

Chart 1: Scandal by Party

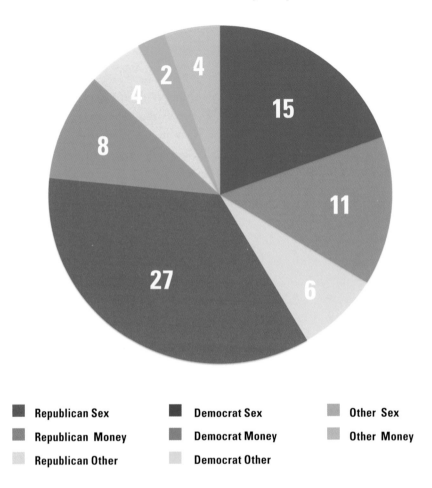

Democrats in total scandals, 39 to 32). The Republican obsession with sex will come as no surprise to anyone familiar with Fox News, which many men watch with the sound off. (Fox News president Roger Ailes admitted, "I hired Sarah Palin because she was hot and got ratings.")

From a geographic standpoint, a few states tower over the others in scandals per capita. The national average is 0.28 Bastards per million, but three are far higher than the rest: Rhode Island (1.89), Connecticut (1.39), and Alaska (1.38). No

Chart 2: Bastards by Office

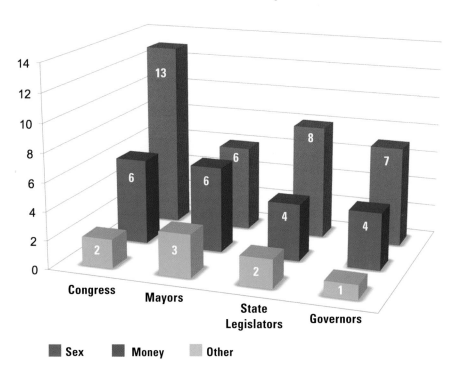

other state reaches 1.0, the next highest (not counting Washington, D.C., which is a special case) being Nevada at 0.73.

Seventeen states have no Bastards, but that could change at any time. For states with low populations, it only takes a few Bastards to charge into contention. Wyoming, Vermont or North Dakota, for example, would jump to the number two spot if the states produced only one Bastard. It will be hard to dethrone Rhode Island, given its low population and long tradition of producing crooked politicians.

Chart 1 clearly shows most Bastards are not minor public officials, but state and federal legislators who make laws (Congress, state legislators, and governors account for 47 of the 77 Bastards, or sixty-one percent). Even the "other" category includes heavy hitters: 4 are federal judges or attorneys general; 3 are senior White House officials.

Table 2: Bastards by State

Rank	State	Bastards	Population	Bastards/Million
1	Rhode Island	2	1,055,247	1.8952909
2	Connecticut	5	3,581,628	1.3960132
3	Alaska	1	721,523	1.3859572
4	D.C.	7	5,582,170	1.2539926
5	Nevada	2	2,709,432	0.7381621
6	New Jersey	6	8,807,501	0.6812375
7	Idaho	1	1,573,499	0.6355263
8	Oregon	2	3,848,606	0.5196687
9	Louisiana	2	4,553,962	0.4391780
10	South Carolina	2	4,645,975	0.4304801
11	Illinois	5	12,864,380	0.3886701
12	Utah	1	2,770,765	0.3609112
13	Kansas	1	2,863,813	0.3491848
14	Ohio	4	11,568,495	0.3457667
15	Mississippi	1	2,978,240	0.3357688
16	Indiana	2	6,501,582	0.3076174
17	Washington	2	6,753,369	0.2961485
18	New York	5	19,421,055	0.2574525
19	Virginia	2	8,037,736	0.2488263
20	Pennsylvania	3	12,734,905	0.2355730
21	Kentucky	1	4,350,606	0.2298530
22	North Carolina	2	9,565,781	0.2090786
23	Alabama	1	4,802,982	0.2082040
24	Georgia	2	9,727,566	0.2056013
25	Minnesota	1	5,314,879	0.1881510
26	Wisconsin	1	5,698,230	0.1754931
27	Maryland	1	5,789,929	0.1727137
28	Florida	3	18,900,773	0.1587237
29	Tennessee	1	6,375,431	0.1568521
30	Massachusetts	1	6,559,644	0.1524473
31	California	5	37,341,989	0.1338975
32	Michigan	1	9,911,626	0.1008916
33	Texas	1	25,268,418	0.0395751
	Total	**77**	**273,181,737**	**0.2818636**

Scandals involving prominent officials, of course, make better headlines, so there may be a built-in bias. But any such bias is completely subsumed by the more serious flaws in this study, and can be safely ignored.

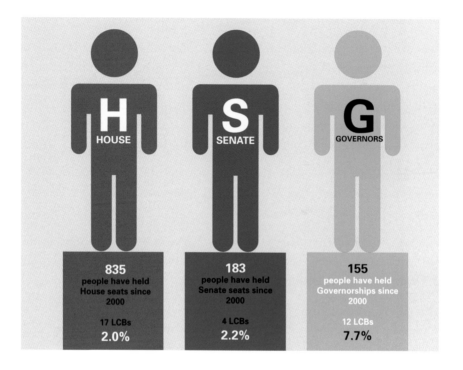

According to the 1992 Census of Governments, there are 513,200 elected officials in the United States, the vast majority of which (493,830, or ninety-six percent) are county, municipal, or town officials (town councils, school boards, etc.). Seventy-seven out of half a million ain't bad (0.01 percent), but the higher up you go the worse it gets.

Governors are clearly a problem, not just because they have the highest Bastard rate, but also because governors often run for president. Prior to Obama, four of the five preceding presidents were governors (G.W. Bush, Clinton, Reagan, and Carter). At least two governor-Bastards were considered presidential candidates at one time (Edwards and Sanford).

THE PROBLEM APPEARS TO BE MEN

The more observant will notice that most of the Bastards are men. Of course there are more men in politics, but, nevertheless, women are not proportionately represented.

If we take a fixed population like Congress, eighty-three percent are men and seventeen percent are women. But all of the Bastards who hold (or held) congressional positions (21) are men—and it's not that the women just didn't make the cut. Not one of the ninety-four women who currently hold these seats are under investigation, have been censured for ethics violations, or have been involved in a scandal during their time in office (their politics notwithstanding).

More remarkable, not a single female representative or senator has resigned in disgrace, or been forced from office, since the first woman, Jeanette Rankin of Montana, was elected to the House in 1917.

Predictably, the majority of male scandals revolve around sex, and even those classified as money and power could probably be thrown into this category since most men try to acquire those things simply to get more sex.

In her CNN article, "Are Men Stupid?," Frida Ghitis concludes, "In the final analysis, if it has to do with sex, some men really are stupid." But she has underestimated the problem: When it comes to sex, all men are really stupid.

It all started a long, long time ago. When it became apparent men were good at throwing things and creating havoc, they were given a lot of high-risk assignments: hunter, warrior, explorer—if for no other reason than to get them out of the house. This made them even more reckless, as they tried to get the attention of the women who watched from a safe distance as they blew things up and built flying machines. If they impressed a woman, they got sex, which of course led to stupider and stupider antics, until here we are today.

If it appears there is no limit to men's stupidity when it comes to sex, it's because there isn't.

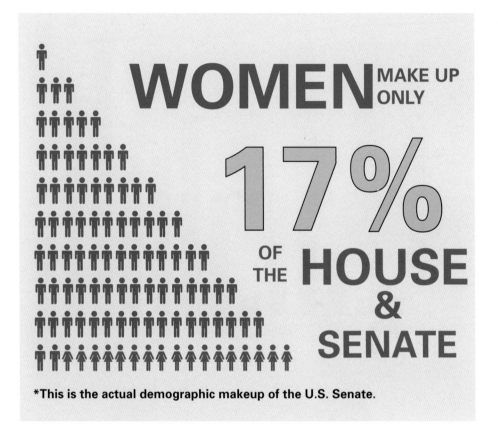

WOMEN MAKE UP ONLY 17% OF THE HOUSE & SENATE

*This is the actual demographic makeup of the U.S. Senate.

To eliminate scandals completely, we would have to vote in only women. But if we did that, the men who would have held political office would have to get real jobs, which they would probably do an equally bad job at, and that would hurt the economy. There's no good answer.

Most alarming, there is an ever-increasing number of Bastards each year (2012 is only a partial year in these calculations). At the current rate (scandals per year increasing by 10 every decade), all members of the House and Senate will be involved in a scandal in the year 2437.

Chart 3: Scandals by Year

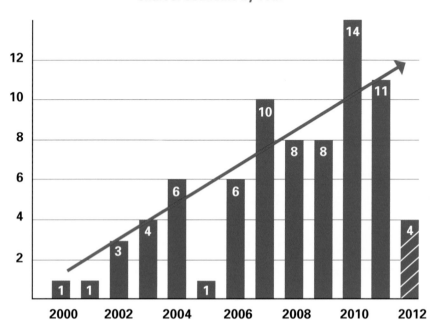

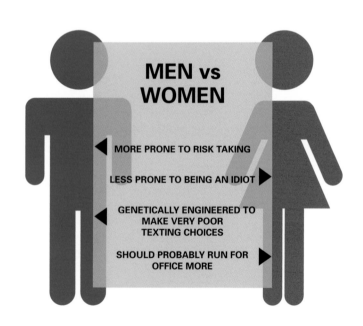

MEN vs WOMEN

◄ MORE PRONE TO RISK TAKING

LESS PRONE TO BEING AN IDIOT ►

◄ GENETICALLY ENGINEERED TO MAKE VERY POOR TEXTING CHOICES

SHOULD PROBABLY RUN FOR OFFICE MORE ►

As this book approached press time, dozens of politicians were queuing up for the next edition. Former Illinois Representative Derrick Smith, for example, was voted out by the Illinois House in August 2012, in the wake of bribery charges. Half the politicians in Arizona seem to be in trouble: Three state representatives and a state senator have resigned amid scandal or been charged with crimes this year. Kerry Gauthier, a state representative from Minnesota has announced he will not seek reelection after he was caught having sex with a seventeen year old man behind a rest stop near Duluth, and, of course, there's Todd Akin (R-MO), who thinks that women can magically avoid pregnancy if the rape is "legitimate."

We're halfway through volume two.

— ANGUS CARROLL, EDITOR

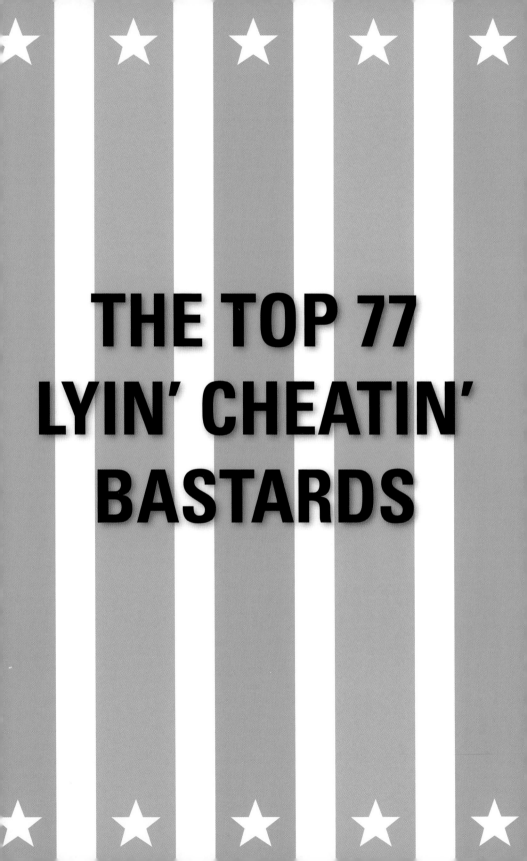

THE TOP 77 LYIN' CHEATIN' BASTARDS

Mike Easley (D)

Governor, North Carolina

Score: 1.0

Pleaded guilty
Retired

FORMER NORTH CAROLINA GOVERNOR MIKE EASLEY has figured out how to beat the system. In late 2010, Easley entered an Alford plea—a plea in which he admitted the state has enough evidence for a conviction, but didn't admit guilt—to avoid facing any jail time for his false campaign finance reports. If only we could all make our problems go away so Easley.

His problems began after he left office when the *Raleigh News & Observer* reported he accepted dozens of free flights on private aircraft and neglected to disclose them on campaign reports or state ethics forms.

The Easley campaign was fined $100,000. Easley himself was only held accountable on one item—that he failed to report a $1,600 helicopter ride—but that made him the only governor of North Carolina ever convicted of a felony.

"I have to take responsibility for what the campaign does," Easley told the judge. "The buck has to stop somewhere. It stops with me, and I take responsibility for what has occurred in this incident." Brave words when the penalty is a $1,000 fine—Easley isn't obligated to pay the $100,000 fine levied against the campaign, even though the campaign paid only $5,335, claiming it had run out of money.

More alarmingly, the free flights were just one of many questionable items. The *Raleigh News & Observer* published a list of gifts and benefits Easley received during his term as governor, but which were not included in his plea agreement. A number of the gift-givers had dealings with the governor around the same time as the gifts were accepted:

1. Easley and his wife, Mary, accepted a $137,000 discount on a coastal waterfront lot in 2005, months after Easley's administration granted environmental permits to the developer.

2. The governor didn't disclose his eight-year waiver for golf dues, worth $50,000, at the Old Chatham Golf Club. The club had trouble with a request for water access, but that problem was cleared up after a call from the governor's office.

3. In 2005, Easley used his influence to get his wife a job at North Carolina State University. She received an eighty-eight percent raise after three years. After this became public, she lost her job and the chancellor and provost of the university resigned.

Easley's attorney stood up for his client's reputation after he was convicted. "He happened to be governor in the 'gotcha age,'" said Joseph Cheshire V. "We live in

this age of 'no matter what you do, someone is going to find fault with it.'" The claim of "gotcha" tactics is a popular refrain among politicians. It's the media's fault. After all, if they didn't look so hard, they wouldn't find anything.

While the former governor's crimes are tame in comparison to the large-scale corruption demonstrated by other *Lyin' Cheatin' Bastards*, any semblance of impropriety is unacceptable.

Easley grimaces as he is grilled over campaign finances. AP Images

76

Roland Burris (D)
U.S. Senator, Illinois

Score: 10.0

Admonished
Did not seek reelection

FORMER U.S. SENATOR ROLAND BURRIS (D-IL) served three terms as Illinois' comptroller, one term as the state's attorney general, and two years in the U.S. Senate—one of only six African Americans to serve in the Senate in the nation's history.

Unfortunately, his term was tainted. He was appointed to the Senate in 2008, three weeks after former Illinois Governor Rod Blagojevich (#3) was arrested on federal corruption charges. These charges included trying to sell President Barack Obama's vacated Senate seat—the seat Burris was appointed to fill. Through the years, Burris had contributed more than $20,000 to Blagojevich's campaign.

> **"I'm from Chicago, and I'll vote twice."**
> —Burris at his farewell speech

Burris came under serious fire in 2009 when, during the trial of the former Illinois governor, he made no mention of trying to raise campaign funds for Blagojevich while seeking the Senate appointment. Burris later admitted he had expressed his desire for the Senate seat to Blagojevich's brother, Rob, and that in exchange, Rob had asked him to help raise campaign funds to the tune of $10,000 to $15,000. Burris tried to put on a fund-raiser, but failed due to the overwhelming disdain for Blagojevich (often referred to by the easier-to-pronounce name "Blago").

Thus, when Burris said in his affidavit, "I did not donate or help raise a single dollar for the Governor from those conversations," he wasn't lyin'. But he wasn't telling the whole truth, either.

When the news came to light, calls for Burris' resignation came from all sides. *The Chicago Tribune* and *The Washington Post* each urged Burris to resign. Members of Congress asked him to step down.

Instead, Burris took a page from Blago's playbook—the one that eventually landed Blago a fourteen-year prison sentence—and urged the investigation on. "I have made an effort to be as transparent as I can, and I'm willing to take a further step as I have nothing to hide," he told the media.

Top Democrats tried to block his path to the Senate—both literally and figuratively—when he arrived in Washington. Burris fought his way through crowds to

Blagojevich (left, with hair) appointed Burris to the Senate. AP Images

get into the Capitol, only to have his credentials rejected by the secretary of the Senate. But in his mind, Burris was already a member of the Senate. After he was rejected, he immediately met with the media. "My name is Roland Burris," he said. "I am the junior senator from the state of Illinois."

Fortunately for Burris, Sangamon County State's Attorney John Schmidt announced on June 19, 2009, that Burris would not face criminal perjury charges because Burris' promise to "personally do something" for Blagojevich (recorded during a wiretap), was too vague to constitute criminal activity. Nevertheless, to be sure that Burris didn't try any more funny stuff, the ethics panel sent him a strongly worded letter of "qualified admonition." In it, the panel called a number of Burris' actions inappropriate and urged him to "meet a much higher standard of conduct," stating, "The Committee found that you should have known that you were providing incorrect, inconsistent, misleading, or incomplete information to the public, the Senate and those conducting legitimate inquiries into your appointment to the Senate."

Due to his ever-changing testimony about his relationship with Blago and how he came to be appointed senator, Burris was added to the "15 Most Corrupt Members of Congress," a list published by the watchdog group Citizens for Responsibility and Ethics in Washington, a group often criticized for primarily targeting Republicans.

After two years, Burris left the U.S. Senate. He delivered his farewell speech to a crowd of four U.S. senators in the Senate chamber, telling them not to be surprised if he comes back, "because I'm from Chicago, and I'll vote twice."

75

Robert A. Watson (R)
State Representative, Rhode Island

Score: 11.0

Pleaded guilty
Still in office

ROBERT A. WATSON (R-30TH DISTRICT) has been serving the state of Rhode Island since 1992. Before he went up in smoke, the state representative wanted to work on the real issues. He thought the General Assembly should focus on the state's fiscal crisis, not social issues, although he observed disdainfully, "I suppose if you're a gay man from Guatemala who gambles and smokes pot, you probably think we're on to some good ideas here."

Odd words from the same representative who cosponsored Rhode Island's medicinal marijuana bill, granted he did later try to overturn the bill he wrote. Twice.

On April 22, 2011, a mere two months after his crack about Guatemalans, Watson was pulled over at a police sobriety checkpoint in Connecticut and charged with possession of marijuana, possession of drug paraphernalia, and DUI. He is currently fighting those charges, although an incident nine months later makes his claim of innocence a bit hard to believe.

On Jan. 22, 2012, Watson was again arrested and charged with possession of marijuana, this time in Rhode Island. The story of his second arrest is quite entertaining.

He was pulled over after he almost hit a snowplow and the driver called the police to report his erratic driving—which included driving around on a rim as he was missing one tire. The police arrived to find Watson and his white Volvo stuck in "deep snow," according to the police report. When two officers approached Watson's car they found him sitting behind the wheel, holding an open can of Natural Ice Beer and saying, "Do you know who I am? I'm the East Greenwich rep."

According to the police report, Watson was "reluctant" to hand over the Natty. The cops also found two bottles of Corona Extra and a pipe full of weed in the car. Watson eventually exited the Volvo, slurring his words and stumbling out before belligerently exclaiming, "Fuck you, whatever, whatever, whatever, whatever, whatever, fuck you," according to one officer. When the police tried to explain to Watson why he was being arrested, he reportedly told them, "Shut up! You got your guy!" Watson was booked and, ironically, released at 4:20 a.m.

Two days later, he checked into rehab.

Watson is not Guatemalan, but he does smoke pot. AP Images

Today, Watson is still serving as a state representative in Rhode Island. He returned to the Statehouse on March 6, 2012, and the Associated Press reported he is "feeling excellent."

But he is not totally out of the woods yet. During his first arrest, the one in Greenwich, CT, Watson blew .05 (.08 is the legal limit), so the DUI charge is unlikely to hold up, but there is still the drug possession charge.

As for his Rhode Island arrest, he pleaded guilty to the marijuana charge and paid a $200 fine, but he was not asked to take a breathalyzer test in that incident (although it sounds like he was hammered and he was holding a beer), so he will skate on that one.

He may end up with no jail time and minimal fines even though he was arrested twice and caught red-handed with pot.

74

John Rowland (R)
Governor, Connecticut

Score: 11.1

Pleaded guilty
Served time

A HOT TUB AND A BOX OF CUBAN cigars have come to symbolize the political career of former Connecticut Governor John Rowland. He was busted for accepting them (and other gifts) from state employees and private contractors. Rowland, a Republican, resigned in disgrace in July of 2004 under the threat of impeachment and served more than ten months in a federal prison on a corruption charge.

"I acknowledge that my poor judgment has brought us here," Rowland said in his resignation speech. But he never apologized.

A two-year investigation led to Rowland admitting he had lied about accepting vacations and work on his cottage from construction firms that had contracts with the state of Connecticut. *The Hartford Courant* broke the story, reporting that a new kitchen and hot tub were installed in his summer home at no charge. The gifts were valued at $107,000.

MSNBC reported he also got cigars, champagne, and a vintage Ford Mustang from employees and friends. Rowland denied for months that he offered any quid pro quo for the gifts.

"I'm not going to sell my integrity or my twenty-five years of public service for a box of cigars. I mean, it's silly to even think that," Rowland said, referring to a state contractor's claim he gave Rowland boxes of Cuban cigars to help speed up payments to his electrical company.

But that's exactly what he did. To avoid serving the maximum of five years in prison, Rowland pleaded guilty to conspiracy to steal "honest service."

"I let my pride get in my way," he said at his sentencing in 2005. He told the judge he lost sight of his ethical judgment and developed a "sense of entitlement and even arrogance."

Rowland's fall from grace was one of the biggest flameouts in Republican Party history. He had been elected to the state House at twenty-three, elected to Congress at twenty-seven, and then won the governorship at thirty-seven—Connecticut's youngest ever. He was elected to three terms as governor, serving nearly ten years. He was the former chairman of the Republican Governors Association.

After getting out of prison in 2006, Rowland got a cushy city management job in his hometown, but now he and a pastor host a radio show called *Church and State*. He's also sharing his tale of adversity and redemption as a motivational speaker. Perhaps he can help his fellow public officials.

Rowland, with his wife, announcing his resignation. AP Images

73

Don Sherwood (R)
Congressman, Pennsylvania

Score: 25.0

Lost reelection bid

FORMER U.S. REPRESENTATIVE DON SHERWOOD (R-PA) had one of the safest seats in Congress, but sex brought him down.

The staunch conservative served four terms in his rural northeastern Pennsylvania district without incident. Then, when the sixty-five-year-old was running for his fifth term in 2005, it was revealed that he'd been having an affair with a woman thirty-five years his junior. On top of that, he settled a lawsuit that claimed he had choked her. Not exactly what voters wanted to hear about a "family values" man, as Sherwood—married with three daughters—was known.

"While I'm truly sorry for disappointing you, I never wavered from my commitment to reduce taxes, create jobs and bring home our fair share," Sherwood said in a campaign ad, apologizing for his behavior at the end of his 2006 campaign.

His mistress, identified by *The Boston Globe* as thirty-year-old Cynthia Ore, wanted her fair share, too. She filed a $5.5 million lawsuit claiming Sherwood had choked her in 2004 in his Washington, D.C., apartment. Police investigated the incident but charges were never filed. Sherwood denied abusing Ore but did admit to having the affair, which lasted five years.

"I made a mistake that hurt my family and has disappointed some of my constituents," Sherwood said in an interview in 2006 (it's not clear which constituents he thought he had not disappointed).

Sherwood signed a confidential agreement with Ore (reportedly paying her $500,000), hoping to limit the damage, but his Democratic opponent, Chris Carney, latched onto the affair and used it against him at every opportunity.

"Don Sherwood is not representing the values of this district," said Carney in one political ad. "Mr. Sherwood went to Washington and he didn't remember the values he took with him." President Bush campaigned with him in Pennsylvania, but to no avail. Voters in the 10th Congressional District listened to Carney and Sherwood lost the election.

According to *Politico*, Sherwood reneged on his deal with Ore after the election, refusing to pay her more than half of the $500,000 he still owed her. Once a cheater, always a cheater.

President Bush campaigned with Sherwood, but It wasn't enough— Sherwood lost.
AP Images

72

Arnold Schwarzenegger (R)
Governor, California

Score: 25.0
Retired

ARNOLD SCHWARZENEGGER ENDED HIS eight-year term as governor of California with a stunning revelation. After leaving office in January of 2011, he confessed to Maria Shriver, his wife of twenty-five years, that he had had an affair with a member of their household staff fourteen years earlier and had fathered her child.

Schwarzenegger's affair with Mildred Patricia Baena happened in 1997 when she was the family's housekeeper. She worked for the family for more than twenty years, retiring in 2011. Baena, then thirty-six, was pregnant with Schwarzenegger's child, Joseph, at the same time Shriver was carrying their fourth child, Christopher. In fact, the babies were born just five days apart.

Schwarzenegger didn't go public until five months later, in May 2011, when *The Los Angeles Times* started asking questions. At that point, he admitted to the affair and said, "I understand and deserve the feelings of anger and disappointment among my friends and family. There are no excuses and I take full responsibility for the hurt I have caused. I have apologized to Maria, my children and my family. I am truly sorry."

Once his secret was out it was "Hasta la vista, baby," as far as Shriver was concerned. She did what any smart, betrayed wife would do: She moved out of their Brentwood, CA, mansion and never looked back.

This was not the first time the former action hero had to apologize for misbehavin'. When he was running for his first term as governor in 2003, "Gropegate" threatened to derail his campaign just days before the election. At least twelve women accused Schwarzenegger of inappropriately touching them without their consent. *The Los Angeles Times* reported that "three of the women described their surprise and discomfort when Schwarzenegger grabbed their breasts. A fourth said he reached under her skirt and gripped her buttocks. A fifth woman said Schwarzenegger groped her and tried to remove her bathing suit in a hotel elevator. A sixth said Schwarzenegger pulled her onto his lap and asked whether a certain sexual act had ever been performed on her."

When the accusations first surfaced Schwarzenegger denied them, but then apologized, admitting, "I have behaved badly sometimes."

"It was on rowdy movie sets, and I have done things that were not right, which I thought then was playful, but now I recognize that I have offended people," Schwarzenegger explained.

Maria Shriver stands by her man as he becomes "the Governator" in 2003.
AP Images

Arnold's Top 7 Nicknames

1. Sperminator

2. Gropinator

3. Impregnator

4. Separator

5. Procreator

6. Marriage Terminator

7. Inseminator

Through all of this, Shriver stood by her man, defending him at every turn. She told Oprah Winfrey in 2003, "I am my own woman ... I look at that man back there in the green room straight on, eyes wide open, and I look at him with an open heart." But there is only so much a woman can take. Shriver filed for divorce in July 2011.

Schwarzenegger didn't find out he was the boy's father until Joseph was a toddler. Baena had listed her then-husband as the baby's father on the birth certificate. The couple separated a few weeks after Joseph was born. Baena told *Hello* magazine that she and Schwarzenegger only slept together "a few times" after "one thing led to another." She said Shriver called her out on Joseph's paternity after realizing he was the spitting image of Schwarzenegger.

Since the affair was exposed, Schwarzenegger has become persona non grata in the political world. "He's radioactive," said Steve Maviglio, former spokesman for former Governor Gray Davis, who lost to Schwarzenegger. But Schwarzenegger has kept his sense of humor. Michael Lewis wrote in *Vanity Fair* magazine that when he was mistaken for Bill Clinton, Schwarzenegger joked, "It's one of those guys who has had a sex scandal." Now known as *Lyin' Cheatin' Bastards*.

71

Jim Gibbons (R)
Governor, Nevada

Score: 25.0

Lost primary
No longer in office

FORMER NEVADA GOVERNOR JIM GIBBONS became the first incumbent governor in state history to lose a primary. The Republican was brought down by a four-year term riddled with scandals and missteps. It was a wonder he was voted into office in the first place—he was involved in three scandals leading up to his election in 2006. According to the *Las Vegas Sun*, these scandals involved: a cocktail waitress claiming he assaulted her in a parking garage after having drinks; a woman saying she was an illegal immigrant who worked for him; and an accusation that he accepted a luxury cruise from a friend lobbying for defense contracts.

Things did not improve once he was in office. According to the *Sun*, he was absent or unavailable so often that his staff had to frequently use an autopen, a device that copies a signature, to get any work done. "The autopen was the busiest employee in the state," a former administration official told the *Sun*.

> ***"I'm living proof that you can survive without sex for that long."***
> —Jim Gibbons

The turmoil escalated in 2008 when he filed for divorce from Dawn Gibbons, his wife of twenty-two years, citing "incompatibility." According to *The Huffington Post*, court documents showed that he wanted her to move out of the governor's mansion because she was "aggressive." The documents stated that living with her was "like being locked in a phone booth with an enraged ferret."

The New York Times reported that until this time, they had been considered one of the state's most politically ambitious couples. He had been a five-term congressman while she had served eight years in the Nevada Assembly. She had even tried to run for his congressional seat while he campaigned for governor.

After the divorce filing, she campaigned heavily against Gibbons, accusing him of extramarital affairs with a former *Playboy* model and the wife of a doctor. Gibbons denied the affairs, claiming the relationships were platonic.

In a sworn deposition in 2010, regarding the cocktail waitress assault (criminal charges were never filed but the waitress filed a civil suit against Gibbons), he told attorneys that he hadn't had sex with his wife or anyone else since 1995. "I'm living proof that you can survive without sex for that long," said Gibbons.

His claim, however, was questioned when state records showed that Gibbons had exchanged more than 850 text messages with the doctor's wife over a six-week period in 2007 on his state cell phone. During one night, between midnight and 2 a.m., they exchanged ninety-one messages. He claimed he was consulting with her about state business.

Despite his denial of any affairs, Gibbons continued to be dogged by the media. In 2010, while running for reelection, a KLAS-TV news crew caught him with the doctor's wife, returning from a trip. He initially denied traveling with her but later admitted it.

Voters weren't apologetic about ousting him from office. "Jim Gibbons is an embarrassment," a lifelong Republican told the *Las Vegas Sun* when he lost the primary.

Jim Rogers, a Republican leader and adversary of Gibbons summed up his tenure this way in the *Sun*. "First of all, he never went to work. Secondly, he had no leadership qualities. You don't get judged well for watching the Titanic sink."

"Hands down, he will be remembered by historians as our worst governor," state historian Guy Rocha told the *Sun*.

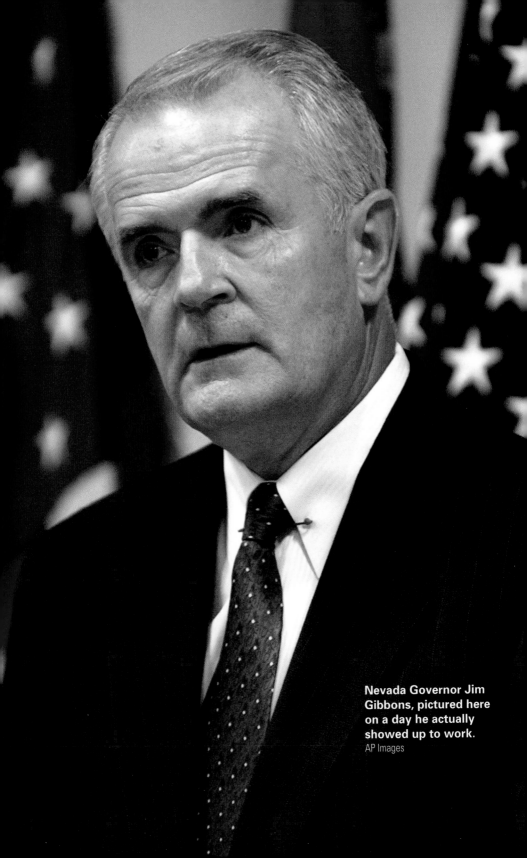

Nevada Governor Jim Gibbons, pictured here on a day he actually showed up to work.
AP Images

70

John Edwards (D)
Senator, North Carolina

Score: 25.0
Disgraced
No longer in office

IN OCTOBER 2007, THE *NATIONAL ENQUIRER* reported that John Edwards, a U.S. senator from North Carolina and a candidate for the Democratic ticket in 2008, was having an affair with a former campaign worker, Rielle Hunter. Later, there were allegations he had fathered a child with her.

Edwards first admitted to the affair while denying he was the father of the child. In a bizarre twist, campaign aide Andrew Young claimed that he, not Edwards, was the child's father. Young later recanted that statement and said Edwards knew all along that he was the child's father and that he had asked Young to take responsibility to cover up the scandal. This and much more is in Young's 2010 book, *The Politician: An Insider's Account of John Edwards's Pursuit of the Presidency and the Scandal That Brought Him Down.*

It was not until January 2010 that Edwards finally admitted he was the father.

ABC News anchor George Stephanopoulos said that members of Edwards' staff (who knew he was having an affair) told him they had a "doomsday strategy" to derail Edwards if it looked like he would win the nomination, but Joe Trippi, a senior campaign advisor, said that was "bullshit."

> **"Falling in love with you could really screw up my plans for becoming president."**
>
> —Edwards to Hunter on the night they met

The affair certainly derailed his marriage. His wife, Elizabeth, left Edwards after he admitted to being the father of Hunter's child. Elizabeth's courage makes the story all the more poignant. She was first diagnosed with breast cancer in 2004, but appeared to recover, and when Edwards decided to run for the 2008 Democratic nomination, she hit the campaign trail with him. Even when her cancer returned while they were on the road in early 2007, he did not drop out of the race. Given that Hunter's child was born in February 2008, Edwards was obviously involved with her at that point.

Edwards originally hired Hunter to make "behind-the-scenes" film documentaries about him in preparation for his run at the presidency, but soon, they were making more than videos together. According to her former boyfriend, the writer Jay McInerney, Hunter was the model for Alison Poole, the lead character in his novel *The Story of My Life.* In an interview, McInerney described the character as "an ostensibly jaded, cocaine-addled, sexually voracious twenty-year-old." Edwards was entranced.

The *National Enquirer* broke the story of Edwards' affair. AP Images

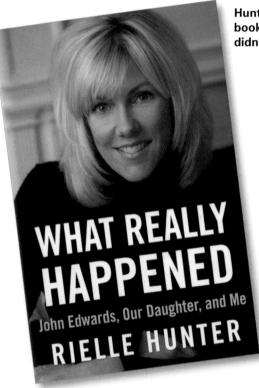

Hunter wrote her own "tell all" book, but no one cared—it didn't sell.

WHAT REALLY HAPPENED
John Edwards, Our Daughter, and Me
RIELLE HUNTER

His troubles, however, turned out to be more than political: he was investigated for using campaign money for personal reasons related to the affair. At issue was about $1 million that was purportedly a campaign donation, but which Edwards allegedly used to support Hunter.

On June 3, 2011, Edwards was indicted by a grand jury on six felony charges, including four counts of collecting illegal campaign contributions, one count of conspiracy, and one count of making false statements. In June 2012 he was found not guilty on one count, but the jury could not reach a decision on the other counts. The judge declared a mistrial and the Justice Department subsequently dropped the charges.

Hunter gave an interview to *GQ* magazine published in the April 2010 issue. During their first night together, Hunter said Edwards told her, "Falling in love with you could really screw up my plans for becoming president."

69

Katherine Bryson (R)
State Representative, Utah

Score 25.0

Did not run for reelection

A BITTER DIVORCE TURNED EVEN NASTIER for former Utah State Representative Katherine Bryson (R-Orem) in 2003 when she was caught on videotape with her lover. The incident put an end to her legislative career.

Bryson and her ex-husband, Kay, had been married for thirty-six years when he filed for divorce in 2003. They were considered quite the power couple in the Utah County Republican Party, but their relationship dissolved quickly into a "he said/she said" amid allegations of adultery, fraud, and domestic violence.

According to *The Salt Lake Tribune*, Kay, who was the Utah County attorney at the time, claimed that Katherine had cheated on him for years. She made a speech on the State House floor that appeared to accuse Kay of domestic violence, implying he had held a gun to her head. He said she had forged his signature on several real estate transactions.

The dispute reached fever pitch when Kay decided to put a surveillance camera in Katherine's condo. He claimed he was doing it at the request of his son, who was renting the condo from her. According to *The Salt Lake Tribune*, the son had told his father he thought someone had broken in because things were out of place. According to Kay, it was just Katherine and her lover using the condo for

"We didn't catch a burglar, what we caught … was an unfaithful wife."
—Kay Bryson, as told to *The Salt Lake Tribune*

Katherine Bryson in happier times. State government photo.

secret trysts. "We didn't catch a burglar, what we caught … was an unfaithful wife," Kay told *The Salt Lake Tribune.*

When Katherine accused Kay of abuse, Kay threatened to share the videotape of Katherine and her lover with her State House colleagues, *The Salt Lake Tribune* reported. He wrote: "Katherine, just wanted you to know that a letter is going out to each member of the House and will begin: Dear Representative, Enclosed you will find a video tape."

Katherine filed for reelection in March of 2004, but withdrew her name from the ballot about a week later with no reason given. She retired at the end of the year from the state legislature and remarried—now going by Katherine Renner.

When she dropped out, Republican opponent Brad Daw told the *Tribune,* "… I think she saw [running again] was going to be a fairly difficult challenge."

68

Roy Ashburn (R)
State Senator, California

Score: 26.0

Did not run for reelection

Special Award
Gay Anti-Gay Legislator

ON MARCH 8, 2010, FORMER CALIFORNIA State Senator Roy Ashburn (R-Bakersfield) came out and said it: "I'm gay." Two words, he said, "that have been so difficult for me for so long."

If only he had managed to come to terms with his sexual orientation before he was arrested for drunk driving after leaving a gay nightclub. Ashburn was sentenced to two days in jail and three years probation after pleading no contest to the DUI charges, but the real fallout was that it forced him to come out.

Fortunately, he didn't hurt anyone other than himself that night, but Ashburn hurt plenty of other people throughout his legislative career. We don't call a politician a Bastard just because of his sexual preference. It's Ashburn's voting record that gets him into the club with so many other anti-gay gay lawmakers.

Equality California Director Geoff Kors told the *TPMmuckraker* blog, "He has voted against every LGBT rights bill that's been introduced in California since he's been in the office." His record includes voting against a resolution to oppose Prop 8, the anti-gay marriage ballot; voting against recognizing out-of-state same-sex marriages; and voting against creating Harvey Milk Day, a holiday to honor the murdered gay rights activist.

At a 2005 anti-gay marriage rally, he said, "Marriage between one man and one woman is fundamental to civilization."

> "I took a position based on what I believed was the will of my constituents, not mine, necessarily."
>
> —Ashburn on why he voted against pro-gay legislation

Before coming out as gay, Ashburn spent much of his time voting against LGBT rights bills. AP Images

The senator was divorced before he came out, but that does not undo the hypocrisy. The *Bakersfield Californian* revealed it had heard gay rumors about Ashburn since his divorce, but had declined to report on the rumors, citing lack of relevance. Ashburn clearly felt the same way. When asked by *Californian* reporter Lois Henry about the gay rumors (before his arrest), Henry dodged the question, asking, "Why would that be anyone's business?"

In an interview with the *Californian* after coming out, Ashburn blamed his constituents for his anti-gay voting record. His district, which makes up most of Bakersfield, is one of the more conservative districts in the state.

"I took a position based on what I believed was the will of my constituents, not mine, necessarily," Ashburn said. "We have a representative form of government ... where citizens select people to cast votes on their behalf." True. But constituents also expect their representatives to be truthful about their own values and beliefs, and masquerading as an anti-gay legislator when you are gay is hypocritical and deceitful. It calls your entire character into question.

Tellingly, once Ashburn came out, the people of California got a much-changed senator. He stayed in office and voted for pro-gay resolutions like the one to repeal the military's "don't ask, don't tell" policy and proclaimed June as Lesbian, Gay, Bisexual and Transgender Month. So much for representing the views of your conservative constituents.

Ashburn did not run for reelection, but he has not completely left the political arena. Ashburn was appointed to the state Unemployment Insurance Appeals Board by Governor Arnold Schwarzenegger (#72), and in February 2012, announced a bid to run for his former job as Kern County supervisor. Can anyone believe what he says?

67

Daniel Gordon (R)
State Representative, Rhode Island

Score: 28.7
Still in office

Special Award
CFA

WHEN RHODE ISLAND STATE REPRESENTATIVE Daniel Gordon (R-71st District) was caught driving with a suspended license, his sordid past caught up with him.

It all started when Gordon was pulled over on Sept. 14, 2011. Police let him go, but later realized he was wanted in Massachusetts for eluding police in April 2008. Two days later, they arrested him.

An investigation revealed that in the earlier incident, Gordon was arrested at gunpoint after leading police on a high-speed chase. The *New England Post* reported that according to the police, when troopers asked Gordon why he refused to stop, he said he "was stupid," quite possibly the last true statement he ever made. Gordon was ordered to appear in court in October 2008, but never did, and a warrant was issued for his arrest. But that's not the half of it.

Turns out Gordon was charged eighteen different times in Massachusetts between 1993 and 2011, and served a total of six months in jail. The representative was charged six times with assault and battery, "twice with a gun," according to Rhode Island's WPRI News. In 1993, he was convicted of operating under the influence. Three years later, he was charged with possession of marijuana.

He served four months in jail in 1999 after being convicted of assault and battery with a dangerous weapon, and one month in 2003 after being convicted again of assault and battery. He was held in 2004 after being charged with attempted murder, although those charges were later dropped.

When the news of his previous arrests came to light, calls for his resignation began. Both the House Speaker and House GOP leader asked for his resignation.

But the real question is: How is it that no one knew about his history of arrests? When we last checked, Massachusetts was right next to Rhode Island.

Gordon's explanation? Alcoholism related to post-traumatic stress disorder (PTSD) from serving in the Middle East, where he said he received a Purple Heart.

"When I returned home from overseas in the Marine Corps, I suffered a lot of issues that returning combat veterans do, namely post-traumatic stress disorder, as well as a physical ailment, and self-medicated it with alcohol. Each and every one of those instances on my Massachusetts' record was directly or indirectly involved with alcohol. I've since received treatment for that ... and continue to

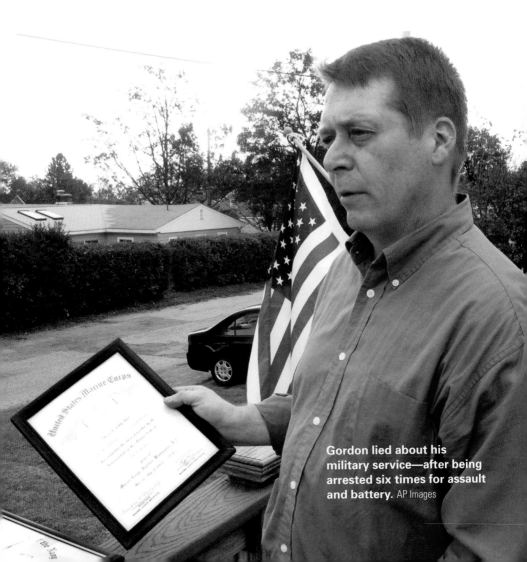

Gordon lied about his military service—after being arrested six times for assault and battery. AP Images

receive counseling for that," Gordon said in an interview with the *Portsmouth Patch* days after his criminal record came to light.

In the same interview, Gordon explained he would not resign because it would be "a disservice to veterans." "The example that I'm giving our veterans who have gone through many of the same things that I have, you can overcome these problems and achieve success ... that's not something I want to take away from them by being a quitter," he said.

There was one slight problem with Gordon's statement: While Gordon claimed he served in the Gulf War and was injured by shrapnel in Baghdad, military records show Gordon never served in the Middle East, let alone received a Purple Heart. He was an aircraft technician and never went near any battlefield.

Gordon has been awarded a special prize. Being a jerk is one thing; fraudulently claiming it's a result of military service is inexcusable. Military professionals deserve to be recognized for their bravery and dedication; Gordon deserves to be recognized for what *he* is: a CFA—Complete F*****g Asshole.

We have not heard the last of Gordon. In January 2012, he tweeted "@RepDanGordon: 2day is as good as any to kick-off my re-election campaign. The tyrants never sleep & some 1 in govt has to fight back." God save us.

66

Paul Patton (R)
Governor, Kentucky

Score: 30.0

Did not run for reelection

BREAKING UP IS HARD TO DO and some people don't take it well. Former Kentucky Governor Paul Patton is one of those people.

In 2002, Patton was sued for shutting down the nursing home of his former mistress, Tina Conner. The two had engaged in an affair for several years and Conner contended that when she ended the relationship the governor went after her business.

Between 1997 and 2001, Patton and Conner were "together" in varying degrees. At forty years old, Conner was fifteen years younger than the governor. She was also the owner and operator of Birchtree Healthcare in Clinton, KY. Just two months after Conner ended the affair with Patton, her nursing home was cited for substandard care, including numerous health and safety violations. The citations caused the nursing home to lose funding and Conner ultimately filed for bankruptcy.

As a result, Conner sued Patton, charging sexual harassment and defamation, arguing he used state legislators to close down her nursing home business after she cut off sex.

It should be noted that Conner did not always think Patton was a Bastard. In her lawsuit, she reminisced about the good old days, noting Patton made sure that extraordinary amounts of state aid were directed to her nursing home while she was sleeping with him.

Initially, Patton denied the affair, but when the *Courier-Journal* in Louisville, KY, reported that five years' worth of telephone records showed 440 phone calls had been made from the governor's office to Conner's personal and business numbers, he changed his tune.

The story of their affair broke exactly one week before Paul Patton and his wife Judi celebrated their twenty-fifth anniversary. In his obligatory news conference, which Judi did not attend, the governor confirmed the affair and offered his regret: "I apologize to the people of Kentucky for my failure as a person."

As for the charges brought by his ex-mistress, the court upheld only one—that he engaged in outrageous conduct. Unfortunately for Conner, the Kentucky Court of Appeals ruled that she could not pursue a case for sexual harassment against Patton because—fun fact—you can't sue someone for sexual harassment unless they were your employer.

But for Patton, the damage was done. In December, the governor's term and his long political career came to an end—another governor brought down by a sex scandal, another *Lyin' Cheatin' Bastard* caught in a web of deceit and corruption.

Patton initially denied allegations of harassment, and his wife Judi initially believed him. AP Images

65

Eddie Perez (D)
Mayor, Hartford, Connecticut

Score: 35.0

Convicted
Out on appeal

YOU WOULD THINK AFTER RISING from meager beginnings and escaping gang life, former Hartford, CT, Mayor Eddie Perez would have tried hard to stay on the straight and narrow. But it wasn't to be. The first Latino mayor of Hartford was convicted on bribery and corruption charges in 2010.

Perez's troubles began in October of 2007, when he was running for his third term as mayor. That's when state investigators started looking into his administration. His home was searched and a grand jury convened. Despite the investigation, Perez was still reelected as mayor.

Over the course of a fifteen-month probe, prosecutors determined that he accepted free home renovations from a city contractor in 2005 in exchange for a city construction contract. The renovations were worth about $40,000 and included a whirlpool and a remodeled kitchen and bathroom. Perez paid $20,000 to the contractor two years later—*after* the grand jury started investigating.

Perez apologized to voters for using a city contractor to work on his home, but he said, "A lapse in judgment is not a crime." He refused to resign from office.

He was arrested for a second time nine months later on new charges of conspiracy and extortion. (He was still facing the original charges). This time prosecutors accused him of trying to extort $100,000 from a developer to pay off a political ally—a former state representative—for his land.

"I want the people of Hartford, the voters, the taxpayers, my friends and neighborhood to know that the truth, the truth is on my side," Perez said at a pep rally after his second arrest.

But the truth really wasn't on his side: He had outright lied to a grand jury when asked if he paid for the renovations, saying he had when he most definitely had not.

His attorney Hubert Santos tried to downplay it as nothing but political expediency. "He lied because if this came out, it would be very politically embarrassing," said Santos. "This was the height of the political season in 2007. He didn't lie because he believed he had committed a crime." No one bought it.

The judge in his case combined all the charges for trial. He was found guilty on five out of six counts on June 18, 2010, including bribery and first-degree larceny by extortion. He resigned from office that same afternoon and asked for forgiveness from the residents of Hartford.

The judge at his sentencing was not feeling very charitable, however. She gave him three years in prison plus three years probation. But so far, he has not served any time. He's currently free on bond, pending appeal. His attorneys are basing his appeal on the fact that other recent political scandals in the state, including one involving the former Governor John Rowland (#74), stacked the deck against him.

It couldn't be that he was just a *Lyin' Cheatin' Bastard* on his own.

Perez looking less than confident at the courthouse. AP Images

64

Marion Barry (D)
Councilman, Washington, D.C.

Score: 35.0

Still in office

Special Award
Tax Evader

IF THERE WAS A *LYIN' CHEATIN' BASTARDS* Hall of Fame, Marion Barry would be one of the first inductees. He served as mayor of Washington, D.C., for four terms (1979-1991, 1995-1999) and is still a D.C. councilman today. Most famously, he was reelected as mayor in 1994 after having been arrested and jailed in a sting operation that showed him, on tape, smoking crack cocaine in a hotel room.

In 2002, U.S. Park Police pulled him over and found traces of marijuana and crack cocaine in his Jaguar. Barry claimed it was a setup. In 2004, he called in to a weekly political talk radio show and explained it wasn't his fault—the cops had it in for him back then.

Barry was lucky in that instance, but he seemed to court trouble. In 2005, the former-mayor-turned-councilman pleaded guilty to two tax charges. Barry admitted he failed to pay taxes on more than $530,000 in income he had earned between the time he left office in 1999 and the trial in 2005. In lieu of jail time, Barry was given three years probation. In January 2009, the probation was extended until May 2011 after he failed to file tax returns for 2007. At the time, he was making more than $90,000 per year as a councilman.

In July 2009, he was arrested and charged with stalking. According to the *Washington City Paper*, Barry pursued his ex-girlfriend, Donna Watts, and her ex-husband in his BMW after the two left Watts' home together. He followed them through a nearby park, flashing his lights and honking his horn, prompting Park Police to arrest him.

Those charges were later dropped, but the incident drew attention to a $15,000 city contract Barry had previously awarded Watts (with kickbacks, of course).

Barry, wearing what must be his lucky tie, speaks to the press after his arrest for stalking in 2009. AP Images

In response, the city council censured Barry and stripped him of committee assignments.

Barry wasn't paying taxes and, apparently, wasn't paying parking tickets, either. In March of 2011, the councilman had nine unpaid parking tickets totaling $705. He may have thought he was above the law—why wouldn't he at this point—but the city booted his car in response. According to the Associated Press, Barry said the booting was "no big thing."

In April of 2012, Barry upped the ante once again when he disparaged Asian-owned businesses in Ward 8. "We got to do something about these Asians coming in and opening up businesses and dirty shops," Barry said after winning the Democratic Primary for his Ward 8 City Council seat, according to ABC News. "They ought to go. I'm going to say that right now. But we need African-American businesspeople to be able to take their places, too."

He apologized two days after the initial remarks, but later insisted the comments were "not racial."

Barry doubled-down later that same week, this time targeting Filipino immigrants. "If you go to the hospital now, you find a number of immigrants who are nurses, particularly from the Philippines," Barry said at a council hearing, according to the *Washington Examiner*. "And no offense, but let's grow our own teachers, let's grow our own nurses ... so that we don't have to be scrounging around in our community clinics and other kinds of places [and] having to hire people from somewhere else."

Somehow, some way, Barry is still serving as D.C.'s Ward 8 councilman.

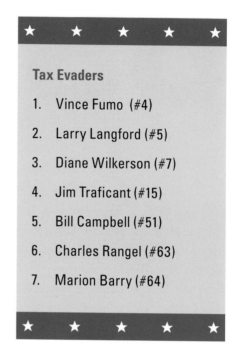

Tax Evaders

1. Vince Fumo (#4)

2. Larry Langford (#5)

3. Diane Wilkerson (#7)

4. Jim Traficant (#15)

5. Bill Campbell (#51)

6. Charles Rangel (#63)

7. Marion Barry (#64)

63

Charles Rangel (D)
Congressman, New York

Score: 46.0

Still in office

Special Award
Tax Evader

AS CHAIRMAN OF THE POWERFUL HOUSE Ways and Means Committee, U.S. Representative Charles Rangel (D-NY) was responsible for writing tax laws—but he didn't think they applied to him. The long-serving Democrat (he's been in Congress since 1971) was censured by the House in December of 2010 for failing to pay all his taxes along with ten other ethics violations. Censure is the most serious form of punishment short of expulsion from the House.

The investigation into Rangel's financial shenanigans began in 2008. According to the *New York Post*, he failed to report rental income and pay taxes on a luxury beachfront villa in the Dominican Republic. Tax avoided: $75,000.

Then *The New York Times* discovered he was renting a rent-stabilized apartment in a Harlem luxury building and using it as his campaign office, which is strictly prohibited by state and city laws. (Regulations require that rent-controlled apartments be used only as a primary residence.)

Shortly after this, *The Washington Post* blew the whistle on Rangel for another big no-no—using congressional stationery and staff to solicit funds for his personal foundation from companies that had business in front of the Ways and Means Committee.

> **"I did not try to have sex with minors."**
> —Charles Rangel

But he didn't stop there. On top of the private donations, totaling close to $25 million, Rangel wrangled $2 million in tax dollars through a special earmark for the Charles B. Rangel Center for Public Policy at the City College of New York. According to the center's brochure, the $30 million building includes the "Rangel Conference Center," "a well-furnished office for Charles Rangel," and the "Charles Rangel Library" for his papers and memorabilia. CBS News reported, "It's kind of like a presidential library without a president." Incredibly, the brochure claims Rangel's library will be as important as the Clinton and Carter libraries.

Rangel was censured for lying and evading taxes, but he's still serving as a U.S. Representative—God Bless America. AP Images

Rangel's Republican constituents quickly dubbed his center the "Monument to Me." When the seventy-eight-year-old Rangel was called out on the House floor by a then-junior congressman about spending taxpayer money on pet projects, Rangel was anything but contrite. "I would have a problem if you did it," Rangel said, "because I don't think that you've been around long enough."

The House also determined that he filed misleading financial statements and failed to report assets and income during a ten-year period, to the tune of $600,000.

On the day of his censure, Rangel offered an apology, telling his colleagues, "I have made some serious mistakes ... I brought it on myself." But he didn't think his conduct was as bad as some others who had previously been censured. "I did not try to have sex with minors," he said. It's good to know he has standards— but he's a *Lyin' Cheatin' Bastard* nevertheless.

62

David Wu (D)
Congressman, Oregon

Score: 50.0

Resigned in disgrace
Facing charges

U.S. REPRESENTATIVE DAVID WU (D-OR) was the first Chinese-American elected to the House. He served from 2008 to 2011—when he resigned in disgrace after it was revealed he had a sexual relationship with the 18-year-old daughter of a close friend.

But long before that, Wu had started to act strangely and had driven most of his staff to quit in despair.

Wu's troubles date to 2004 when *The Oregonian* broke the news that Wu had sexually assaulted a former girlfriend while at Stanford in the summer of 1976. According to the report, the woman told an assistant dean it was an attempted rape and Wu used a pillow to muffle her screams. He was never charged, but he admitted it was "inexcusable behavior on my part," according to *The Oregonian*. Despite the scandal, Wu was reelected.

> **"... There are Klingons in the White House..."**
> —David Wu

But in 2007, his behavior became more and more erratic. First, he delivered his famous analysis of the government's actions in Iraq: "... unlike the Vulcans of Star Trek who made their decisions based on logic and fact, these guys make it on ideology. These aren't Vulcans. There are Klingons in the White House, but unlike the real Klingons of Star Trek, these Klingons have never fought a battle of their own. Don't let faux-Klingons send real Americans to war—it's wrong."

By 2010, Wu was clearly living in a parallel universe. His staff became so worried they arranged an intervention with his psychiatrist, but Wu refused to attend.

His staff left him and his wife left him. In late October, he gave a loud, angry speech at a Democratic meeting, accusing the media of being "unfair," and his Republican opponent, Rob Cornilles, of being a lousy tipper. Wu also made it a point to tell the audience he had stopped drinking as of July 1, though that was less believable than his other claims. His speech was so out of place that a leader of his own party wrote him a letter condemning it.

On October 29, 2010, Wu badgered a TSA officer at the Portland airport into giving him access to a restricted area where Wu greeted off-loading passengers and asked for their votes. The cranky passengers were not impressed—one filed a complaint with the TSA.

But the best was yet to come. The next day, members of Wu's staff received a series of bizarre e-mails. The first message contained no text, only the infamous photo of Wu dressed in a tiger suit (2010 was the Year of the Tiger, but the suit did not bring Wu good luck). Shortly afterward, a message with the subject line "Not funny" arrived in staffer's inboxes. This one was signed by his daughter and read, "You're the best, but my Dad made me say that, even though you threatened to shut down his campaign."

The third e-mail was sent a few minutes later. The subject line was "Wasted" and it said, "My Dad said you said he was wasted Wednesday night after just three

Wu's staff was likely surprised to recieve a photo of their boss dressed as a furry.

sips of wine. It's just that he hasn't had a drink since July 1. Cut him some slack, man. What he does when he's wasted is send e-mails, not harass people he works with. He works SO hard for you … Cut the dude some slack, man. Just kidding." It was signed by Wu's young son. A final e-mail said, "My Dad says you're the best because not even my Mom put up with him. We think you're cool."

Wu's staff and the media speculated the e-mails were sent from him and made to appear as though they'd come from his children.

The proverbial straw that broke the camel's back came in July 2011, when the eighteen-year-old daughter of one of Wu's longtime friends accused him of sexual assault. Wu didn't deny a relationship with the girl, but insisted the sexual encounter was consensual. The young woman did not agree with that assessment. Wu announced his resignation less than a week after the scandal broke, citing his inability to focus on his job or care for his family while also fighting the allegations.

61

James West (R)
Mayor, Spokane, Washington

Score: 50.0

Recalled

Special Award
Gay Anti-Gay Legislator

IN 2004, THE LOCAL SPOKANE, WA, newspaper, *The Spokesman Review,* targeted Mayor Jim West in a sting operation after reporter Bill Morlin received a tip that the real identity of the persona "Cobra82" on gay.com was in fact Mayor West. To find out if it was true, *The Spokesman Review* hired a professional investigator to create a false online persona named "Motobrock." The newspaper then used this persona to arrange a meeting with Cobra82. When Jim West turned up for the meeting at a Spokane golf course, the cat was out of the bag.

If that were the end of the story, West would not be a *Lyin' Cheatin' Bastard.* Being gay does not get you into the elite LCB club. It is West's legislative record that earns him a place on the list.

Before becoming mayor of Spokane, West was a member of the State House and Senate, where he gained a reputation as an anti-gay legislator. He supported one bill that would have banned gays and lesbians from working in schools or day care centers. (See sidebar on GAGL, the Gay Anti-Gay Legislators).

When he was "outed," calls for his resignation came from all sides. On May 30, 2005, West defended himself on *The Today Show,* where he explained his support for anti-gay laws: If someone hires you to paint their house red, then you paint it red. Even if you think it would look better green.

At a Spokane City Council meeting immediately afterward, the council unanimously passed a resolution requesting that he step down (7-0), yet West announced he intended to continue on as mayor. In a rare show of bipartisan solidarity, the Spokane County Republican Party, the Washington State Republican Party, and Spokane County Democratic Chairwoman Katie Kirking all called for West's resignation.

Although West refused to step down, organizers of a recall gathered a sufficient number of signatures to force a recall vote, and a special mail-in election was held on Dec. 6, 2005. West was recalled by the voters with sixty-five percent in favor of ousting him versus thirty-five percent in favor of keeping him. His term ended on Dec. 16, 2005, the day the final votes were certified.

Mayor West's resignation was the one thing that Washington Democrats and Republicans could agree on. AP Images

60

Thomas Porteous (D)
Federal Judge

Score: 50.0

Impeached
Removed

ON MARCH 11, 2010, THE HOUSE VOTED to impeach Thomas Porteous, a federal judge. On Dec. 8, the Senate convicted him of Article I of the articles of impeachment, thus removing him from the bench.

The Senate subsequently convicted him on three additional articles of impeachment and then, for good measure, voted 94-2 that he be "Forever disqualified to hold any office of honor or profit under the United States." Article I of his impeachment read, "Engaging in a pattern of conduct that is incompatible with the trust and confidence placed in him as a Federal judge." It passed the House (impeachment) by a vote of 412-0 and the Senate (conviction and removal) by a vote of 96-0.

Porteous had a gambling problem and was deep in debt (he declared bankruptcy in 2001). The impeachment certificate stated that there was substantial evidence that Porteous "repeatedly committed perjury by signing false financial disclosure forms," thus concealing "cash and things of value that he solicited and received from lawyers appearing in litigation before him." In a specific case, "he denied a motion to recuse based on his relationship with lawyers in the case … and failed to disclose that the lawyers in question had often provided him with cash," thus depriving "the public of its right to his honest services."

Removing a federal official through impeachment is rare: since 1797, the House of Representatives has impeached only sixteen federal officials (two presidents, a cabinet member, a senator, a justice of the Supreme Court, and eleven federal judges). Of those, the Senate has convicted and removed only seven, all of them judges. (Not included in this list are those who resigned rather than face impeachment, most notably President Richard M. Nixon). The last two federal judges removed were Alcee L. Hastings and Walter M. Nixon, who were impeached, found guilty by the Senate, and removed from office in 1989. Hastings is currently the U.S. representative for Florida's 23rd Congressional District, proving that no matter what you do, you can still be a member of Congress. (Former federal judge Samuel Kent was impeached in 2009, but resigned before being removed by the Senate, see LCB #12).

"I am deeply saddened to be removed from office but I felt it was important not just to me but to the judiciary to take this fight to the Senate," Porteous said in a statement after his impeachment. In other words, he dragged it out to the end, hoping against hope to get acquitted, wasting everyone's time.

The Senate voted 94-2 that Porteous be "Forever disqualified to hold any office of honor or profit under the United States." AP Images

59

Chip Pickering (R)
Congressman, Mississippi

Score: 50.0

Retired

Special Award
Hypocrite

FORMER U.S. REPRESENTATIVE CHIP PICKERING (R-MS) is a member of the notorious Capitol Hill club known as "C Street." He is one of three Republican politicians associated with a Christian home caught in a sex scandal. Pickering spent time at the well-known "C Street Complex" in Washington, D.C., with Nevada Senator John Ensign (#39) and South Carolina Governor Mark Sanford (#26).

Pickering retired from Congress in January of 2009 after serving six terms, saying he wanted to spend more time with his family, which includes five sons. However, about seven months later, his estranged wife Leisha (he had filed for divorce the year before) accused Pickering's alleged mistress of ruining their marriage and ending Pickering's political career.

The alienation of affection lawsuit (when an outsider interferes with a marriage) claimed that Pickering and the woman—Elizabeth Creekmore Byrd—dated in college, hooked back up after Pickering was married, and had an affair before and while he was living at the C Street home and while serving in Congress. Leisha said in the lawsuit the extramarital relationship ended both of their marriages. Creekmore Byrd divorced her husband in 2007.

Leisha also blamed Creekmore Byrd for Pickering's retirement from politics. The suit alleges that when Trent Lott (R-MS) resigned from the U.S. Senate in December of 2007, Mississippi Governor Haley Barbour offered the seat to Pickering, who turned it down. Leisha charged that Creekmore Byrd gave Pickering an ultimatum that they couldn't be a couple if he moved to the Senate because he'd have to stay married.

"Creekmore Byrd gave Pickering the option to remain a public servant or become a private citizen and continue relations with her," the lawsuit said.

He chose his mistress over his family despite his reputation as a "defender of decency," according to CBS News. He had pushed former President George W. Bush to adopt legislation declaring 2008 "the National Year of the Bible."

Pickering, a model for Christian values, stands next to his now ex-wife and announces he will not run for reelection. AP Images

Pickering, Ensign, and Sanford all fell from grace within a month of each other, prompting Peter J. Boyle from *The New Yorker* to call the home on C Street a "boys-gone-wild house of pleasure." The building is affiliated with a Christian group called "The Fellowship," which sponsors the annual National Prayer Breakfast attended by the president, members of Congress, and other dignitaries.

Pickering now works as a lobbyist for Cellular South, conveniently owned by Creekmore Byrd's family.

The C Street Complex in D.C., where Pickering, Ensign, and Sanford all stayed, is owned by a Christian organization called The Fellowship.

58

Tim Mahoney (D)
Congressman, Florida

Score: 50.0

Lost reelection

Special Award
Hypocrite

SEX SCANDALS HAUNT FLORIDA'S 16TH Congressional District. Just two years after Republican Representative Mark Foley (#40) resigned when he was caught sending sexually suggestive texts to male pages, U.S. Representative Tim Mahoney (D-FL)—who replaced Foley—admitted to having numerous affairs.

"I showed complete bad judgment on my part," he said during an interview with Tampa TV station WPBF News 25. "To allow myself to be put into that position was just stupid on my part."

Mahoney's 2008 confession came just days after ABC News revealed that Mahoney had secretly paid off a former mistress and campaign staffer, fifty-year-old Patricia Allen, after she threatened him with a sexual harassment lawsuit. The fifty-two-year-old Mahoney said the affair with Allen started in 2006 when he was running for Foley's seat under the (in retrospect) ironic slogan "Restoring America's Values Begins at Home." (Mahoney was married at the time, with a daughter.)

ABC News reported that Mahoney first met Allen at a campaign stop and fixed it so she could be a volunteer. She was later hired as a campaign staffer. According to ABC, she broke off their relationship after learning that Mahoney was having other affairs. Shortly afterward, Mahoney fired her.

At that point, Allen hired an attorney and threatened to sue Mahoney for more than a million dollars. ABC News reported that in a letter sent to the congressman, Allen alleged sexual harassment, intimidation, and humiliation, and charged that Mahoney's behavior masked a "dark and depraved personality."

Mahoney said he fired her for performance issues, but he still ended up settling with her. He paid her $121,000 out of his own pocket, he says: $61,000 for her and $60,000 in legal fees.

He also admitted to having a relationship with a second woman in 2007, a high-ranking official in a nearby Florida county.

Not surprisingly, Mahoney's wife filed for divorce soon after his confession and he lost his reelection bid.

Nor have things improved for Mahoney recently. He is currently awaiting trial on a DUI arrest in 2011. CBS4 in Miami reported that police found him asleep behind the wheel of his parked car on a South Florida road at 3 a.m.

Mahoney gives his victory speech in 2006, with his wife (center) and daughter (right) standing behind him. AP Images

Hank Johnson (D)
Congressman, Georgia

Score: 50.0

Still in office

Special Awards
Stupidity, Caught on Tape

AT A MARCH 2010 HOUSE ARMED Services Committee hearing on the defense budget, U.S. Representative Hank Johnson (D-GA) expressed concerns about plans to move "thousands of Marines and their families, about 8,000 people in all, to the small island of Guam, which has a current population of about 180,000."

The plan already had its critics. At its peak (during construction of a new base), the plan would increase Guam's population by 79,000 people, or about forty-five percent. According to *The Washington Post*, the buildup "could trigger island-wide water shortages that would fall disproportionately on a low income, medically underserved population," and possibly overload sewage treatment systems in a way that could "result in significant adverse public health impacts." In short, adding thousands of people to Guam's population would strain the island's infrastructure, resulting in disease and possible deaths.

But these problems paled in comparison to the impending catastrophe foreseen by Johnson. After a long, disjointed prologue in which he established the approximate size of the island (twenty-four miles long by about seven miles wide "at its least widest place"), Johnson concluded, "My fear is that the whole island will become so overly populated that it will tip over and capsize."

In an incredible display of self-control, Admiral Robert Willard replied calmly, "We don't anticipate that."

After the hearing, Johnson's office tried to claim the statement was a metaphor. In a follow-up e-mail Johnson said, "I wasn't suggesting that the island of Guam would literally tip over, I was using a metaphor to say that ... the addition of 8,000 Marines and their dependents—an additional 80,000 people during peak construction on the tiny island with a population of 180,000—could be a tipping point which could adversely affect the island's fragile ecosystem and could overburden its overstressed infrastructure."

Unfortunately, that explanation is not believable; one has only to watch the video. The government is so embarrassed by the episode it has removed the video from the House Armed Services website. Clicking on the video for March 25, 2012 (a so-called "permanent link") results in no file found (all other video links work fine). But removing it from the official website accomplishes nothing: the video is on YouTube.

Although the video came out the week before the 2010 congressional reelections, Johnson successfully defended his seat.

Johnson is included in *Lyin' Cheatin' Bastards* not because of his statements about Guam (that's just dumb), but because of his attempt to portray his stupidity as metaphor. That's lyin'.

Johnson explains how he thinks Guam might "... tip over and capsize ..." The video is now memorialized forever on YouTube. U.S. Government video

The 7 Stupidest

Arguably all *Lyin' Cheatin' Bastards* are stupid, but these seven deserve special recognition:

1. Hank Johnson (#57)
Thought the island of Guam might tip over.

2. Eliot Spitzer (#11)
Asked his bank if there was any way to secretly send wire transfers.

3. Anthony Weiner (#25)
Sent photos of his 'package' out on Twitter.

4. Vito Fossella (#47)
Called his mistress to get him out of jail.

5. Michael Duvall (#13)
Told racy stories while the mic was on during a council meeting.

6. John Lake (#35)
Tried to bribe his opponent to drop out of the race.

7. Chris Lee (#23)
Used his real e-mail while cyber-cheating on his wife.

56

James W. Holley (D)
Mayor, Portsmouth, Virginia

Score: 50.0

Recalled Twice

JAMES W. HOLLEY III WAS THE FIRST African American to serve on the Portsmouth, VA, City Council and the city's first black mayor. He was also the first Portsmouth mayor to be recalled from office and the first (and only) mayor in U.S. history to be recalled from office a second time.

Holley served in World War II, went to college on the G.I. Bill, held city office for 42 years, twice hosted Martin Luther King Jr. at his home and helped desegregate part of Virginia. But he has left a mixed legacy.

His first term as mayor was marked by abuse of power and ended in disgrace. After holding several city positions, Holley was elected mayor in 1984 at the age of sixty-one. Foreshadowing trouble to come, he took his election as an opportunity to get a vanity license plate on his Corvette: "Hizonor."

The combination of an expense account scandal—he used city money to pay for phone calls, magazines, and travel—and a piece of hate mail tracked back to Holley spelled the end of his first term.

After a heated debate over a high school closing in 1987, anonymous hate mail, complete with profanities and racist statements, was sent to black community leaders. Eventually, the letters were linked to Holley. His fingerprints were found on them—literally. He was recalled.

Remarkably, eight years later, he ran for mayor again and won—and he was reelected three more times.

In 2007, *Esquire* magazine crowned him one of America's best-dressed mayors, but beneath the old-school style, Holley was just getting old. In 2005, he gave a rambling speech at the State of the City address, forcing his aides to switch to prerecorded videos for speeches. In 2008, he declared that Portsmouth needed "a black hotel" to balance out the white hotel in town (which has his picture hanging in it and a ballroom that bears his name). The City Council was forced to revoke the eighty-one-year-old's driving privileges after he wrecked three city cars in two-and-a-half years.

Unfortunately, not all Holley's idiosyncrasies were harmless. His assistant, Lorraine Stokes, drafted a formal complaint against the mayor citing he was verbally abusive and required her to undertake personal tasks during workdays. She told WAVY TV that four of those tasks included shopping for a stun gun, printing labels for his socks, filling out sweepstakes entries, and canceling his subscription to *Playboy* magazine. If she failed to complete one of these tasks—like finding his favorite cologne at the store—Stokes claims Holley would berate her, saying, "If you have a problem with it, then quit you chicken! I am going to burn you out like I did the rest of them."

The City Council fined Holley $2,500 for what they deemed was a pattern of mistreating his assistants, and asked him to retire. He declined. But Stokes' complaint triggered another recall and Holley was removed as mayor for the second time, at age eighty-three.

Holley (right), pictured here with Democratic presidential candidate John Kerry (center) in 2004, may be the first African-American mayor ever to send racist hate mail to black community leaders. AP Images

55

Thad Viers (R)
State Representative, South Carolina

Score: 51.0
Resigned in disgrace

LADIES, FORMER SOUTH CAROLINA State Representative Thad Viers (R-68th District) is back on the market. But beware: If his past relationships are any indication, he's not good at breaking up. If you leave him, there's bound to be phone calls, stalking, and threats against future boyfriends.

Viers resigned from the South Carolina House of Representatives on March 21, 2012, saying he needed to focus on his defense. Stalking and harassment charges came down the day after his resignation. At his indictment Viers said, "I'm facing jail time and I've lost my political career over something nothing more than love letters." That's not exactly how his ex-girlfriend sees it.

Viers turned himself in to Myrtle Beach Police in January after Candace Bessinger told police she broke off their relationship six months earlier, but Viers continued to call, text, e-mail, and show up at her home and work.

She wasn't exaggerating. She gave police a three-ring binder that describes phone calls, texts, e-mails, and stalking after their breakup. A police report from the previous December records a detective telling Viers to stop bothering her. Bessinger also sent letters to Viers asking him to stop, as did her father and her lawyer.

"#11 WINE – Don't go to a gas station – but if u do – pickot (sic) the chepest (sic) & then try to sell it as expensive! It will improve ur skills."
—One of the romantic tips Viers posted on Twitter

The ex-State Representative has a history of bad break-ups. According to The Associated Press, Viers pleaded no contest four years ago to threatening to beat up a man dating his estranged wife. He paid a $500 fine for unlawful communication.

Although Viers has resigned from the State Legislature, faces harassment charges and has had his law license suspended by the South Carolina Supreme Court—all due to his disastrous personal relationships—he took to the cybersphere to offer romantic advice just in time for Valentine's Day giving tips on dates, gifts, and other topics. The mind reels.

Viers in court where he pleaded no contest to charges he threatened his estranged wife's boyfriend.
AP Images

He may just be worried about his investment. Viers reportedly paid $6,000 for Bessinger's implants.

54

Larry Craig (R)
Senator, Idaho

Score: 51.0

Did not run for reelection

Special Awards
Gay Anti-Gay Legislator, Tackiness

FORMER U.S. SENATOR LARRY CRAIG (R-ID) was arrested June 11, 2007, at the Minneapolis-St. Paul International Airport for "lewd conduct." Initially, Craig denied he was soliciting the police officer in the stall next to him, claiming he simply had "a wide stance" and was picking up a piece of paper off the floor. Later, however, he pleaded guilty to the lesser charge of "disorderly conduct."

Although Craig signed a plea that specifically stated, "I understand that the court will not accept a plea of guilty from anyone who claims to be innocent ... I now make no claim that I am innocent of the charge to which I am entering a plea of guilty ..." he later attempted to withdraw his guilty plea.

In an unusual strategy, his lawyer argued his guilty plea was "not intelligent." The judge, while quite possibly agreeing with that statement, denied the motion.

When his arrest was made public, Craig announced he would resign, but he later reversed his decision and finished out his term (he left office Jan. 3, 2009). He did not run for reelection. Post-Senate, he started a consulting firm with Mike Ware, his ex-chief of staff.

Craig has been awarded two special designations: first, GAGL Award because of his record of voting against gay rights and his holier-than-thou attitude toward his fellow *Lyin' Cheatin' Bastards*.

He was one of the original sponsors of the Federal Marriage Amendment, which would bar gay marriage (to protect the sanctity of the "union of a man and a woman"). He later voted against the Local Law Enforcement Hate Crimes Prevention Act, which extended the federal definition of hate crimes to cover sexual orientation. Craig joins a number of others in the not-so-exclusive "Gay Anti-Gay Legislators (GAGL)."

"I have a wide stance."

—Craig's explanation of why the undercover police officer thought Craig was trying to signal him in the next stall

(Top) Craig's mug shots from his arrest at the Minneapolis airport. Minneapolis Airport Police file photo. **(Bottom) The scene of the crime—the men's room at the airport.** Editor's file photo

In addition, he was sharply critical of former President Bill Clinton for the Monica Lewinsky scandal. Speaking on NBC's *Meet The Press,* Craig told Tim Russert, "The American people already know that Bill Clinton is a bad boy—a naughty boy. I'm going to speak out for the citizens of my state, who in the majority think that Bill Clinton is probably even a nasty, bad, naughty boy." Yes, he actually said that. It was recorded. (Clinton is not in the Top 77 *Lyin' Cheatin' Bastards* because his lyin' and cheatin' took place prior to 2000, the cutoff year for the list).

Craig's second special award is for Tackiness. It's one thing to fool around or steal money—half our politicians are engaged in such activities. But an airport bathroom? Hath the man no dignity?

Gay Anti-Gay Legislators (GAGL)

Everyone's entitled to their opinion. If you are anti-gay and vote that way, that's one thing. If, however, you're anti-gay and vote that way, but meanwhile are running around with other men when no one's looking, that's different. It's a special category of hypocrisy. All Republicans. Go figure.

1. Larry Craig (#54)
Solicited a male undercover police officer in the men's room at the Minneapolis airport. Sponsored the Federal Marriage Amendment, which would bar gay marriage to protect the sanctity of the "union of a man and a woman." Called Bill Clinton, "a nasty, bad, naughty boy."

2. Bob Allen (#22)
Solicited a male undercover police officer in a public park. Suggested they go to the men's room. Cosponsored (mere months before his arrest) a bill that would have increased the charges for, "unnatural and lascivious acts or exposure or exhibition of sexual organs within 1,000 feet of a park, school or child care facility," from a misdemeanor to a felony.

3. Richard Curtis (#16)
Dressed in red stockings and a black sequined top, Curtis met a man at the Hollywood Erotic Boutique and the two went to a hotel. Exactly what happened there is not clear, but it was almost certainly not a discussion of public policy. Curtis voted against a bill to grant civil rights protections to gays and lesbians and against a bill to create domestic partnerships of same-sex couples.

4. Phillip Hinkle (#48)

Responded to a Craigslist ad by a young man looking for a "sugar daddy." Ended up in a hotel room with same. Voted for an amendment to the Indiana State Constitution to define marriage as between a man and a woman only. Co-authored the bill that created a new license plate, "In God We Trust."

5. Ed Schrock (#30)

Called a male prostitution service and left a message: "Uh, hi, I weigh 200 pounds, uh, six-foot-four, hazel eyes, blond hair, very muscular, very buffed-up, uh, very tanned, um, I'd just like to get together with a guy from time to time just to—just to play." Cosponsored 2004's Federal Marriage Amendment that aimed to constitutionally ban gay marriage and oppose other rights for gay citizens, including non-discrimination in employment.

6. Roy Ashburn (#68)

Arrested for drunk driving leaving a gay club and forced to come out in 2010. Equality California Director Geoff Kors said, "He has voted against every LGBT rights bill that's been introduced in California since he's been in the office." His record includes voting against a resolution to oppose Prop 8, the anti-gay marriage ballot, and voting against recognizing out-of-state same-sex marriages.

7. James West (#61)

Caught in a sting operation when the local paper figured out he was Cobra82 on gay.com. Known as an anti-gay legislator, he supported one bill that would have banned gays and lesbians from working in schools or day care centers. Claimed he was representing the views of his constituents, not his own. On *The Today Show* he explained his support for anti-gay laws: If someone hires you to paint their house red, then you paint it red. Even if you think it would look better green.

53

Claude Allen (R)
Special Assistant to the President

Score: 51.0
Resigned in disgrace

REPUBLICAN LAWYER CLAUDE ALLEN served as the assistant to the president of the United States for domestic policy under George W. Bush. Allen was appointed in January 2005 and supervised the government's response to one of the worst national disasters in U.S. history—Hurricane Katrina.

One year later, in February 2006, Allen resigned his post, citing his desire to "spend more time with his family." But that wasn't the whole story.

A month after his resignation, Allen was arrested in Maryland for allegedly stealing more than $5,000 from Target and Hecht's stores in a refund fraud scheme. Allen was gaming the system.

According to the police's initial reports to the media, Allen was caught on camera at a Target store on Jan. 2, 2006, putting merchandise from a shelf into his bag. He then walked to the customer service desk and requested a refund. A store employee stopped him, police were called to the scene, and he was charged with a misdemeanor.

The misdemeanor charge was dropped when detectives realized it wasn't an isolated case. As it turned out, Allen had developed an elaborate scheme. He would purchase an item and bring it out to his car. He would then return to the store, select the same item from a shelf and "return" the item to receive a refund based on his receipt for the item sitting out in his car, thereby getting the item for free.

Investigators found Allen had sought $5,000 in fraudulent refunds during the year he was working for the Bush administration, for items ranging from a Bose home theater system to things worth as little as $2.50.

In March 2006—one month after his resignation and two months after the original misdemeanor charge—Allen was arrested in Maryland on two counts: felony

Allen leaves court with wife Jannese after pleading guilty to charges of theft.
AP Images

theft scheme and theft over $500. Each charge carried with it a possible fifteen years in prison. Allen's salary at the time was $161,000.

Four months later Allen pleaded guilty to a single count of misdemeanor theft in a plea deal that required him to pay a $500 fine, reimburse Target for $850 in stolen merchandise, and perform forty hours of community service in lieu of jail time. The judge also ordered Allen to complete two years of supervised probation. According to the terms of the deal, after successfully completing the two-year probation and paying the fines, Allen's record would be expunged and he could continue practicing law.

Allen's lawyer, Gregory B. Craig, said in a statement that the judge's probation sentence showed the bar association that "this court believes that Claude Allen has a future in our profession, as a respected member of the bar." Well, of course. Why would something as silly as a criminal record exclude someone from the legal profession?

But what would cause a man with a high-level job in Washington, D.C., and a salary of more than $160,000 to steal from Target? Allen insisted it was a potent mix of sleep deprivation, family problems, and stress. "Something did go terribly wrong," Allen said in court. "I lost perspective and failed to restrain myself. At the time, I did not fully appreciate what was going on."

In September 2011, Allen's law license was suspended in D.C. for one year after an ethics action brought by the D.C. Office of Bar Counsel decided the suspension was necessary due to the "dishonesty, fraud and deceit" surrounding the thefts. Nevertheless, the Bar found Allen's actions did not amount to moral turpitude, defined as a "gross violation of standards of moral conduct," for which attorneys are often disbarred. Lucky for him, his actions constituted only moral "stupitude," so he just has to sit out for a while until everyone forgets what an idiot he is.

52

Sharpe James (D)
State Senator, New Jersey

Score: 52.5

Convicted
Served time

"SHARPE JAMES" MAY SOUND LIKE the name of a private detective from the 1970s, but it's actually the name of a former New Jersey politician. James served as mayor of Newark from 1986-2006, and simultaneously as state senator from 1999-2008.

In July of 2007, after retiring from his position as mayor but still serving as a state senator, seventy-one-year-old James was indicted on fraud charges. According to the indictment, brought by U.S. Attorney and soon-to-be-Governor Chris Christie, James used city-issued credit cards to pay for lavish trips for himself and a number of female companions, and to devise a kickback scheme that involved one of his so-called "companions," thirty-eight-year-old Tamika Riley.

The scheme, according to the indictment, involved steering cheap properties to Riley, who then resold them for a steep profit. This wasn't ordinary flipping though—James directed the properties to Riley under a redevelopment program that allowed developers to buy devastated city land and rehabilitate it. Riley allegedly did no rehab to the properties, yet sold them for up to $619,000 more than she paid for them. In return, she accompanied James on trips, bought him tickets to events, and carried on a "relationship" with him.

The eighty-nine-page indictment also included more than 150 instances of James using the city credit card for travel and entertainment, adding up to roughly $58,000 in total charges, including $3,500 for a Labor Day getaway to Martha's Vineyard with one of his "companions," and $167 of "nightclub expenses" for two days in Rio's Red Light District.

James was convicted in July 2008 and sentenced to twenty-seven months in prison and a $100,000 fine for his role in the land-deal scheme. That's a long time to spend in jail at seventy-two, but far less time than the twenty years the prosecution was seeking.

Riley was sentenced to fifteen years for her part in the scheme and, even worse, had to face James' wife of forty-four years and his ninety-four-year-old mother in court.

James served nearly two years of his twenty-seven-month sentence. One of his corruption convictions was reversed in appeals court, but James had already served his sentence. The reversal of his conviction for "theft of honest services" was prompted by the U.S. Supreme Court narrowing the definition of the statute to apply only to cases of defendants taking bribes or receiving kickbacks. James' other convictions on fraud and conspiracy charges were unchanged.

Looking Sharpe. James leaves the courthouse after his indictment. AP Images

Bill Campbell (D)
Mayor, Atlanta, Georgia

Score: 53.0

Convicted

Special Award
Tax Evader

HE'S CREDITED WITH REJUVENATING the economy and bringing the Olympic games to Atlanta, GA, during his eight years in office (1994-2002), but those accomplishments weren't enough to keep former mayor Bill Campbell out of prison. He was convicted of tax evasion in 2006. At his sentencing, the judge praised his record but said he couldn't ignore his crimes.

A six-year-long federal investigation into Campbell's administration led to him being charged in 2004 with eleven counts of accepting bribes, tax fraud, and racketeering, including taking more than $160,000 in payoffs and $137,000 in illegal campaign contributions. According to the forty-eight-page indictment, the payoffs from city contractors included a trip to Paris, gambling junkets, and a free air conditioning system for his home. The *Atlanta Journal-Constitution* said allegations leveled against him painted "a portrait of a City Hall awash in corruption, bribery, fraud, obstruction of justice and illegal campaign contributions."

"We are here today because of a pervasive pattern of government corruption which victimized the citizens of the city of Atlanta and deprived them of the honest services of their public officials," said FBI Special Agent Gregory Jones when the indictment was announced.

Campbell emphatically denied the charges and pleaded not guilty. "The only thing correct in this indictment is the spelling of my name," said Campbell after his arraignment. "Everything else is false."

By the time his trial started in 2006, however, the *Journal-Constitution* reported that twelve other people targeted by the investigation had been convicted, including two top officials in Campbell's administration.

After a three-month trial, filled with more than a thousand pieces of evidence and nearly one hundred witnesses, Campbell was found guilty of three counts of tax evasion, but acquitted on four charges of corruption.

The *Journal-Constitution* reported that despite believing that Campbell had taken money from city contractors—at one point prosecutors said he used them as "human ATMs"—jurors weren't convinced from whom or how much, so they found him innocent of the racketeering and bribery charges. The tax charges

Campbell at the court house with his wife Sharon. AP Images

relate to Campbell intentionally failing to report nearly $150,000 in income over three years—income prosecutors said he got from the city contractors.

Campbell said after the verdict that he was vindicated. But the judge didn't see it that way. He sentenced him to two and a half years in prison. Campbell also had to settle the nearly $63,000 tax bill he owed the IRS. In laying out his sentence, the judge said he "was overcome, almost appalled, at the breadth of misconduct in your administration."

Campbell ended up serving a little over two years in a minimum-security prison in Miami, FL. According to the *Journal-Constitution*, he tried to shorten his sentence even further by admitting he was an "alcoholic." Being an "alcoholic" would gain him admittance to the prison's drug rehab program, which, upon completion, would shave four months off his sentence. When prosecutors heard about his ploy, however, they raised hell. Prison officials then determined Campbell was faking and tacked the four months back on.

He was released in October of 2008 and as of 2011, according to the *Journal-Constitution*, he was trying to reestablish himself in the Atlanta community. Longtime friend Tom Houck told the *Journal-Constitution* that Campbell deserved a second chance.

"He wasn't smoking crack in a hotel room like Marion Barry (#64)," Houck said. "He wasn't like the governor of New York (#11) who got hookers and ended up with his own television show. I am convinced there are a lot of people in this town who like Bill Campbell." Drugs and hookers bad—ripping off the government, not so bad.

50

Vincent Cianci, Jr. (I)
Mayor, Providence, Rhode Island

Score: 54.3

Convicted

VINCENT "BUDDY" CIANCI, JR.'S reign over Providence, RI, ended in 2002 when he was convicted on federal racketeering charges. The flamboyant "Prince of Providence" served as mayor for twenty-one years during two separate terms. He was known for talking tough, wearing distinctive toupees, and marketing a pasta sauce bearing his name. During his second stint as mayor in the 1990s, Cianci took more than $1.5 million in cash in exchange for jobs, leases, contracts, promotions, and other favors, according to prosecutors.

The ninety-seven-page indictment came down in April of 2001, following a lengthy corruption investigation nicknamed "Operation Plunder Dome." Federal prosecutor Richard Rose said during the trial that Cianci was the head of a "corrupt, criminal enterprise" run out of City Hall.

Allegations included taking a $250,000 "campaign contribution" from tow truck operators who wanted to keep working for the police department and threatening to turn the city's exclusive University Club into a "BYOB" establishment if he wasn't given an honorary membership (he held a grudge because they refused to admit him years before).

"Look, I'm no hero. Mother Teresa's not going to come and give me an award."
—Cianci after his arrest for attacking his estranged wife's lover

Cianci addresses the media after being indicted on charges of bribery and racketeering. AP Images

Cianci had a history of harboring hard feelings. He was first elected mayor of Providence in 1974. Ten years later, he was forced to resign after being charged with assaulting his estranged wife's lover with an ashtray, lit cigarette, and fireplace log. He pleaded no contest and received a five-year suspended sentence and five years probation.

"Look, I'm no hero," Cianci said of the event. "Mother Teresa's not going to come and give me an award." He's right about that.

While on probation for the assault charges, Cianci became a popular radio talk show host—but the call of the mayor's office was just too great. He ran again in

1990, and despite his criminal record he returned to City Hall, winning reelection by just 317 votes.

The former mayor's corruption trial lasted seven weeks in 2002 with more than fifty witnesses taking the stand. After nine days of deliberations, the sixty-one-year-old was found guilty on one charge of racketeering conspiracy while being acquitted on eleven other public corruption charges.

"I didn't do this stuff," he said at a news conference after the verdict was read. "I will go all the way to the Supreme Court, The Hague, wherever they want to go."

He went as far as the federal correctional facility in Fort Dix, NJ. He was sentenced to five years and four months in prison. At his sentencing, the judge compared him to Dr. Jekyll and Mr. Hyde. He said one Buddy Cianci was a "skilled and charismatic political figure, probably one of the most talented politicians Rhode Island had ever seen." The other Buddy Cianci, he said, "presided over an administration rife with corruption at all levels."

Cianci served four and a half years. During that time, Providence didn't forget about him—in fact, the city celebrated him. *The New York Times* reported that in 2006 The Providence Preservation Society inducted Cianci into its Hall of Fame. His life and career were also the subject of a book, *The Prince of Providence*, and a musical, *Buddy Cianci: The Musical*.

Some Providence residents told *The New York Times* in 2003 that they would love to have him back in City Hall. They said the new administration didn't have the same pizzazz. "He's a crook," one woman said, "but I'd vote for him again."

So far, Cianci hasn't given her a chance. Though he went back to Providence when he got out of prison in 2007, he took a job as a radio talk show host after a bidding war. He was voted the "Best Radio Talk Show Host" in 2008, 2009, and 2010. In 2011, he wrote his autobiography: *Politics and Pasta: How I prosecuted mobsters, rebuilt a dying city, dined with Sinatra, spent 5 years in a federally funded gated community, and lived to tell the tale.*

He's eligible to run again for office in 2012.

49

Tom Anderson (R)
State Representative, Alaska

Score: 57.0

Convicted
Served time

ALASKA DIDN'T BECOME A STATE until 1959, but it quickly became a major player in corruption scandals. "Polar Pen," the most notable investigation into political wrongdoings in the state, began in 2003 and resulted in the indictment of a senator and five current and former Alaska state legislators.

Alaska State Representative Thomas T. Anderson (R-19th District) was one of those arrested, charged with extortion, conspiracy, bribery and money laundering. According to the indictment, Anderson and a lobbyist created a fake company known as Pacific Publishing through which they funneled money back to Anderson. The company supposedly managed a website that posted articles on Alaskan politics. The bribe money was reported as payments for banner ads.

In the end, there was a certain poetic justice to it all. The bribes came from a private prison company and that's exactly where Anderson ended up—in prison—when he was convicted in July of 2007. He was sentenced to five years and did his time at a work camp in Sheridan, OR, and was released to a halfway house in February of 2011.

With his political career squashed, the new bachelor—his wife, Alaska State Senator Lesil McGuire (R-N District), left him in 2010—had to start fresh. Anderson joined his father's public relations firm as a general manager and strategist. According to the Optima Public Relations website, the former state representative "brings a wealth of advocacy, campaign management and political experience."

He certainly has public relations experience. Anderson did his own PR during his trial, though that did not go so well. It is not known how many clients have sought Anderson's guidance on public communications strategies.

When he's not spouting questionable PR advice, Anderson is on the Alaskan airwaves dissecting the moral fiber of current issues. He is the host of *Ethically Speaking with Tom Anderson*, a political radio show on Fox News Talk KOAN 95.5 FM. Here, the former state representative and felon discusses a plethora of hot-button issues, ranging from the race for the Republican presidential nomination to the necessity of the Alaskan Moose Federation.

Anderson and his attorney looked pretty happy leaving the courthouse after closing arguments—but when the verdict came in it was a different story.
AP Images

48

Phillip Hinkle (R)
State Representative, Indiana

Score: 60.0

Still in office

Special Award
Gay Anti-Gay Legislator

IF YOU'RE LOOKING FOR A COMPANION to talk baseball, the going rate is $80. At least that's what Indiana State Representative Phillip Hinkle (R-92nd District) paid a young man he met through Craigslist in 2011.

Hinkle denied he is gay, but responding to an ad by a man looking for a "sugar daddy" is an odd way to make a new friend if all you want to do is talk sports.

Conflicting reports from the two parties make it hard to pin down exactly what happened, but according to the *Indianapolis Star*, it went something like this: Hinkle responded to a Craigslist ad posted by eighteen-year-old Kameryn Gibson in the section for "casual encounters" between men. They exchanged a few e-mails, and then met at a hotel. According to Gibson, Hinkle had offered the young man $80 for "a good time," and in an e-mail "Sent from Phil's iPad," wrote, "For a really good time, you could get another 50, 60 bucks. That sound good?"

Gibson claims Hinkle tried to prevent him from leaving the hotel room, exposed himself, and tried to pay him off with cash, an iPad, and a Blackberry. Hinkle sticks to his story that they chatted about "baseball." He went to use the restroom and when he came back, Gibson was gone and had stolen the money, the iPad, and the Blackberry.

Regardless of exactly what happened, why was Hinkle paying a young man to meet him in a hotel room? Hinkle, who is married with two children and has a long record as an anti-gay legislator, offered no real insight into the situation. He told reporters, "I don't know what was going through my mind. I don't know why I did what I did."

Indiana Governor Mitch Daniels called it "a personal family tragedy." Indiana House Speaker Brian Bosma (R-Indianapolis), said, "If the circumstances are as reported, it is an extremely sad and disappointing situation for all of us, especially the families involved." The governor didn't immediately call for Hinkle's resignation, saying it was between Hinkle and his constituents—but other legislators, including Bosma, did. Hinkle refused to resign, claiming he did nothing illegal with Gibson, but said he would not seek reelection in 2012.

While Gibson maintained he didn't know what to do when Hinkle revealed himself—figuratively and literally—his sister reportedly took matters into her own hands.

Megan Gibson says she got a call from her brother when he escaped to the bathroom and that she went to the hotel to pick him up. After a confrontation with Hinkle, she made it out with her brother, Hinkle's iPad, Blackberry, and $100 cash. She told the *Indianapolis Star* she started receiving calls on the Blackberry almost immediately from Hinkle's wife.

"I was like, 'Your husband is gay,'" Megan said she told her. "And then she was like, 'You have the wrong person.'" After Megan read her the e-mail address, Hinkle's wife quickly changed her tune. According to Megan, "The first thing she said was, 'Please don't call the police.'" After Hinkle's wife offered Megan $10,000 not to say anything, she received a call from Hinkle, still at the hotel. When Megan said she had already told his family he was gay, he said, "You just ruined me."

No, Phil, you did that all by yourself.

Hinkle never could explain what he was doing that night. AP Images

Vito Fossella (R)

Congressman, New York

Score: 61.0

Did not run for reelection

Special Award
Stupidity

WHEN YOUR TEAM WINS THE SUPER BOWL, things tend to get a little crazy—especially if you're a Giants fan. U.S. Representative Vito Fossella (R-NY) got caught up in the moment on May 1, 2008. True, the Giants had won Super Bowl XLII months before, but the forty-three-year-old politician had just left a Giants' victory celebration at the White House.

After the five-term Staten Island congressman departed the "official" party, things got more interesting. Fossella went barhopping in downtown Washington, D.C. According to *The New York Times*, Fossella and his friend were asked to leave one D.C. pub because they were too drunk. What does a congressman do when cut off at a bar? Get behind the wheel of a car.

Thankfully, Fossella was pulled over by police for running a red light before killing anyone. *The Daily News* reported his blood alcohol content level at 0.17—more than double the legal limit.

According to the police report, Fossella "had a strong smell of alcoholic beverage," and failed a field sobriety test. The report went on to say, "he was unsteady on his feet, unable to recite a section of the alphabet." They tossed him in jail for the night and slapped him with a DUI.

But that's not the story. Fossella used his one phone call to get bailed out by the woman he loves, the mother of his child. Only problem? It wasn't his wife. It was retired Air Force Lt. Col. Laura Fay, a single mother raising her daughter in the D.C. area. Fossella was not only in town to celebrate the Giants victory, but also to check in on his secret family.

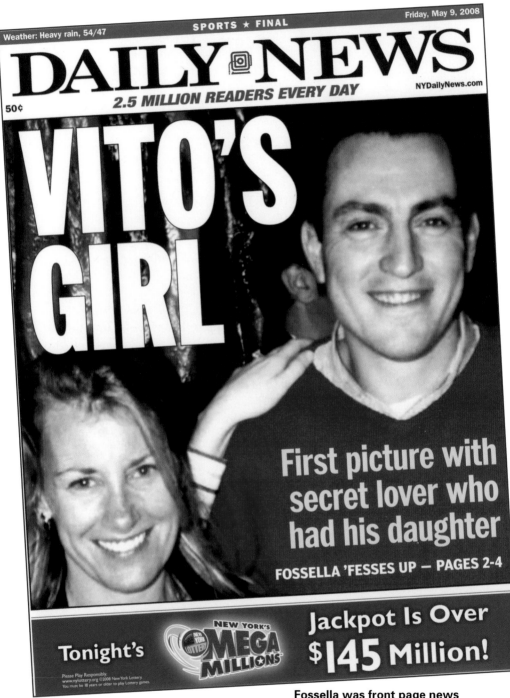

Fossella was front page news when his affair with Laura Fay came to light. Copyright *New York Daily News*

According to court reports, Fossella told the police at the time of his arrest that he was rushing to get home to see his sick child. He did not mention it was the child he fathered with his mistress, but then again, no one asked.

The bailout by Fay raised many questions, and a week later Fossella was holding one of those all-too-familiar press conferences where a political figure admits to an extramarital affair.

"My personal failings and imperfections have caused enormous pain to the people I love, and I am truly sorry," he said. He was probably referring to his three children and wife of eighteen years, Mary Pat, who was there, but standing nowhere near him.

He tried to deny the charges of blowing 0.17, claiming the equipment was faulty, but he was convicted, sentenced to five days in jail, had his Virginia driver's license revoked, and was forced to attend an alcohol education program. Nevertheless, Fossella refused to resign his congressional seat.

The sole Republican Congress member in New York City represented an area dubbed "the most conservative-leaning district in the city," by *The New York Times*. Fossella had always played to the family values crowd, but it turns out a mistress and illegitimate child don't poll great with a largely Catholic constituency. Republicans saw him as a liability and wanted him to resign, but he refused and served out his term.

For the record, Fossella was arrested in May 2008 and convicted in October. He "retired" the following January and reported to jail in April.

But even that wasn't the end of it. Fossella ended up in trouble with the Federal Election Commission (FEC), which fined Fossella $6,450 for failing to return campaign contributions. Once you say you're not going to run for office, you have to stop taking money from people to fund a campaign. It's only right. Fossella, however, had accepted more than $160,000 after he "retired," and as a result, the FEC stepped in to shut down his election committee and force it to return all the money.

46

Bruce Barclay (R)

County Commissioner, Cumberland County, Pennsylvania

Score: 70.0

Resigned in disgrace

WHEN TWENTY-YEAR-OLD MARSHALL McCURDY accused Bruce Barclay, Cumberland County Commissioner, of rape, police obtained a warrant to search Barclay's house. What they found proved he was innocent—but at a price.

When the police searched Barclay's home, they discovered a network of hidden cameras concealed in AM/FM radios, motion detectors, and intercom speakers. The cameras covered virtually every area of the house, including the bathrooms. Police also found hundreds of sex tapes. One of those tapes showed McCurdy having consensual sex with Barclay.

Matthew Gover, Barclay's attorney, said that the tape proved the accusation of rape was false. Reading a prepared statement, Gover said, "It is clear in my client's private life he has made an error of judgment. What is striking is this very same lack of judgment exonerates him from a rape allegation." Saved by his own perversity. (McCurdy later recanted his story and was sentenced to twenty-four months probation for filing a false report).

Vindicated, but humiliated, Barclay admitted he taped hundreds of sexual encounters without permission and that he hired prostitutes from harrisfratboys.com on a "weekly basis."

Barclay resigned when the rape charge first surfaced—perhaps knowing trouble lay ahead—but that would not get him off the hook. As a result of what the police found at his house, he faced seventeen charges ranging from invasion of privacy to wiretapping.

To avoid a three-ring circus, he opted not to have a jury trial and put his fate in the hands of York County Judge Michael Bortner. The judge heard from both sides before handing down his ruling: Barclay was guilty of two felonies and a number of misdemeanors. He escaped with no jail time, but was sentenced to nine months of electronic monitoring, eight years probation, $18,000 in fines, and 200 hours of community service.

In this real-life version of *Sex, Lies and Videotape*, the sword cut both ways.

Barclay did not want to talk as he left the courthouse. *Patriot News*

45

Peter Cammarano (I)
Mayor, Hoboken, New Jersey

Score: 71.0
Convicted

AT THIRTY-ONE, PETER CAMMARANO BECAME the youngest mayor of Hoboken, NJ. He also had one of the shortest terms of any government official in recent memory.

In 2009, he won a runoff election by 161 votes to become the city's new mayor. He was sworn in on July 1, 2009, with his wife and young daughter by his side. Governor Jon Corzine called him the new, young face of the Democratic Party and it seemed he was preparing for a long, successful career in politics.

Unfortunately, his career ended before it ever really began. On July 23—a mere three weeks after taking office—the newly elected mayor was arrested, along with forty-three others, in a corruption and money-laundering sting.

Among those arrested were three other New Jersey mayors, two state assemblymen, and five Jewish rabbis.

According to the FBI's investigation, Cammarano's exploits began when he was a councilman running for mayor. He accepted $25,000 in illegal campaign contributions from an FBI informant who posed as a crooked real estate developer. The informant promised Cammarano cash in return for his support of the informant's phony real estate projects.

The young councilman was so sure he'd be mayor he told the informant, "I could be, uh, indicted, and I'm still gonna win."

He was right. But after his arrest, he was forced to resign.

Like most other politicians convicted of corruption, Cammarano ran for mayor as a "fiscal watchdog and family man," according to *The Star-Ledger*. Turns out he was neither—he was taking bribes the entire time he was running. His wife left him after he was arrested.

Ultimately, Cammarano was sentenced to two years in prison after pleading guilty to charges of felony extortion.

Now thirty-four, Cammarano still has plenty of time to pursue a political career. Looking at the careers of Marion Barry (#64), Daniel Gordon (#67), and others, there's no reason to think we have seen the last of Cammarano.

Cammarano leaves federal court on July 23, 2009. AP Images

44

Paul Stanley (R)
State Senator, Tennessee

Score: 75.0
Resigned in disgrace

BORN-AGAIN EVANGELICAL CHRISTIAN and former Tennessee State Senator Paul Stanley (R-Memphis) "fell short of God's standard" (his own words). Stanley resigned in 2009 after an extortion investigation revealed he was having an affair with twenty-two-year-old intern McKensie Morrison.

Stanley was brought down by blackmail when Morrison's boyfriend allegedly got hold of photos of the senator and the intern in compromising positions and demanded $10,000 to keep quiet. Stanley confessed his sexual relationship to agents investigating the blackmail, but was planning to stay in office until the details became public.

As with so many LCBs, Stanley's legislative actions do not align perfectly with his personal actions. He opposed funding for Planned Parenthood, for example, because he said unmarried people should not have sex. (To be fair, he did not specifically say married people should not have sex with interns, but he did say, "When you're married, there's a commitment there.")

"Whatever I stood for and advocated, I still believe to be true," Stanley told Memphis radio station WREC-AM. "And just because I fell far short of what God's standard was for me and my wife, doesn't mean that that standard is reduced in the least bit."

Importantly, Stanley has learned from his mistakes. He offered this hard-earned insight to Politico.com: "There need to be some ground rules in relationships— you don't ever need to be alone with someone of the opposite sex after 5 p.m. or after business hours. There's nothing good that can come of it." Thus, not a failing on his part, really, but rather the inevitable outcome of circumstances beyond his control.

Stanley during an interview with WMCTV, says he has "moved on." AP Images

Intern McKensie Morrison says she regrets the affair and is praying for Stanley.

While Stanley did confess to his misdeeds, he told reporters that he was different from disgraced officials like Eliot Spitzer (#11) because his apology was genuine. "I never really saw them truly say they were sorry and ask for the public's forgiveness at the time. When you do that, people are extremely forgiving," Stanley said. "All of us have done things in our life we don't want things on the front page of the paper. But people are very forgiving when you ask. I know people are just very forgiving overall."

His wife wasn't very forgiving—she divorced him. Stanley currently works as the politics editor for *The Christian Post* and is writing a memoir (oddly) titled *The Extortion of Forgiveness.*

43

Paul Morrison (D)
Attorney General, Kansas

Score: 75.0

Resigned in disgrace

HOLDING A GRUDGE RARELY PAYS OFF. Case in point—former Kansas Attorney General Paul Morrison. He was forced to resign after only one year when he revealed he'd had a two-year affair with a former staffer. It might never have come out except he drove her crazy. She worked for the district attorney who Morrison hated and he constantly badgered her for information about him. When she could take it no more she filed a sexual harassment suit and it all came crashing down.

Morrison had himself been the district attorney for eighteen years before winning the attorney general's seat in 2006. He switched parties to run as a Democrat against his nemesis, Republican Phil Kline. Morrison beat Kline soundly, becoming attorney general, but Kline was given Morrison's old district attorney job, which upset him to no end. The *Topeka Capital-Journal* reported Morrison went as far as to send a letter to Kline's bosses suggesting he get paid $30,000 less than he himself had earned because Kline was not as qualified.

> "Infidelity is not a Democratic problem. It's not a Republican problem. It's a human problem."
>
> —Former Kansas Governor Mark Parkinson

Morrison and his mistress, Linda Carter, had been seeing each other about a year when he was sworn in as attorney general. She was a top administrator in the district attorney's office. Both were married with children when their affair started in 2005. That didn't stop them from having sex at the Johnson County

Courthouse and motels all over Kansas. Always the gentleman, Morrison rarely stayed the night and never paid for a room. Carter signed for the rooms and paid cash, according to the *Capital-Journal*.

As their relationship progressed, so did Morrison's demand for sensitive information on Kline's activities as district attorney, according to Carter's statement. She said he wanted to know details about criminal prosecutions and even tried to coerce her into writing letters on behalf of eight former Morrison employees who

Morrison announces his resignation on December 14, 2007. AP Images

got fired by Kline the day he took office. (They had filed a wrongful termination lawsuit against Kline.) Eventually, it became too much for Carter. According to the *Capital-Journal*, she told him to "Go home and make peace with Phil Kline." She also said that Morrison's "hatred of Kline was going to destroy him."

Carter filed a sexual harassment complaint against Morrison with the Federal Equal Opportunity Commission. In addition, she accused him of trying to influence a federal lawsuit involving a political opponent.

Morrison admitted the affair with Carter but denied any harassment or misconduct. He also said he would not resign—but he quickly changed his mind. He resigned on Dec. 14, 2007, telling reporters, "I have held others accountable for their actions, and now I must be held accountable for my mistakes."

According to former Kansas Governor Mark Parkinson, who was lieutenant governor at the time, Morrison's mistake is one that anyone can make—it's not confined to one political party. "Infidelity is not a Democratic problem. It's not a Republican problem. It's a human problem," Parkinson said.

It's certainly true for *Lyin' Cheatin' Bastards*—almost 42 percent (32 out of 77) of our subjects were caught cheating on their spouses (20 Republicans, 11 Democrats, and 1 Independent).

42

Jim McGreevey (D)
Governor, New Jersey

Score: 75.0
Resigned in disgrace

JIM McGREEVEY SERVED AS GOVERNOR of New Jersey from January 2002 to November 2004. He resigned when news broke that he had an affair with Golan Cipel, an Israeli citizen and a member of his staff. The revelations came after Cipel filed a sexual harassment lawsuit against McGreevey.

The then-governor and father of two came out in a press conference, saying the affair was wrong, but openly declaring he was "a gay American." His wife of four years stood by his side, expressionless. The two separated shortly after and eventually divorced.

An affair is bad for a governor, gay or not, but it went beyond just a fling. McGreevey had appointed Cipel as special counsel to the governor—a position that paid $110,000 per year.

When questioned, McGreevey's aides could not list the responsibilities that Cipel's new job entailed, but rumors swirled he was in charge of domestic security, a position he was clearly not qualified to hold (he has degrees in communications arts from the New York Institute of Technology). McGreevey reassigned Cipel to a position as an advisor on government operations when Cipel could not obtain a security clearance from the FBI.

In August of 2002, Cipel gave up his government position and McGreevey helped him land a job at a prominent PR and lobbying firm at $120,000 per year. The next month, just before the firm planned to fire Cipel, McGreevey helped him land a position at another lobbying firm. This one was run by McGreevey's best friend, and came with a $30,000 raise.

Instead of going ahead with his sexual harassment claim after McGreevey resigned, Cipel returned to Israel. Cipel's lawyers denied there ever was an affair and said Cipel chose not to pursue sexual harassment charges because "he only wanted justice and got it when the governor announced his resignation."

McGreevey's camp said Cipel tried to blackmail the governor and that McGreevey resigned instead of succumbing to threats.

After his resignation and eventual divorce, McGreevey began a relationship with Australian-American businessman Mark O'Donnell. In 2010, McGreevey graduated with a master's degree in divinity from the General Theological Seminary in Manhattan and requested to join the priesthood of the Episcopal Church. He was turned down.

With now ex-wife Dina at his side, McGreevey announces his resignation. AP Images

41

Amy Koch (R)
State Senator, Minnesota

Score: 75.0
**Resigned position as majority leader
Still in office**

ONE OF THE MOST POWERFUL women in Minnesota politics was forced
to resign her leadership post in 2011 after she was caught sleeping with a staffer.

State Senator Amy Koch (R-19th District) was the first female senate majority
leader in Minnesota history. She was credited with helping Republicans take back
control of the Senate in 2010 for the first time in nearly forty years. But apparently she couldn't control herself when it came to her communications chief
Michael Brodkorb. Forty-year-old Koch is married and has a teenage daughter.

She was first elected to office in 2005 and had been majority leader for less than
a year when word of her affair with Brodkorb spread through the legislature,
setting off an investigation by Senate leaders. Four of her colleagues confronted
her in December of 2011 about the inappropriate relationship.

"We don't want the Minnesota Senate to have that kind of work environment for
our employees," Deputy Senate Majority Leader Geoff Michel (R-41st District)
told reporters at a news conference after Koch's resignation was announced. "And
so that's why we felt we had to act."

According to the Minnesota *StarTribune*, Koch neither confirmed nor denied the
allegations during the meeting.

"Her response to the conversation was ... 'I think I need to consider resigning,'"
Assistant Senate Majority Leader David Hann (R-42nd District) told the
StarTribune after their meeting with Koch.

On Dec. 15, 2011, Koch said she would not seek reelection and resigned from her
leadership post immediately, ending one of the shortest terms as majority leader
since the 1930s. According to Minnesota Public Radio, Koch's resignation letter

did not mention the affair—instead, she said she was "resigning because she felt it was time, that she wanted 'to explore some other options' and spend time with her daughter."

The day after Koch resigned, Brodkorb was fired. He is threatening to sue the Senate for more than half a million dollars for defamation and illegal termination based on gender discrimination. He told *The Huffington Post* that there are plenty of female staffers who had affairs with legislators and were not let go.

Less than a week after she quit her post, Koch issued a statement, admitting to the affair and apologizing for her behavior.

"I have made some mistakes and errors in judgment, for which I am deeply sorry, by engaging in a relationship with a Senate staffer," Koch

Koch immediately resigned her position as Majority Leader when it was revealed she was having an affair with a staffer. AP Images

wrote. "I regret more than words can express the hurt that I have caused to the people that I love, and to those who have worked and served with me over the past years."

A big proponent of family values, Koch did not live up to her own words.

40

Mark Foley (R)
Congressman, Florida

Score: 75.0

Resigned in disgrace

Special Award
Hypocrite

HE WASN'T CHEATING ON HIS WIFE. That's about all that can be said for former U.S. Representative Mark Foley (R-FL), who resigned Sept. 29, 2006, after being questioned about inappropriate e-mails and IMs (instant messages) sent to underage boys.

Six weeks before the 2006 congressional elections, ABC News reported e-mail messages and IMs of a sexual nature had surfaced between Foley and a former congressional page. These communications included queries such as, "How my favorite young stud doing?" and, "Did you spank it this weekend yourself?"

Foley stepped down immediately once the risqué messages came out—no surprise, since more pages stepped forward with allegations of inappropriate communications dating back several years.

> **"Did you spank it this weekend yourself?"**
>
> —Foley in an IM to a male congressional page

Just months before the accusations surfaced, Foley had introduced legislation to protect children from exploitation over the Internet. In his role as chairman of the Missing and Exploited Children's Caucus, Foley spoke before Congress in 2004, and decried the Internet as "a new medium for pedophiles to reach out to our most vulnerable citizens—America's children."

When the House passed the Children's Safety Act in 2005, Foley said, "We track library books better than we do sexual predators." For someone so concerned with tracking pedophiles on the Internet, he didn't do a very good job of hiding his tracks with the AOL screen name MAF54 (Mark Adam Foley, born 1954).

Foley's fondness for the pages (who entered the congressional page program as high school juniors) seems to have been an open secret. According to *The Washington Post*, a former page said he knew of "three or four" pages from his 2001-2002 class who were sent inappropriate messages. The former page said he remembered saying at a 2003 reunion, "If this gets out, it will destroy him."

According to CNN, some members of Congress may also have known about Foley's interactions with pages long before the messages were revealed to the public. In the weeks following Foley's resignation, conflicting statements were released regarding who knew what, and when. According to MSNBC, an internal report from House Speaker J. Dennis Hastert's office claims his staff knew about "overly friendly" e-mail messages only in the fall of 2005. Foley's former top aide, however, said he told Hastert's chief of staff about the former congressman's behavior in 2002 or 2003.

U.S. Representative John Shimkus (R-IL), who oversaw the congressional page program, said he learned about Foley's e-mails in late 2005 and "took immediate

In an interview two years after the scandal, Foley still could not explain why he sent inappropriate text messages to underage pages. AP Images

action to investigate the matter." Apparently his idea of "immediate action" was to tell Foley "to be especially mindful of his conduct."

After Foley's resignation, top Republican leadership—Majority Leader John Boehner, Hastert, and Majority Whip Roy Blunt of Missouri—released a statement calling for a full investigation of Foley's misconduct. "[Foley's] immediate resignation must now be followed by the full weight of the criminal justice system."

Foley was investigated by the House Ethics Committee, the FBI, the Justice Department and the Florida Department of Law Enforcement (FDLE), but no criminal charges were filed. According to FDLE Commissioner Gerald Bailey, "FDLE conducted as thorough and comprehensive [an] investigation as possible considering Congress and Mr. Foley denied us access to critical data. Should additional information arise which is pertinent to this case, we will ensure it is appropriately investigated."

After a nine-week investigation, a bipartisan four-member House Ethics subcommittee issued a report that recommended no disciplinary action be taken against the congressmen or senior staffers for their roles in the Foley scandal. The report did take congressional leadership to task for not being more proactive regarding rumors surrounding Foley's behavior. "Some may have been concerned that raising the issue too aggressively might have risked exposing Foley's homosexuality. ... There is some evidence that political considerations played a role in decisions that were made by persons in both parties." The incident says as much about Congress as it does about Foley.

Foley tried to return to the spotlight with a talk radio show titled *Inside the Mind of Mark Foley*, but apparently that wasn't a place anyone wanted to go and the show was cancelled.

Online is Forever

Even kids know better—be careful what you post on the Internet; it will come back to haunt you. Many *Lyin' Cheatin' Bastards* are just learning that lesson—the hard way.

1. Anthony Weiner (#25)
Anyone who uses Twitter has accidentally sent a message to the wrong person, but it's usually not as serious a mistake as Anthony Weiner's. In what appeared to be a direct message gone wrong, a picture of his 'package' was sent out, then quickly deleted. Now the entire world is familiar with Weiner's, well, you know.

2. Carmen Kontur-Gronquist (Poor Judgment)
While we sympathize with her fitness goals and her search for love, she wasn't thinking. Even though her name and town weren't listed on her MySpace profile that hosted racy photos of her on a fire truck, *of course* someone printed them off and shared them with the entire town/world.

3. Hank Johnson (#57)
The House Armed Services Committee tried to help: They deleted the video of Johnson talking about Guam tipping over from the official record, but it doesn't matter. It's on YouTube. And always will be.

4. Chris Lee (#23)

Here's the thing about e-mail: you have a copy, and so does your recipient. Chris Lee seemed to have forgotten that crucial fact when corresponding with potential girlfriends on Craigslist. Lucky for us, one lady sent all of her e-mails from Lee (including shirtless pics) to Gawker. He might have gotten away with it if he had used a fake name. Too late now.

5. Mark Foley (#40)

Text messages do not just disappear into the ether. IMing underage boys about sex leaves a record. And in Foley's case, his signature. His screenname? His initials and his age: MAF54.

6. James West (#61)

While West was supporting legislation to keep gays from working in schools or daycares, he was flushed out because he had an online handle on gay.com: Cobra82.

7. Mark Sanford (#26)

Sanford's e-mails to his Argentinian mistress are just a one facet of the saga, but they're keepers. In one e-mail that has since gone around the world, Sanford waxes romantically about his then-mistress, Maria Chapur, "... the curve of your hips, the erotic beauty of you holding yourself (or two magnificent parts of yourself) in the faded glow of night's light ..."

39

John Ensign (R)
Senator, Nevada

Score: 75.9
Resigned in disgrace

U.S. SENATOR JOHN ENSIGN (R-NV) won his Senate seat in 2001 and served until 2011—when he resigned in disgrace amid an ethics investigation related to an extramarital affair.

Ensign was a staunch advocate of traditional values. He opposed gay marriage, and called for President Bill Clinton's resignation after his affair with Monica Lewinsky came to light, saying Clinton had "no credibility left." In 2004, Ensign spoke to the Senate about the Federal Marriage Amendment and said, "Marriage is the cornerstone on which our society was founded. For those who say that the Constitution is so sacred that we cannot or should not adopt the Federal Marriage Amendment, I would simply point out that marriage, and the sanctity of that institution, predates the American Constitution and the founding of our nation."

Turns out he was talking about other people's marriages, not his own. In November 2007, he began an affair with his political treasurer, Cynthia Hampton. Cynthia's husband, Doug, was Ensign's administrative assistant. Cynthia, Doug, and the Ensign family were close friends—Cynthia and Ensign's wife Darlene were friends from high school and the couples often vacationed together with their children.

On Dec. 23, 2007, Doug Hampton discovered what was going on. The next day, Christmas Eve, the couples met to talk things over. Ensign promised to stop the affair, and the couples met up with their children and celebrated Christmas together (that must have been a tension-filled dinner).

Despite his promises to the contrary, Ensign continued to pursue Cynthia. In January 2008, he began calling her again. According to the Senate ethics report, Cynthia pleaded with Ensign to stop, but he persisted. At the National Prayer Breakfast in Washington, D.C., he told Cynthia he wanted to marry her.

Doug discovered that the affair had resumed while on a congressional trip with Ensign in Iraq in early February. During the four-day trip, Ensign made $1,000 worth of calls to Cynthia back in the United States. He tried to disguise the calls by referring to Cynthia as "Aunt Judy," but fooled no one.

Ensign, with his wife Darlene at his side, announces he will not run for reelection after the scandal broke. AP Images

Back in the United States, Doug confronted Ensign again. This time, Ensign confessed his love for Cynthia and, in what can only be called an act of poor sportsmanship, fired Doug. Ensign told his wife about his feelings, and then moved out of their home and in with his parents. Ensign bought secret cell phones and created fake e-mail addresses he used to correspond with Cynthia. She entered therapy.

All of this happened out of the public eye. But in June of 2009, Doug Hampton threatened to tell the media everything. But Ensign beat him to the punch and did it himself. "Last year, I had an affair. I violated the vows of my marriage. It's absolutely the worst thing I've ever done in my life," Ensign told the media in the press conference in mid-June 2009.

Unfortunately, there was more going on than just an affair. According to the Senate Ethics Committee's report, Ensign helped Doug Hampton get a job as a lobbyist with a consulting firm run by Ensign's top political advisors. Hampton alleged Ensign helped him line up his first lobbying clients, who all happened to be donors to Ensign's political committees. The report also found Ensign's wealthy parents paid the Hamptons $96,000 after he fired them. The money was labeled gift income for tax purposes, "the precise amount legally permissible without triggering taxes," according to *The Washington Post*.

Ensign resigned in April 2011, one month before the results of the ethics investigation were released.

A Justice Department investigation into possible criminal activity by Ensign resulted in no charges. Doug Hampton, however, was indicted and arraigned on seven counts of violating the one-year ban on lobbying imposed on senior congressional staffers after terminating their employment.

Cynthia and Doug Hampton divorced, and Cynthia filed for personal bankruptcy. She described her life as "ruined" in the Senate Ethics Committee report. Incredibly, the Ensigns are still married.

Amy Brewer (I)
Mayor, Milford, Ohio

Score: 75.0
Resigned in disgrace

Special Award
Caught on Tape

MILFORD, OH, IS A SMALL TOWN just outside Cincinnati. The city website boasts attractions like the Frontier Days festival and recreational activities on the Little Miami River. Small-town life may have gotten too cozy, however, when Milford police officer Russell Kenney was suspended for having sex with the town's mayor while on duty.

Amy Brewer joined the Milford City Council in 2005 and was elected mayor in January 2010. A few months later in May 2010, a police investigation revealed Kenney and Brewer met several times for sex while the officer was on night duty between November 2009 and mid-January 2011. At first, both parties denied the affair, but when confronted with GPS tracking reports and audio recordings from Kenney's car, they realized they had been caught red-handed.

Compared to some of the tawdry sexual encounters detailed elsewhere in this book, their affair seems almost sweet. Nevertheless, audio recordings from Kenney's squad car show their meetings were not about public safety. "I can think of a lot of little things I like to do to you ..." Brewer tells Kenney. There to serve, the police officer tells her, "... I like to have your legs wrapped around my waist, or my shoulders. It don't bother me."

Still, a *Lyin' Cheatin' Bastard* is a *Lyin' Cheatin' Bastard*. First and foremost, Kenney was on duty during several of their trysts and no one should have that much fun while at work. Second, Brewer and Kenney were both married—although Brewer was separated at the time of the affair, Kenney, not surprisingly, soon afterward.

When their relationship first came to light, Brewer intended to stay in office. "If I have done something in my personal life that has offended anyone or

103

Brewer explains the rules of chicken wing eating contest at the Quaker Steak & Lube. Mary Dannemiller

embarrassed the City of Milford in any way, I sincerely apologize. However, my personal life is just that, personal, and I am not going to comment on it further," Brewer said in a statement. "I will continue my efforts to make Milford a great place for everyone to live and work."

The people of Milford, however, weren't willing to overlook the matter no matter how hard she wanted to work. A week after the affair was revealed, Brewer resigned as mayor (although she will stay on the city council until her term expires in 2014).

"While I remain capable of doing the job as mayor, and it is evident that the council does not have enough votes to remove me from office," Brewer said in a statement, "I feel it would be in the best interest of the City of Milford and the citizens to voluntarily resign as mayor."

Small-town residents appear to be quick to forgive (once you step down). Milford resident Betty Henry spoke at the city council meeting where Brewer resigned. "I respect Ms. Brewer for what she did, for resigning," Henry said. "I feel hopefully that we can get things back on track."

A quick look at the Milford website indicates things are getting back to normal: The town was preparing for its 50th annual Frontier Days, featuring a parade and spaghetti-eating and frog-jumping contests.

37

Robert Levy (D)
Mayor, Atlantic City, New Jersey

Score: 76.0

Convicted
Resigned in disgrace

Special Award
CFA

ROBERT "BOB" LEVY SERVED as mayor of Atlantic City, NJ, from January 2006 to October 2007. He was elected by an overwhelming majority, due in part to claims about his military service. In his bid for mayor, Levy claimed he was awarded the Combat Infantryman and Parachutists Badges, completed Airborne School, served with the Green Berets, and was abandoned in the jungle by his troops for several weeks.

Not true. Though Levy served two tours in Vietnam, he was not a Green Beret and did none of the things he said he did. The mayor owned up to some of his lies on Veterans Day in 2006, saying he was an enlisted soldier but did not serve with the elite Special Forces unit. An investigation revealed Levy's claims about receiving the badges were also false.

Lying to your constituents about your military service is bad enough, but it didn't stop there. Levy filed a false report with the Department of Veterans Affairs in an effort to increase his veteran's benefits. It worked, and he pocketed more than $25,000.

It all caught up with Levy when the Feds figured out he was defrauding the VA. He couldn't take the pressure, and in late September of 2007 he disappeared. For two weeks, Levy was nowhere to be found, and speculation about his whereabouts swirled. His office released a statement a few days after he disappeared citing medical problems as the reason for his absence, but no further details were given. Atlantic City was left without a mayor.

It wasn't the first time. In December of 2006, Levy mysteriously vanished for eleven days. According to the *New York Daily News*, a political ally said he had a bad reaction to medication.

Levy not only made up part of his military record, he filed for benefits based on his fictitious claims. AP Images

On Oct. 10, 2007, Levy resigned. It was later revealed he'd checked into a rehab facility for help with dependence on prescription drugs.

The investigation continued after his resignation, and Levy eventually pleaded guilty to defrauding the Department of Veterans Affairs. He was sentenced to probation and a $5,000 fine, and ordered to pay back the $25,198 in extra benefits he received based on his false claims.

Despite Levy's admission of guilt, he continued to exaggerate his military service, telling U.S. District Court Judge Jerome Simandle he was a member of "the Pathfinders," a group that set up drop zones and made other combat preparations behind enemy lines. Although the Pathfinders are real—known for being "First In, Last Out"—there is no record that Levy ever was one.

36

Bob Ney (R)
Congressman, Ohio

Score: 76.0

Convicted
Resigned in disgrace

U.S. REPRESENTATIVE BOB NEY (R-OH) took all sorts of gifts from lobbyist Jack Abramoff—free trips, meals, concerts and luxury boxes at sporting events—all in exchange for his vote. After being named by Abramoff and others involved in the scandal, he pleaded guilty to conspiracy and making false statements. He was sentenced to thirty months in prison.

Ney was elected to the Ohio House of Representatives in 1980 at the age of twenty-six, defeating Wayne Hays, who had resigned from Congress in 1976 over a sex scandal. Ney served one term and was then himself defeated. In 1984, he was appointed to the Ohio Senate and managed to hold that seat until 1994. By then, he had a taste for bigger things and jumped to Congress, where he stayed until he resigned in disgrace in 2006.

> **"These mofos are the stupidest idiots in the land for sure."**
>
> —Abramoff in an e-mail referring to his clients, but he was the one who went to jail

During his tenure at the Capitol, Ney took on a number of tough issues. It was he (along with fellow U.S. Representative Walter B. Jones (R-NC)) who changed the name of French fries to Freedom fries at the House cafeteria to express displeasure with France's position on Iraq. Unimpressed by Ney's provocative move, a spokesperson for France's embassy in Washington pointed out that French fries come from Belgium, adding, "We are at a very serious moment dealing with very serious issues and we are not focusing on the name you give to potatoes." (It wasn't until 2006 that the name French fries was reinstituted in House restaurants.)

Ney (far right) at Carnoustie golf course in Scotland, a trip paid for by lobbyist Jack Abramoff (far left). AP Images

But Ney had his fingers in more than just fast food. He quickly became embroiled in the Abramoff scandal. Abramoff, a Washington lobbyist, swindled an estimated $85 million out of American Indian tribes that were trying to set up casinos and hired Abramoff to lobby on their behalf. At one point, Abramoff hired other lobbyists to campaign *against* his clients so his clients would pay him more to fight back. Abramoff did not think much of his clients. In one e-mail to Michael Scanlan (one of his co-conspirators, also sentenced to prison time), Abramoff wrote, "These mofos are the stupidest idiots in the land for sure." They, however, did not end up in prison, begging the question: Who are the real idiots?

Although Ney had pleaded guilty to several charges—admitting he received "tens of thousands of dollars' worth" of gifts from Abramoff—he did not immediately resign. Apparently, he thought that was just business as usual and saw no reason to quit. But even his fellow Republicans wanted him out and he was forced to resign on Nov. 4, 2006.

Ney's conviction triggered a domino effect and many corrupt legislators and public officials were implicated. He was just the tip of the iceberg.

In a brief statement to Judge Ellen Segal Huvelle, Ney apologized to his family and his former constituents and suggested that his crimes had resulted in part from alcoholism. He said he was continuing to "battle with the demons of addiction that are within me," and requested through his lawyers that he serve his sentence at a federal prison in West Virginia that has a rehabilitation program. He was sentenced to two years, six months.

But there is no need to worry about Ney—he served his time, he gets to keep his $30,000-per-year congressional pension, and he got his own talk radio show on WVLY. And if you want more details, the entire scandal is documented in the movie, *Casino Jack and the United States of Money*.

35

John Lake (R)
Mayor, Carneys Point, New Jersey

Score: 78

Convicted

Special Award
Stupidity

IN NOVEMBER OF 2006, JOHN "MACK" LAKE, mayor of Carneys Point, NJ, was indicted on charges of trying to bribe his opponent in the race for town committee.

The grand jury indicted Lake on one count of second-degree official misconduct and two counts of second-degree bribery. Allegedly, Lake approached his opponent, Anthony Rullo, at least twice and offered him paid city appointments in return for dropping out of the race.

The first position Lake offered Rullo was a part-time position with the Carneys Point Sewer Authority. The pay was a whopping $1,500 per year. Not surprisingly, Rullo didn't take the bait. Lake then upped the ante, offering his opponent a job as assistant to the township housing inspector at a yearly salary of $15,000.

Unfortunately for Lake, Rullo was more interested in a position with the town council than anything the former mayor offered him. Not only that, Rullo brought the offers to the attention of the county's prosecutor, who referred the matter to the state to investigate.

On Nov. 7, 2006, Rullo defeated Lake in his bid for the town council's open seat. Fourteen days later, Lake was indicted. In December 2007, Lake was found guilty on all counts. He was sentenced in April 2008 to three years in prison. The prosecution wanted seven years, but more than ninety constituents wrote letters to the judge in support of Lake, which the judge took into account during sentencing.

Attorney General Rabner said, "This case involves political corruption at its most venal and brazen. Lake basically told his opponent, 'You keep me in power and

I'll use that power to reward you financially.' That's the kind of cynical attitude that we reject and why we intend to significantly increase our resources to root out public corruption."

Once again, luck was not on Lake's side. In July 2009, an appeals court ordered Lake's sentence be increased from three years to five years, saying the original judge did not have the authority to downgrade the sentence.

Lake breaks down in tears as the judge sentences him to three years in prison.
Lori M. Nichols/*Today's Sunbeam*

34

Scooter Libby (R)
Chief of Staff to the Vice President

Score: 79.0

Convicted
Pardoned

IRVE LEWIS "SCOOTER" LIBBY SPENT many years in government positions, but it was his last—chief of staff and national security advisor for the vice president—that brought him down.

Libby worked for Vice President Dick Cheney from 2001 to 2005 but his career ended abruptly when he was indicted on five charges related to leaking CIA agent Valerie Plame's identity. The charges included one count of obstruction of justice, two counts of perjury, and two counts of making false statements. He resigned immediately.

On July 14, 2003, Plame's name was published in a syndicated newspaper column by Robert Novak, effectively ending her CIA career and putting an entire network of covert agents in danger.

Only eight days earlier, Plame's husband, former Ambassador Joe Wilson, had criticized President George W. Bush in *The New York Times* for claiming Iraq was trying to buy uranium from Niger. Wilson had investigated the matter himself and found the claims to be false, and his reports to the Bush administration reflected that conclusion. The outing of Wilson's wife looked like retaliation.

Ultimately, no one was convicted of any crime in connection with the leak itself (in October of 2003, Richard Armitage, the deputy secretary of state, told the FBI he "was the inadvertent leak"), but prosecutors went after people they believed had lied during the investigation. On March 6, 2007, nearly four years after the leak and two years after his indictment, Libby was found guilty of four felony counts of making false statements to the FBI, lying to a grand jury, and obstructing a probe into the leak. Three months later, he was sentenced to thirty months in prison and fined $250,000.

The lyin' may have gone all the way up to the president. At Libby's trial, evidence came out indicating Bush knew more than he claimed (he always maintained he was completely unaware of any attacks on Wilson by White House staff). In September 2003, Cheney wrote a number of notes for then-White House Press Secretary Scott McClellan, which Libby's lawyers introduced into evidence. One of them read, "Not going to protect one staffer [meaning Rove] and sacrifice the guy [meaning Libby] ~~the Pres~~ that was asked to stick his neck in the meat grinder [meaning the press] because of the incompetence of others." The words "the Pres"

Our little pal Scooter, shown here at the courthouse, wearing his big boy clothes. AP Images

are scratched out but clearly legible. The implication is that Bush is the one who tasked Libby with refuting charges the administration had misrepresented intelligence to justify the war with Iraq (throwing him into the battle with Wilson), and that Cheney felt Bush was sacrificing Libby to protect Rove (who had also confirmed Plame was a CIA agent in a phone conversation with Novak on July 8).

In a final turn of events, Bush commuted Libby's sentence because he "concluded that the prison sentence given to Mr. Libby [was] excessive." Bush did not pardon him of the charges and did not commute the $250,000 fine. Libby served two years probation.

Despite the commutation of his prison sentence, Scooter was disbarred until at least 2012 and his career tarnished as a result of the charges. Whatever his role in the Plame affair, he lied to a grand jury and deliberately misled investigators, which is certainly lyin', if not cheatin'.

Libby (and others) outed Plame, ruining the career of America's best looking spy. AP Images

33

Kyle Foggo (R)
Executive Director, CIA

Score: 81.8

Pleaded guilty
Served time

KYLE FOGGO BECAME THE HIGHEST-RANKING CIA official in history to be convicted of a crime when he pleaded guilty to wire fraud in 2008. He was sentenced to three years in prison.

The only charge to which Foggo admitted guilt was helping a friend secure a delivery contract, but prosecutors claim his history of misconduct spanned his entire career.

"Foggo insists upon portraying himself as a patriot. This is a self-image he cultivated throughout his scheme," prosecutors wrote, as reported by the *San Diego Union-Tribune*. "His ability to ascend up CIA ranks, despite a record of misconduct, demonstrates how good he was at deceiving others."

His big break came when he was running a supply base in Germany and was asked to build prisons to house terrorists after 9/11. His work was rewarded with a promotion back in Washington. Foggo was named the CIA's executive director in 2004, essentially running the operations of the nation's spy agency.

Slick, Foggo was not. He took advantage of his new position to award contracts to his childhood friend, Brent Wilkes. Foggo claimed the contracts were not granted inappropriately, but that he "needed something done by someone I trusted in private industry." "Trust" is an odd word to describe the relationship between Wilkes and Foggo, which included lavish vacations and expensive dinners paid for by Wilkes, not to mention the promise of a post-retirement job. Indeed, the original indictment against Foggo included charges of fraud, conspiracy and money laundering in connection with his dealings with Wilkes. Twenty-seven of the twenty-eight charges were dropped when Foggo pleaded guilty to wire fraud.

Wilkes appears elsewhere in *Lyin' Cheatin' Bastards:* He is co-conspirator No. 1 in government documents filed in the Duke Cunningham (#10) investigation. Two former CIA officials told ABC News that Foggo oversaw the contracts for at least one of the companies accused of paying bribes to Cunningham.

Jim Olson, a former CIA counterintelligence chief and one-time supervisor of Foggo's, wrote in an affidavit that he was "flabbergasted" when Foggo was named executive director of the CIA. "I was not surprised when I learned of his guilty plea," Olson wrote. "I knew Mr. Foggo was a person who was seriously flawed, ethically and morally, who would cut corners to achieve his aims."

Court records also spelled out Foggo's political aspirations. His plan was to run for Cunningham's seat after Cunningham retired. He knew he belonged in Congress—he was just practicing at the CIA.

Foggo turns away from the cameras as he leaves the courthouse after his arraignment on charges of corruption. AP Images

32

Tom DeLay (R)
Congressman, Texas

Score: 82.0

Convicted
Served time

FOR ALL THE SCANDALS FORMER U.S. Representative Tom DeLay's (R-TX) name has been linked to, he's only been convicted of money laundering.

In January 2011, DeLay was sentenced to three years in prison for laundering money related to campaign financing. He was sentenced to another five years on a second count, but the judge agreed to let him serve ten years of community service instead.

While DeLay insisted he was the victim of political persecution and "everybody was doing" what he was doing, prosecutors say he hurt his chances for probation by showing a lack of contrition. "I can't be remorseful for something I don't think I did," said DeLay, shooting himself in the foot.

Lead prosecutor Gary Cobb claimed DeLay's refusal to accept responsibility went against conservative values. Fellow prosecutor Steve Brand argued probation would give the wrong signal to other members of Congress and said DeLay's claims in his memoir that he did nothing improper were "the equivalent of a 'screw you' to the system."

He was also investigated for six years as part of the Abramoff scandal, but eventually the Justice Department declined to bring charges against him. Abramoff himself pleaded guilty to five counts of fraud and corruption and twenty people pleaded guilty or were convicted in connection with the Justice Department's investigation, including two senior aides to DeLay. Still, he insisted all of his dealings with Abramoff were above reproach, including the golf trip he took with Abramoff to Scotland, which was charged to Abramoff's American Express card. DeLay classified the trip on mandatory disclosure reports as "educational."

In the years between his indictment in 2006 and his conviction in 2010, DeLay published his memoir, *No Retreat, No Surrender*. DeLay used the book to assert his innocence. But defending himself wasn't enough and the former legislator, who earned the nickname "The Hammer" for his forceful legislative style, compared his liberal critics to Hitler. From the book:

"I believe it was Adolf Hitler who first acknowledged that the big lie is more effective than the little lie, because the big lie is so audacious, such an astonishing immorality, that people have a hard time believing anyone would say it if it wasn't true. You know, the big lie—like the Holocaust never happened or dark-skinned people are less intelligent than light-skinned people. Well, by charging this big lie [that DeLay broke campaign finance laws] liberals have finally joined the ranks of scoundrels like Hitler."

Comparing anyone to Hitler is idiotic, but DeLay has never demonstrated much common sense. While awaiting trial, he appeared on *Dancing with the Stars*, at one point dancing the ChaCha to "Wild Thing" while wearing a leopard print vest and two-inch heels.

DeLay, pictured here awaiting sentencing, still doesn't think he did anything wrong. AP Images

31

George Ryan (R)
Governor, Illinois

Score: 83.0

Convicted
In prison

FORMER ILLINOIS GOVERNOR GEORGE RYAN was found guilty in April 2006 on 18 counts of racketeering and fraud charges. Prosecutors accused him of abusing the power of his office, selling out the state of Illinois, and then trying to cover it up. They say he directed big state money contracts and leases to his friends and lobbyists while he was Illinois Secretary of State in the 1990s and then as governor starting in 1999.

"Basically the state of Illinois was for sale," said Patrick J. Fitzgerald, U.S. attorney for the northern district of Illinois, at the time of Ryan's indictment in 2003.

Ryan's favoritism was well-rewarded. He was given luxury vacations, lavish gifts, and thousands of dollars in cash. He was known for carrying wads of money, which he apparently got from his own staff. They would give him 'Christmas gifts'—cash stuffed in cards that said what a great boss he was. Janitors, receptionists, and other low-level staffers all "voluntarily" contributed to the annual collection. Being a conscientious boss, Ryan kept track of who gave what.

An investigation into corruption under Ryan began while he was secretary of state. A tragic, fiery crash that killed six children in 1994 led to Operation Safe Road and an investigation determined that the trucker who caused the accident had obtained his Illinois driver's license illegally. Employees were selling commercial driver's licenses to truckers, with the money going into Ryan's campaign fund. Prosecutors said the payoffs were in the thousands of dollars. Deeply concerned about the allegations, Ryan quashed the internal probe and fired the investigators.

Federal authorities got involved in 1998 when Ryan was running for governor. They began indicting state employees. Ryan repeatedly denied he knew anything about the matter.

"Was I involved in selling driver's licenses to people illegally? Hell no I wasn't. Would I have tolerated it? Hell no," said Ryan, according to WLS-TV in Chicago.

For some reason, voters believed him and he won the election. Nevertheless, his term was plagued by the arrests of former employees, friends, and close confidants, including his longtime aide Scott Fawell. In the end, seventy-nine former state officials, lobbyists, truck drivers, and others were charged. Seventy-five people were convicted with no acquittals. Ryan announced he would not seek a second term due to the growing scandal.

But he couldn't dodge his past. He went on trial in 2005 on eighteen counts of corruption, including lying to the FBI. He was convicted in 2006 and sentenced to six and a-half years in prison. He's expected to be released on July 4, 2013. Independence Day.

"He says he's going to jail with a clear conscience," Fitzgerald said when Ryan reported to prison. "Well, after all that's been proven ... it shows that some people just don't get it."

Illinois has had a string of governors who don't get it. The state is the only one to send four former governors to prison: Otto Kerner, Dan Walker, George Ryan and Rod Blagojevich (#3). That's a lot of lyin' and cheatin' in the land of Honest Abe.

Ryan arrives at the courthouse for his bribery and corruption trial.
AP Images

30

Ed Schrock (R)
Congressman, Virginia

Score: 85.0

Did not seek reelection

Special Awards
Gay Anti-Gay Legislator,
Caught on Tape

WHENEVER YOU COME ACROSS a vehement anti-gay legislator, look for a gay prostitute lurking in the shadows.

U.S. Representative Ed Schrock (R-VA) was a family values man. His twenty-four-year career as a Naval officer included two tours of Vietnam. Fitting that he represented Virginia's 2nd Congressional District, a conservative stronghold, home to numerous military bases and Pat Robertson's Regent University. According to the *Daily Kos*, Schrock tied Dennis Hastert as the second most conservative person in the entire 2003 Congressional class based on voting stats from the *National Journal*.

The married father of one was a cosponsor of 2004's Federal Marriage Amendment. The law aimed to constitutionally ban gay marriage and oppose other rights for gay citizens, including non-discrimination in employment.

The retired officer also favored ending the "don't ask, don't tell" policy; he just wanted to get rid of all the gays in the military whether they told or not. In 2000, Schrock told *The Virginian-Pilot*, "You're in the showers with them, you're in the bunk room with them, you're in staterooms with them. You just hope no harm would come by folks who are of that persuasion. It's a discipline thing."

> **I'd just like to get together with a guy from time to time just to—just to play.**
>
> —Schrock as recorded on MegaMates answering service

Enter Michael Rogers, who runs the Washington, D.C.-based website *Blog Active*, which reports on hypocrisy in the U.S. government over sexual equality issues. In 2004, *Blog Active* released a tape that allegedly featured Schrock soliciting sex from a male prostitution service.

According to Rogers, Schrock often used MegaMates/MegaPhone Line, "an interactive telephone service on which men place ads and respond to those ads to meet each other."

Schrock at the commissioning ceremony of USS Virginia. US Navy

The Washington Post notes the recording was from "several years" before it was leaked, but as soon as it was out, Schrock announced he was ending his campaign for a third term in Congress. On Aug. 30, 2004, sixty-three-year-old Schrock said, "In recent weeks, allegations have surfaced that have called into question my ability to represent the citizens of Virginia's 2nd Congressional District … After much thought and prayer, I have come to the realization that these allegations will not allow my campaign to focus on the real issues facing our nation and region."

According to rawstory.com, Schrock received a ninety-two percent rating from the Christian coalition, a one hundred percent voting record from the right to life movement, and a zero percent rating from the Human Rights Campaign.

The audio recording is available online, but be prepared—it's schrocking.

The transcript reads:

"Uh, hi, I weigh 200 pounds, uh, six-foot-four, hazel eyes, blond hair, very muscular, very buffed-up, uh, very tanned, um, I'd just like to get together with a guy from time to time just to—just to play. I'd like him to be, uh, in very good shape, flat stomach, good chest, good arms, well-hung, cut, uh, just get naked, play, and see what happens, nothing real heavy duty, but just a fun time, go down on him, he can go down on me, and just, uh, take it from there. Hope to hear from you. Bye."

29

Bob Ryan (I)
Mayor, Sheboygan, Wisconsin

Score: 85.0

Recalled
Facing Charges

Special Award
Caught on Tape

BOB RYAN DIDN'T FINISH HIS TERM as mayor of Sheboygan, WI. Voters recalled him from office after a series of escapades rendered him unacceptable to Midwesterners—and to basically all other people as well.

The first incident was a sexual harassment lawsuit involving Ryan and Angela Payne, the city's human resources director. Payne alleges that on July 9, 2009, while they went to dinner and then for drinks at a bar called the End Zone tavern, a drunk Ryan tried to kiss her and "repeatedly looked her body up and down," implying he wanted a sexual relationship. Payne made it clear he was not going to get to the end zone with her. When she was fired less than a month later, Payne claimed the sexual rejection was the reason for her dismissal. Ryan claimed Payne was let go for "unsatisfactory services"—sounds like semantics. In any case, in October 2009 Payne filed a sexual harassment and wrongful termination claim.

> **"I've heard she gives a hell of a hummer."**
>
> —Ryan talking about his wife's sister

According to the *Sheboygan Press*, "Payne said Ryan became 'extremely distant' after the incident, refusing to call her by name or speak to her directly, and rolling his eyes when she talked." The *Sheboygan Press* also referenced a letter Payne sent to the city which claimed Ryan told her at the End Zone that he had been getting more oral sex from "young girls" since being elected mayor.

The second strike against Ryan occurred on Sept. 22, 2009, when a YouTube video was posted showing a drunken Ryan spouting sexually explicit comments about his sister-in-law. In the video, the inebriated cheese head says, "My wife's

If you think his wife looks angry, you should see her sister. AP Images

sister, she's more fun than my wife ... she's got red hair, she's a little bit meaty around the edges, but I've heard she gives a hell of a hummer." Another patron had recorded it all on his iPhone. The video went viral, even making Jay Leno's monologue on *The Tonight Show*.

Ryan said he didn't know the video was being shot (clearly) and apologized in a press conference with his wife by his side. His sister-in-law was not in attendance.

Drunk in a bar, Ryan was caught on video talking about his wife's sister.

After the video incident, Ryan managed to lay low for a while, but in July 2011 a third alcohol-fueled scandal emerged. According to the Associated Press, it began as "a three-day drinking binge" at Elkhart Lake which produced photos of Ryan passed out face down at a bar and culminated in sexual assault charges.

A woman named Andrea was sitting at the bar of Siebkens Resort talking to a friend when she claims she felt two hands reach from behind her, touch her stomach, and grab her breasts. She asked a male friend for help and he immediately recognized the mayor, saw Ryan grab her a second time, and told the police he heard Ryan say, "he could do what he wanted because of who he was." Ryan's group carted the "very intoxicated" mayor who "reeked of alcohol and was very unsteady on his feet" out of the bar.

The married father of three admits to being at the Siebkens bar hammered beyond all reason, but denies touching the woman. Two witnesses confirm they saw Ryan grab Andrea. Ryan was charged with two counts of fourth-degree sexual assault.

A week after the Elkhart story broke, Payne's case was abruptly settled. Payne got $310,000 (of city/taxpayer money) to drop her sexual harassment complaint. Ryan and the city admitted no wrongdoing.

The weekend in Elkhart proved to be too much for Wisconsinites and they recalled him.

Conceding, Ryan said, "Our city is in good hands, I have nothing to be ashamed of." The first part of that statement may be true, but the second part certainly is not.

Ryan left office on March 5, 2012, but it's not over yet. If convicted on the sexual assault charges, Ryan faces up to eighteen months in jail and $20,000 in fines.

Caught on Tape

Almost all *Lyin' Cheatin' Bastards* try to deny everything when they get caught. It's harder, of course, when you're literally caught on tape.

1. Michael Duvall (#13)
During a break in the proceedings, California Assemblyman Duvall turned to one of his colleagues and started telling him about his sexual escapades. Unbeknownst to him, the mic was still on. One of his alleged mistresses was a lobbyist.

2. Hank Johnson (#57)
It's awful when you something really stupid like you think an island might tip over if too many people stand on one side—it's worse if it's video-taped. Johnson expressed his concern during an Armed Services Committee hearing which was recorded. The Committee has kindly taken the video off their website, but it's on YouTube.

3. Amy Brewer (#38)
If you're thinking of making out in a squad car, don't. Everything is recorded. Mayor Brewer initially denied she was having sex with one of the town's policemen until they played the tape. Eager to serve, he was recorded saying, "... I like to have your legs wrapped around my waist, or my shoulders. It don't bother me."

4. Ed Schrock (#30)

Left a voicemail for a gay prostitution service. Describing his perfect mate, he said, "I'd like him to be, uh, in very good shape, flat stomach, good chest, good arms, well-hung, cut, uh, just get naked, play, and see what happens, nothing real heavy duty, but just a fun time, go down on him, he can go down on me, and just, uh, take it from there. Hope to hear from you. Bye."

5. Rod Blagojevich (#3)

Famously caught on an FBI wiretap trying to sell Barack Obama's vacated Senate seat. "I've got this thing and it's fucking golden. I'm not just giving it up for fucking nothing."

6. Dianne Wilkerson (#7)

Hard to deny something funny is going on when you're caught on a surveillance tape stuffing hundred dollar bills into your bra. Turns out she had taken over $20,000 in bribes.

7. Bob Ryan (#29)

Drunk in a bar, Ryan told whoever would listen that his wife's sister was pretty hot and he had heard, "she gives a Hell of a hummer." Unfortunately, the guy next to him was recording it all on his iPhone. It could not have gone well when he got home.

28

Christopher Myers (R)
Mayor, Medford, New Jersey

Score: 85.0
Resigned in disgrace

BROKEN PROMISES OFTEN LEAD TO TROUBLE. Former Medford, NJ, Mayor Christopher Myers learned this firsthand in December of 2011, when he resigned after a male prostitute accused him of welching on a payment for sex.

Myers, a married father of two, had been mayor for ten years and ran unsuccessfully for Congress in 2008. He also worked full-time for Lockheed-Martin as vice president of international business development and traveled frequently.

It was on a business trip to California in 2010 that an anonymous man claimed Myers paid him $500 for a sexual encounter in his hotel room. The man said Myers set it up through rentboy.com, a website that offers escorts around the country. The *Burlington County Times* first reported the allegation in October 2011 after the man started a website outing Myers because he said Myers had gone back on his promise of a car and other gifts. The man never identified himself, but the website (which was quickly taken down after news coverage began) included an alleged photo of Myers asleep, wearing nothing but a pair of blue Calvin Klein underwear. Myers insisted the photo was fake.

"The Internet is a murky place," he told the Medford Township Council after the photo surfaced. "I categorically deny the allegation." He told the *Times*, "I've been down that road before, where a photo has been Photoshopped to look like something it wasn't." His theory was that someone sneaked into his hotel room and took the pictures while he was sleeping. But instead of trying to figure out who might have done it to clear his name, Myers brushed off the incident as if it didn't matter.

"I've been told to ignore it and not investigate," Myers told the *Times*. "I'm thoroughly disgusted at the lengths people will go to." He blamed dirty politics for the website.

This photo was posted online by a man who claimed Myers did not pay him the agreed amount for an encounter in a California hotel.

Many residents in Medford were thoroughly disgusted as well and called for him to resign. "He's such an arrogant son-of-a-gun that it would be justice if it were true," one resident told the *Courier-Post.*

He refused to resign, however, ignoring calls for him to step down. When asked by the *Courier-Post* if he was gay or bisexual, he said, "I'm not commenting on my personal life."

But the pressure got to be too much. He gave notice in December of 2011, two months after the sex scandal broke and just a week after he left his job at Lockheed-Martin. According to the *Courier-Post*, he'd been put on administrative leave by the company to "avoid workplace distractions," soon after the compromising photo was leaked.

He kept mum about the allegations in his resignation letter. After seven paragraphs dedicated to his achievements, he concluded, "At this time, I feel it's time to pass the baton, and allow others to take the reins and lead our town forward."

Probably a good idea.

27

Jack & Leslie Johnson (D)
Executives, Prince George's County

Score: 85.7

Convicted
In prison

MOST PHONE CONVERSATIONS BETWEEN husbands and wives revolve around mundane topics like "What's for dinner?" or "Who's picking up the kids?" not, "Should I flush the check down the toilet?" or "Where should I hide the cash?" But that's the conversation the FBI caught on tape between Jack and Leslie Johnson, former officials of Prince George's County, MD.

The two were arrested in November of 2010 on charges of destroying evidence in connection with a federal corruption probe. The FBI had wiretapped the Johnsons' phone because they suspected sixty-one-year-old Jack Johnson of accepting more than a million dollars in bribes while serving as Prince George's county executive. Fifty-nine-year-old Leslie had been elected to the Prince George's County Council a week before their arrest. Jack's term was ending due to term limits and according to prosecutors he intended to continue his corruption schemes through his wife.

> ## "Put it in your panties."
> —Johnson telling his wife where to hide $80,000 in cash

When the FBI showed up at their home following a five-year investigation, Leslie made a frantic phone call to Jack, not knowing the Feds were listening. Jack told Leslie not to answer the door. Then, according to the recording, their conversation took an almost comic turn. Jack told Leslie to destroy a $100,000 check from a real estate developer.

"Do you want me to put it down the toilet?" Leslie asked.

"Yes, flush that," Jack responded.

Then she asked about the cash they had stashed in their home—nearly $80,000, according to the FBI.

"What do you want me to do with this money? They are banging," Leslie said.

"Put it in your panties and walk out of the house," Jack instructed.

"I have it in my bra," she said. And that's where the FBI found it when she tried to leave. (That had to be an interesting exchange, but it was not recorded.)

Three months later, Jack Johnson was indicted on conspiracy, extortion, and bribery charges. Prosecutors accused him of running a "pay to play" game that had business developers offering bribes—everything from money, to rounds of golf, to mortgage payments, to campaign contributions—to him and other state

Johnson talks to reporters after his arrest on charges of witness tampering and destruction of records. AP Images

and local government officials. In exchange, Johnson steered millions of dollars in federal and local funds their way.

"I'm innocent of these charges," Johnson said after his indictment. "I just can't wait for the facts to come out. When they come out, I'm absolutely convinced I'll be vindicated."

Not exactly. He ended up pleading guilty to two felony charges: one count of extortion and one count of evidence tampering. Six other charges were dropped.

"Under Jack Johnson's leadership, government in Prince George's County literally was for sale," according to the prosecutors' seventy-six-page sentencing memo. More disappointing is that Jack had been the county's state's attorney prior to being elected county executive.

Jack was sentenced to just over seven years in prison, three years supervised probation, and a $100,000 fine. His lawyers asked for leniency, saying that he suffered from Parkinson's disease, but prosecutors challenged that claim, showing pictures of Johnson carrying his bag during a recent round of golf. Johnson is serving his sentence at Butner Federal Prison in North Carolina with Ponzi king Bernie Madoff.

Leslie pleaded guilty to one felony count of conspiracy to commit witness and evidence tampering and resigned from the county council. She was sentenced to twelve months and one day in prison and is currently serving her term at Alderson Federal Prison Camp in West Virginia. "Camp Cupcake," as it's called, is the same minimum security women's prison that housed Martha Stewart.

26

Mark Sanford (R)
Governor, South Carolina

Score: 97.0

Did not run for reelection

Special Award
Hypocrite

FROM JUNE 18 TO JUNE 24, 2009, no one knew where former South Carolina Governor Mark Sanford was. He told his staff he was hiking the Appalachian Trail, but he was, in fact, in Argentina, visiting his mistress Maria Belen Chapur.

News of the affair first broke when a reporter met Sanford at the Atlanta airport as he stepped off a flight from Buenos Aires. Realizing the jig was up, Sanford quickly held a press conference at which he admitted he had been unfaithful to his wife. Sanford, who was married with four children, was encouraged to resign but refused to do so.

After the affair was revealed, Sanford said, "There's been a lot of speculation and innuendo on whether or not public moneys were used to advance my admitted unfaithfulness. To be very clear: No public money was ever used in connection with this."

Except that when a reporter used the Freedom of Information Act to seek records of what public funds were used to pay for Sanford's trip to Argentina, Sanford elected to reimburse taxpayers for expenses he had incurred one year earlier while meeting Chapur in Buenos Aires. "I made a mistake while I was there," he said,

"If there's one thing that's abundantly clear, it's that I ain't running for president."
—Sanford at a Republican Party meeting

"meeting with the woman who I was unfaithful to my wife with. That has raised some very legitimate concerns and questions, and as such I am going to reimburse the state for the full cost of the Argentina leg of this trip."

It was certainly a steamy relationship, as their e-mails demonstrated. One of Sanford's read, "... I love the curves of your hips, the erotic beauty of you holding yourself (or two magnificent parts of yourself) in the faded glow of night's light ..." That was, understandably, too much for Sanford's wife, Jenny, who divorced him on Feb. 26, 2010.

Don't cry for me, Argentina: Sanford tears up during a rambling news conference in which he admits to having an affair, ignoring Andrew Lloyd Weber's advice. AP Images

In his defense, Sanford never claimed to be a cartographer.

Sanford has been awarded the Hypocrite Award because of his prior statements regarding people in similar situations. During former President Bill Clinton's scandal, for example, Sanford said, "I think it would be much better for the country and for him personally [to resign]. ... I come from the business side. ... If you had a chairman or president in the business world facing these allegations, he'd be gone."

Not only is that statement patently false—plenty of CEOs carry on inappropriate relationships with underlings—but blatantly hypocritical. Sanford did not resign, but served out his term, just as Clinton did.

Although never charged with any crime, Sanford pleaded no contest to thirty-seven ethics violations and was censored by the State Legislature.

On Jan. 4, 2010, at a Republican party meeting, Sanford said, "If there's one thing that's abundantly clear, it's that I ain't running for president." Good to get that cleared up.

25

Anthony Weiner (D)
Congressman, New York

Score: 100.0

Resigned in disgrace

Special Award
Stupidity

ANTHONY WEINER SERVED AS A U.S. representative for New York's 9th Congressional District from January 1999 to June 2011, when he resigned in disgrace. He was a golden boy of the Democratic party until news of his "sexting" scandal broke.

The saga began in May 2011 when a photo of a man's "package" was tweeted from his account. The tweet was quickly removed, but it was too late. The photo was captured and conservative blogger Andrew Breitbart wrote about the tweet on his website. The rest of the media soon picked up the story. Weiner's camp denied he sent the photo, claiming his account had been hacked.

> **"I need to highlight my package."**
> —Weiner in an e-mail discussing his wardrobe needs

When the media didn't let up, Weiner began to crack under the pressure. He lost his cool with a CNN reporter who questioned why he wouldn't refer the alleged hacking to the FBI. He called the reporter "a jackass."

It got worse on June 1, 2011, when Weiner gave an interview with MSNBC News. The reporter asked point-blank if the person in the photo was him. He replied, "You know, I can't say with certitude. My system was hacked. Pictures can be manipulated. Pictures can be dropped in and inserted." Weiner's refusal to deny it was him confirmed in most people's minds what they'd thought all along: Weiner had sent the photo of himself and thought he wouldn't get caught.

As it turns out, the photo of Weiner's wiener was just the beginning. A few days after Weiner said he couldn't be certain about who was in the photo, Breitbart said he had more incriminating pictures he planned to release. Hours later, Weiner called a press conference at which he admitted the photo was of him. "I take full responsibility for my actions," Weiner said at the press conference. "The picture was of me, and I sent it." Weiner admitted to inappropriate online relationships with six women over the course of three years, including Meagan

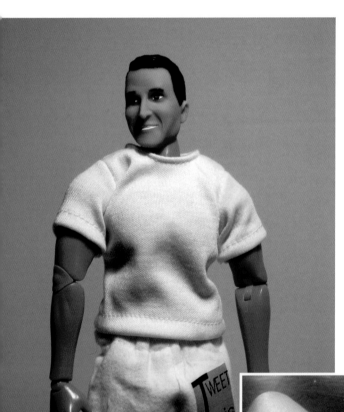

(Left) Weiner has now been immortalized with his own doll. AP Images

(Bottom) Weiner tweeted this photo of his "package" to his followers.

Broussard, who sat for an interview with ABC News, and Ginger Lee, a former porn star.

Days after Weiner admitted his indiscretion, it was revealed that his wife, Huma Abedin—deputy chief of staff and aide to U.S. Secretary of State Hillary Clinton—was pregnant. The couple had been married for eleven months when the scandal broke.

Top Democratic leaders called for him to resign. President Obama said Weiner should quit, citing his inability to properly focus on his job amid the scandal. Despite all the opposition, Weiner insisted he would not step down. "I am sorry, and I continue to be, but I don't see anything that I did that violates any rule of the House. I don't see anything I did that certainly violated my oath of office," he said at a press conference.

The straw that finally broke the camel's back was former porn star Ginger Lee's news conference. She told the media Weiner initiated sexually explicit talk with her after she followed him on Twitter, then asked her to lie about it once the scandal broke. According to Lee's lawyer, Gloria Allred, the messages often mentioned his "package."

"My package and I are not going to beg," Weiner e-mailed Lee, according to Allred. Another explicit e-mail said, "I have wardrobe demands too—I need to highlight my package."

One day after Lee's press conference, Weiner announced his resignation to a mixed crowd of media and hecklers. Former Speaker of the House Nancy Pelosi applauded the move, saying Weiner "made the right judgment in resigning," though he clearly showed little judgment in the first place. His wife did not stand beside him at his resignation speech.

It goes without saying that Weiner gets a special award for stupidity.

Stand By Your Man

Scandals can be hard on a marriage. Some survive; some don't. There are a lot of different routes to take when you discover your bastard spouse has been lyin' and cheatin' in front of the watchful eye of the American public. The response of spouses falls across a wide spectrum, but there's a general pattern of emotion from hot to cold:

1. Silda Wall Spitzer (wife of #11 Eliot Spitzer)
She had to be disappointed that her husband was screwing prostitutes, but she took it well. To some degree she blamed herself, saying, "The wife is supposed to take care of the sex. This is my failing; I wasn't adequate."

Status: Still married.

2. Huma Abedin (wife of #25 Anthony Weiner)
Still a relative newlywed when her husband got caught with his wiener out, Huma Abedin had been married just eleven months, and was pregnant—they all say the first year of marriage is the hardest. Abedin did not attend the press conference where he admitted to his online trysts, but she and Weiner have not divorced. They now have a son who will one day be able to Google his father's sexting escapades.

Status: Still married.

3. Mary Pat Fossella (wife of #47 Vito Fossella)
Arrested for drunk driving, Vito called his mistress, Laura Fay, to get him out of jail. Turns out they also had a three-year-old child. His wife, Mary Pat, attended the press conference where he owned up to it—but she stood nowhere near him. We picture her sitting somewhere in the back of the room, arms crossed, shaking her head, muttering, "Yea, tell them what you did you stupid son of a…"

Status: Still married.

4. Maria Shriver (wife of #72 Arnold Schwarzenegger)
When Arnold first ran for office a number of women came forward claiming he had harassed them, but Maria shrugged it off. She told Oprah in 2003, "I am my

own woman ... I look at that man back there in the green room straight on, eyes wide open, and I look at him with an open heart." But she had her limits. When Arnold had a child with the housekeeper, she left.

Status: Not yet divorced, but headed that way.

5. Dina Matos McGreevey (wife of #42 Jim McGreevey)

Jim McGreevey held a press conference and told the world he was gay. He informed his wife by cheating on her with a man. Dina stood with him at the podium, but it wouldn't last. She later divorced him and wrote a memoir (*Silent Partner*), and promoted it on TV shows like *Oprah* and *Good Morning America*. Speaking about that fateful day, she told Oprah "[McGreevey] said, 'You have to be Jackie Kennedy today,' And I'm thinking, 'Jackie Kennedy—her husband was murdered. You lied and cheated on me, and I have to be Jackie Kennedy?'"

Status: Divorced.

6. Jenny Sanford (wife of #26 Mark Sanford)

A manhunt for her "missing" husband revealed he was quite comfortable in the arms of his Latin American lover. When erotic e-mails between the two were released to the press, Jenny Sanford took her four boys and moved out of the governor's mansion. She divorced Mark, and in an interview with Vogue, said God would deal with him: "If you don't forgive, you become angry and bitter, I don't want to become that. I am not in charge of revenge. That's not up to me. That's for the Lord to decide…" Them's smiting words.

Status: Divorced

7. Leisha Pickering (wife of #59 Chip Pickering)

When your husband cheats on you with his college girlfriend and it results in the death of your marriage and his political career, one option is to sue that woman for ruining your life. And that's just what Leisha Pickering is doing. In Mississippi the "alienation of affection" law has a pretty good history of netting a decent bag for those cheated on. Looks like Chip should've used more caution, because Leisha ain't dickering around.

Status: Divorced.

24

Mark Souder (R)
Congressman, Indiana

Score: 100.0

Resigned in disgrace

Special Award
Hypocrite

MARK SOUDER SERVED IN THE HOUSE for fifteen years before his resignation in 2010. He was a fundamentalist Christian who kept a copy of the Ten Commandments on his desk. "Read the Ten Commandments and understand why some people don't want them posted," Souder said in a 2004 interview. "It's because they are a warning that the Lord is God, and do not take his name in vain, and honor him, and put no other gods before him. That is a rebuke to much of what happens in our society."

The family values representative apparently missed the seventh commandment: Thou shalt not commit adultery.

In May of 2010, Souder resigned after admitting to an extramarital affair with Tracy Jackson, a part-time member of his staff. At the time, Souder and his wife Diane had been married for more than thirty-five years. "I wish I could have been a better example," he said in his resignation speech. "In the poisonous environment of Washington, D.C., any personal failing is seized upon, often twisted, for political gain. I am resigning rather than ... put my family through that painful, drawn-out process ... by stepping aside, my mistake cannot be used as a political football in a partisan attempt to undermine the cause for which I have labored all my adult life."

One of those causes, ironically, was abstinence education. In November of 2009, Souder recorded a video with Jackson in which he discussed his appearance at a congressional hearing on the subject. In the video, Souder asserts there is no type of sexual education that works very well to keep kids from having sex.

"They [the Democrats] did have a number of witnesses that suggested that abstinence education increased teen sexual activity, increased teen pregnancy, even though there wasn't any evidence of that," Souder told Jackson in the video.

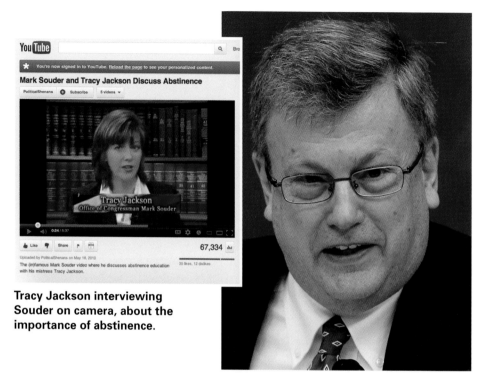

Tracy Jackson interviewing Souder on camera, about the importance of abstinence.

Souder wanted everyone else to stop having sex, but he couldn't stop himself. AP Images

Evidently, it increases sexual activity between Washington politicians and their aides.

In an interview with the Fort Wayne, IN, *Journal Gazette*, Souder responded to the issue of the pro-abstinence video he shot with his mistress: "Just because a Christian says something and fails does not mean their words are wrong. If you took that principle, you should never advocate something where you're doing less than you think you should be doing. But it hurts the cause."

Souder also said the fallout from the affair made him question if life was worth living, but that he was "not a suicidal guy, for religious reasons."

In an interview with the Christian *World Magazine*, Souder blamed loneliness for the affair. His family was back in Indiana for his entire fifteen years in office.

The 7 Biggest Hypocrites

They're all hypocrites to some degree, but here are the best of the best. *Lyin' Cheatin' Bastards* who have taken hypocrisy to a whole new level.

1. Mark Souder (#24)
Getting caught having an affair with one of your staff is not that unusual. What is unusual is that they had made a video on abstinence together. You can't make this stuff up.

2. Randall Tobias (#17)
As global AIDS coordinator, Tobias made organizations take an anti-prostitution oath before they could get funding—while on the other line he was ordering hookers.

3. Eliot Spitzer (#11)
While attorney general, Spitzer spearheaded the prosecution of two prostitution rings. There's nothing to add to that.

4. Chip Pickering (#59)
According to a lawsuit filed by his ex-wife, Pickering left her when his mistress, Elizabeth Creekmore Byrd, told him he had to choose between the two women. This after he had pushed President Bush to declare 2008 as The Year of the Bible.

5. Mark Sanford (#26)

You shouldn't cheat on your wife when you've made such a ruckus about other people doing it. During the Clinton scandal, Sanford said, "... I come from the business side. ... If you had a chairman or president in the business world facing these allegations, he'd be gone." Of course, Sanford didn't resign when his affair hit the news, he served out his term—just like Clinton.

6. Mark Foley (#40)

Not long before his inappropriate texts to under-age Congressional pages made news, Foley had introduced legislation to protect children from exploitation. He warned that the Internet was, "a new medium for pedophiles to reach out to our most vulnerable citizens—America's children." And then he proved it.

7. Tim Mahoney (#58)

Speaking of Mark Foley, Mahoney picked up where he left off. After winning Foley's old seat, campaigning under the slogan, "Restoring America's Values Begins at home," Mahoney, married with a daughter, had an affair with one of his staffers.

23

Chris Lee (R)
Congressman, New York

Score: 100.0

Resigned in disgrace

Special Award
Stupidity

THE INTERNET HAS CHANGED THE WORLD. News goes viral in seconds. What you could get away with a few years ago now will destroy you before you can say "Google." Indeed, 2011 brought us the fastest political resignation in U.S. history, and the smoking gun was not missing millions or a dead body—it was a photo of U.S. Representative Chris Lee's (D-NY) rock-hard abs.

In a sign of the times, the congressman went looking for love on Craigslist—just a "very fit, fun, classy guy," looking for a connection. Only one small problem: He was married.

Lee, also the father of a young son, posed as a divorced, thirty-nine-year-old lobbyist, sending flirty messages and half-naked pictures of himself to lucky ladies. One woman, Yesha Callahan, Googled Lee after receiving the racy snaps (who wouldn't?), to learn more about this brazen Casanova, and found that he had lied about his marital status, age—he was forty-six—and occupation—he was a congressman from New York.

Callahan turned over their correspondence to Gawker, which posted the e-mails in full. One gem came when, discussing their most recent dates, Lee expressed disbelief that people lie in their online profiles:

> **From: Christopher Lee**
>
> **To: [redacted]@yahoo.com**
>
> **Date: Sat, Jan 15, 2011 3:41:30 AM**
>
> **Lol... last Monday.... She was not as advertised. Lol... how do people think you aren't going to figure it out once you see them in person.**

Or when you Google them, Lee.

Initially, his camp had all sorts of explanations for the salacious solicitations, at first claiming his e-mail account had been hacked, stating, "The Congressman is happily married. The only time [he] posted something online was to sell old furniture."

Good times. Lee, with his wife Michele, staged a mock swearing-in ceremony a month before the scandal broke. AP Images

Lee showing off his abs.

But Gawker had done its homework and proved the "in-the-buff" photo was taken with Lee's government-issued Blackberry (tax dollars hard at work). Furthermore, the e-mail address Lee used on Craigslist matched the one he used to create his congressional Facebook page—which featured a photo of him and his wife and son. Three hours later, Lee resigned.

During its investigation, Gawker also pointed out Lee's inherent hypocrisy, "whose support for 'Don't Ask, Don't Tell' and vote to reject federal abortion funding suggests a certain comfort with publicly scrutinizing others' sex lives." In his resignation statement, the congressman said, "The challenges we face in Western New York and across the country are too serious for me to allow this distraction to continue, and so I am announcing that I have resigned my seat in Congress effective immediately."

What Lee did pales in comparison to what other politicians are up to, so one has to wonder why he threw in the towel so fast. Well, ten days after Gawker broke the story, two more people came forward. Lee had also conducted online flirtations with a transgender woman and a transvestite hooker. That would explain it.

Resigning was the only smart move made by a man who didn't even use a fake name to cybercheat on his wife.

22

Bob Allen (R)
State Representative, Florida

Score: 101.0

Resigned in disgrace

Special Awards
Gay Anti-Gay Legislator, Tackiness

EVEN THOUGH FLORIDA STATE REPRESENTATIVE Bob Allen (R-32nd District) offered to perform oral sex on an undercover police officer in a public bathroom, it's not what you think. He can explain.

"This was a pretty stocky black guy and there was nothing but other black guys around in the park," Allen said during his taped police interrogation, adding, "Oh, I'm about to be a statistic here." In short, Allen's defense was that he offered to pay the cop $20 to perform fellatio on him, not because he wanted to, but because this was a big scary black guy and he was afraid. Well, OK then. That's different.

The timing of the incident wasn't great for the seven-year legislator, who had recently been named a Florida co-chairman of U.S. Senator John McCain's (R-AZ) presidential campaign. The arrest also came just one month after U.S. Senator Larry Craig (R-ID, a fellow Republican crusader), was arrested for soliciting sex in a men's airport bathroom in Minneapolis (#54).

Timing was perfect, however, for Titusville Officer Danny Kavanaugh, who, according to *The Orlando Sentinel*, "was staking out a nearby condo hoping to catch a burglar," when Allen approached him. It should also be noted that it was 3:30 p.m. on a Wednesday. Why Allen wasn't at his desk working, no one knows.

Married, father of one daughter, Allen was also quoted in the police report asking, "I don't suppose it would help if I said I was a state legislator, would it?" as he was being put into the police car. "No," the officer told him, it wouldn't.

As a lawmaker, Allen worked to create tougher punishments and tighter restrictions for public lewdness. In addition to his "Sexual Predator Elimination Act"

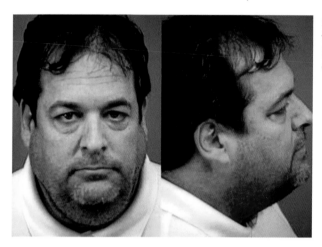

Few mug shots are flattering, but Allen looks particularly disheveled in his.

bill, Allen also cosponsored (mere months before his arrest) a bill that would have increased the charges of "unnatural and lascivious acts or exposure or exhibition of sexual organs within 1,000 feet of a park, school or child care facility," from a misdemeanor to a felony. Apparently, he wanted to get one in under the wire.

Allen publicly denied the charges for months, but on Nov. 9, 2007, he was convicted of solicitation of prostitution and sentenced to six months' probation and a $250 fine. He resigned from the Florida House of Representatives one week later on Nov. 16, 2007. Once voted "Lawmaker of the Year" by a Florida Police Association, Allen is now persona non grata in law enforcement circles.

He had a lot going for him, but he blew it.

21

Marc Dann (D)
Attorney General, Ohio

Score: 102.0
Resigned in disgrace

IT WAS A LOT LIKE A FRAT PARTY—inappropriate relationships, late-night drinking, and threatening behavior—except it was the attorney general's office. Marc Dann was elected Ohio's attorney general in 2007, but he didn't last long. He was forced to resign in 2008.

The debauchery came to light when two staffers filed a sexual harassment case against one of Dann's senior aides, Anthony Gutierrez. Not long after, Leo Jennings III, Dann's communications director, was accused of urging a colleague to lie to investigators. By the time the dust settled, Gutierrez and Jennings were fired and a top advisor, Edgar C. Simpson, had resigned.

Dann wasn't the subject of the initial investigation, but when one of the plaintiffs claimed she saw Dann's scheduling assistant at his apartment in her pajamas, he quickly became the main story. Twenty-eight-year-old Jessica Utovich was apparently handling more than his calendar.

Nevertheless, Dann refused to resign, saying his admission was punishment enough. When it was pointed out he had fired an agent in his investigative division for having an affair with a female subordinate, he said the circumstances were different.

Ohio lawmakers did not see it his way. Every state-level Democratic lawmaker signed a letter asking Dann to resign, and Governor Ted Strickland personally asked him to do so. When he refused, Ohio Democrats filed articles of impeachment (sponsored by forty-two of forty-five House Democrats) on May 13, 2008, charging him with nine counts relating to the sexual harassment scandal. Finally, Dann resigned from office on May 14.

He had only managed to stay in office seventeen months—not surprising, given the townhouse he shared with disgraced cronies Jennings and Gutierrez was nicknamed Animal House and Marc was referred to as "The Dannimal."

Ohio newspapers, while eager to endorse Dann in his 2006 election, were quick to turn on the attorney general. An editorial in *The Columbus Dispatch* said,

Dann resigns at the Governor's office on May 14, 2008. AP Images

"Ohio's attorney general must be able to provide leadership, command respect and exercise strong judgment. Marc Dann has failed miserably in all three and is not fit to serve." An editorial in the *Cleveland Plain Dealer* claimed, "By his own actions and by those of the people he trusted the most, Dann has turned the attorney general's office into a laughingstock."

Even after resigning, however, Dann was not out of the woods. In March 2009, Dann was found guilty of violating election laws for misspending political campaign funds on personal items. Instead of being referred for criminal charges, the Ohio Elections Committee fined him $1,000.

Dann claims to have found enlightenment after leaving the political spotlight. In a 2012 profile of sex scandals by *Politico*, Dann said he was thankful for his fall from the top. "How often in life do you get a hard stop? And have an opportunity to reassess the kind of things that are important to you and put those into priority." He credits time with his family, but since his wife divorced him in 2010, it's not clear exactly what he meant.

20

Rita Crundwell (I)
Treasurer, Dixon, Illinois

Score: 103.0

Facing charges

Special Award
Audacity

RITA CRUNDWELL STOLE MORE THAN $53 MILLION in public funds over a thirty-year career as comptroller and treasurer of Dixon, IL. Originally, the FBI thought she pocketed a mere $30 million, starting in 2006, but soon discovered the town's treasurer had been dipping into the till for decades.

Appointed comptroller in 1983, and earning an annual salary of $80,000, Crundwell was also well-known in the international horse-breeding game. Her champion horse ranch in Beloit, WI, (one of two), produced fifty-two world champions. At the time of her arrest, Crundwell had 311 registered quarter horses.

Most of the money she stole was funneled into the horses, so she typically took off four months per year (three of which were paid, according to the *Chicago Tribune*) to run the business. It was while she was away that a city employee discovered the fraud.

The FBI says Crundwell opened a bank account in the name of the city of Dixon and one named "RSCDA." She would then create fictitious invoices and move funds from the city's various bank accounts to the ones she created through a series of wire transfers and checks payable to "Treasurer." According to ABC News, these checks were written "C/O Rita Crundwell. And if the city was low on funds, Crundwell would tell the mayor and City Council that the state of Illinois was late in its payments to Dixon.

According to the *Tribune*, Crundwell moved $2.8 million from the city's accounts to her own account between September 2011 and February 2012—that's nearly $470,000 per month. The *Tribune* reports that "by March, she had written nineteen checks totaling more than $3.5 million from the account, payable to the 'Treasurer'"—about a third of the city's entire budget.

With these funds, the fifty-nine-year-old purchased a $2.1 million motor home, "the highest-end motor home you can get," according to a company spokesperson. It had marble flooring, Viking appliances, HD flat-screen TVs with a Bose sound system, and custom-made leather furniture.

In addition to horsing around, Crundwell spent more than $2.5 million on her personal American Express credit card, dropping $339,000 on jewelry and

Crundwell leaves court after pleading not guilty. How she plans to explain 400 horses on her comptroller salary of $80,000 is anybody's guess. AP Images

Seizure of Leisure

It was great while it lasted, but Uncle Sam repossessed it all in the end: homes, cars, cash, and more than 400 horses. Here's a breakdown of loot Crundwell amassed during one of the greatest embezzlement schemes in U.S. history:

Real Estate: Single-family residence located at 1679 U.S. Route 52, Dixon, IL; the horse farm property located at 1556 Red Brick Road, Dixon, IL; a single-family residence located at 1403 Dutch Road, Dixon, IL; approximately eighty acres of vacant land located in Lee County, IL; single-family residence located at 821 East Fifth Street, Englewood, FL.

Cars: 2009 Liberty Coach Motor Home ($2.1 million), 2012 Chevrolet Silverado 3500 pickup truck, 2005 Chevrolet Silverado, 2010 GMC Terrain, 2009 Kenworth T800 Tractor Truck ($146,787), Ford Thunderbird Convertible, 1967 Chevrolet Corvette Roadster, 2009 Chevrolet Silverado Pickup Truck ($56,646), 2007 Chevrolet Silverado 3500 Pickup Truck, 2009 Freightliner Truck ($140,000).

Boats: 2000 20' Playbuoy Pontoon Mfg. pleasure boat, a 1998 Cobalt 25 LS Deck Boat.

Other Vehicles: 2009 Featherlite Horse Trailer ($258,698), 2012 Featherlite 40' gooseneck car trailer, 2009 Heartland Cyclone 3950 5th Wheel Trailer, 2004 Elite Horse Trailer, 2009 Eliminator Trailer, 2010 Elite Trailer, 2004 Featherlite 6 Horse Trailer, 2004 Featherlite 4-Horse Bumper Pull Trailer, 2007 John Deere Model XUV 6201 Gator/Utility Vehicle, 2007 John Deere Model XUV 850 Gator/Utility Vehicle, 2007 John Deere Model 757 Z-Track 60" mower, 2009 John Deere Model 5065E Tractor, 2011 John Deere Model X324 Riding Mower.

Cash: $191,357.75 seized from her RSCDA account and $33,540.82 seized from her account at The First National Bank, Amboy, IL.

averaging more than $5,380 per month, according to ABC News, see sidebar for a list of what Crundwell bought, which the FBI subsequently confiscated.)

Following her arrest on April 17, 2012, the Dixon City Council rejected Crundwell's resignation letter, voting unanimously to fire her, and stipulating that she won't be entitled to any pension. Goods she purchased with the embezzled funds were repossessed, and the horses were put into the care of the U.S. Marshals Service.

On June 15, 2012, a judge approved the sale of Crundwell's 400 horses, thirteen saddles, twenty-one horse embryos, and frozen stallion semen. Proceeds of the sale will be used to pay for the horses' upkeep, according to the *Rockford Register Star.*

For now, Crundwell remains free pending her trial where 17,000 pages of evidence are waiting for her (in May she pleaded not guilty). She is charged with wire fraud, which, according to the FBI, carries a maximum penalty of twenty years in prison, and a $250,000 fine, or an alternate fine totaling twice the loss or twice the gain, whichever is greater.

Touchingly, Crundwell named one of her horses Have Faith in Money.

19

Joseph Ganim (D)
Mayor, Bridgeport, Connecticut

Score: 106.5

Convicted
Served time

ON MARCH 20, 2003, JOSEPH GANIM, the mayor of Bridgeport, CT, was found guilty of racketeering, extortion, bribery, and several other felonies.

Like many LCBs, Ganim had leveraged his power to grant contracts for his personal benefit. According to the twenty-two-count indictment, Ganim had a taste for the finer things in life. He received more than $425,000 in cash, but also tailored suits, jewelry—including a $1,600 pair of diamond earrings—and bottles of "investment-quality wine."

Ganim was originally indicted in 2001. Not surprisingly, he denied the charges and refused to step down.

According to John W. Olsen, Connecticut's Democratic Party chairman, the indictment was no reason for Ganim to consider resigning. "Democrats don't have to walk around with our heads down," Olsen told *The New York Times*. "I mean, look, Phil Giordano is still the mayor of Waterbury." (See entry #1.)

Despite his best efforts to prove he was set up, Ganim was convicted on sixteen of twenty-two counts and sentenced to nine years in prison. Not bad, considering he faced up to 126 years in prison, $500,000 in restitution, and $4 million in fines. It wasn't until nine days later—March 29, 2003—that Ganim resigned from office. At the time of his arrest, a mayor in Connecticut could not be removed from office until he or she was imprisoned.

Ganim served his time in jail until Jan. 21, 2009, when he was released to a halfway house. In July of 2010, he received a supervised release. In November of 2011, Ganim argued for an early end to this supervision, citing his good behavior in jail. To support his case, he presented more than two dozen letters from other inmates he'd helped during his sentence.

Jeffrey Gold, who previously ran a New York real estate management company, said he appreciated Ganim's fitness training and advice. Ironically, when Ganim was mayor, one of the illegal gifts he received was a $2,000 piece of exercise equipment.

Robert Mauri, who was in prison for misappropriating more than $3 million when he was director of a Wall Street investment bank, said Ganim's advice was "very informative and helpful in how I may approach the job market when I leave here." Uh oh.

Ganim speaks to the media after pleading not guilty in court. AP Images

7 Worst Mayors

Mayoral misconduct runs rampant. There are, of course, a lot of mayors in the United States—more than 15,000 according to the 1992 Census of Governments—so there's bound to be a few bad apples. Connecticut certainly got its fair share: Three of the seven worst mayors are from the Constitution State.

1. Phil Giordano (#1), former mayor of Waterbury, CT. Currently serving 37 years for child molestation.

2. Larry Langford (#5), former mayor of Birmingham, AL. Currently serving a 15-year sentence for corruption.

3. Joseph Ganim (#19), former mayor of Bridgeport, CT. Served seven years in prison on corruption charges.

4. Vincent Cianci, Jr. (#50), former mayor of Providence, RI. Served four and a half years in prison for corruption.

5. Eddie Perez (#65), former mayor of Hartford, CT. Sentenced to three years in prison for corruption and bribery. (Currently free on bond, awaiting appeal.)

6. Bill Campbell (#51), former mayor of Atlanta, GA. Served two years in prison for tax evasion.

7. Kwame Kilpatrick (#6), former mayor of Detroit, MI. Served 14 months for violating probation relating to a 2008 case.

7 More Mayors Behaving Badly

Although these mayors did not make the *Lyin' Cheatin' Bastards* list, they all deserve a dishonorable mention:

1. Sheila Dixon, former mayor of Baltimore, MD. Resigned from office after she was convicted of embezzlement for misusing holiday gift cards for the poor.

2. Roosevelt Dorn, former mayor of Inglewood, CA. Resigned from office after he pleaded guilty to a misdemeanor conflict of interest charge. He was sentenced to two years probation and barred from holding public office again.

3. Kevin Jackson, former mayor of Rio Rancho, NM. Resigned after he was accused of misusing the city credit card, charging more than $5,000, including $1,600 for Willie Nelson concert tickets.

4. Brent Warr, former mayor of Gulfport, MS. Pleaded guilty to one felony count related to Hurricane Katrina fraud.

5. Frank Kessler, former mayor pro tem of Canyon Lake, CA. Pleaded guilty to felony embezzlement for using his city-issued credit card to buy thousands of dollars in casino tokens and alcohol on a Hawaiian cruise.

6. Jim Nehmens, former mayor of Adelanto, CA. Sentenced to six months in jail, along with his wife, for stealing $20,000 from the city's Little League fund.

7. Michael Stotts, former mayor of Barrow, AK. Resigned after he was accused of running up the city's credit card with personal charges, including bail for a drunk driving charge.

18

Bell Council (D)
City Council, Bell, California

Score: 106.7

Special Award
Audacity

CORRUPTION ON STEROIDS—that's how the Los Angeles County district attorney described what was going on in the small town of Bell, CA. After a Pulitzer Prize-winning report by the *Los Angeles Times* uncovered that city officials and council members in one of the poorest cities in the state (one in six lives in poverty) were making some of the highest salaries in the nation, all hell broke loose.

Initially, the *Times* reported that Robert Rizzo, Bell's city manager, was pulling in nearly $800,000 per year, its police chief almost $500,000, and the assistant city manager about $400,000. Those salaries were at least fifty percent higher than what their counterparts were making in much larger cities, such as Los Angeles or New York City. In addition, the *Times* reported that top officials routinely received significant yearly raises—twelve percent for Rizzo alone.

> ## "He was like a little dictator."
> —Bell resident talking about city manager Robert Rizzo

The mayor and city council members were not above getting their cut either. The *Times* reported they received $100,000 per year for their part-time positions. They also were assigned to various committees and received compensation of nearly $8,000 per month for "attending" committee meetings that were never held or lasted only minutes. State officials said normally, council members in a city the size of Bell would get about $400 per month. Only one council member, Lorenzo Velez, was making a realistic salary of $8,000 per year. He had just recently joined the council.

According to the *Times*, the council had exempted itself from state salary limits in 2005 by getting voters to approve a "charter city" designation in a special election. Fewer than 400 ballots were cast—less than ten percent of Bell's population. The switch was touted as a way to give the council more local control. Council members failed to mention it would give them a way to rip off the town.

In the meantime, Bell's population of mainly Latino and foreign-born residents was paying some of the highest tax rates in the county. According to the *Times*, a state audit showed the city illegally overcharged residents and businesses by $5.6 million in taxes and fees.

A little more than a week after the *Times* story broke, Rizzo, his assistant, and the police chief were forced to step down. Council members kept their jobs but slashed their pay by ninety percent. The L.A. district attorney and federal and state authorities began investigating whether the high salaries were legal and if other financial transactions could be considered theft of public funds.

After a two-month probe, the state attorney general first filed a lawsuit against the city, accusing leaders of scheming to increase their salaries and trying to hide it from the public. Then the big bust happened—eight current and former Bell city leaders were arrested, including Rizzo, his Assistant City Manager Angela Spaccia, and Mayor Oscar Hernandez. They were all charged with misappropriating more than $5.5 million dollars from the working-class community.

"They used the tax dollars collected from the hardworking citizens of Bell as their own piggy bank which they then looted at will," District Attorney Steve Cooley said at the time of the arrests. (Sound familiar? See Rita Crundwell, #20 and Betty Loren Maltese, #14.)

Rizzo was charged with fifty-three criminal counts that include misappropriating public funds, conflicts of interest, and falsifying public records to keep his salary a secret. According to prosecutors, he wrote fraudulent contracts that enriched their salaries and made it nearly impossible to determine how much they were being paid. Prosecutors determined that Rizzo's salary and benefits package added up to $1.5 million dollars. In addition, the *Times* reported that he gave city loans to more than fifty city officials (including himself) that totaled nearly $2 million. Prosecutors said he lent the money to buy loyalty so he could keep his monster paychecks.

From left; Robert Rizzo, former city manager; Angela Spaccia, former assistant city manager; Victor Bello, former council member; and Oscar Hernandez, mayor, appear in Los Angeles County Superior Court in matching outfits and handcuffs. AP Images

Rizzo, called the "unaccountable czar" by Cooley, claimed all along that he deserved the salary since he had been working for the city since 1993. His attorney said his salary was approved by the council members so they could keep him from retiring. Residents did not feel quite the same way.

"He ran the show. He was like a little dictator," one resident told *USA Today* after Rizzo's arrest. "The city council would do whatever he said."

Residents formed a group called the Bell Association to Stop the Abuse, or BASTA, which means "enough!" in Spanish. In March 2011, the group forced the recall of the city council members who had been charged in the scandal but had not resigned. According to *The Huffington Post*, more than ninety-five percent of voters in Bell cast ballots in favor of giving them the boot. A new mayor was elected a month later—he vowed to restore integrity to the city.

But as Bell was trying to get back on its feet, more shocking details were being revealed about the depths of corruption going on in the town. The *Times* revealed that grand jury testimony showed Rizzo had set up a secret pension fund holding $4.5 million to avoid retirement limits for state employees. The *Times* also reported that before the scandal broke, Rizzo was on course to receive a $650,000-per-year pension—making him the highest-paid pensioner in the state's system.

Rizzo and his cohorts are currently awaiting trial. Three of them, including former Mayor Hernandez, tried to bill the city for their legal bills. They claim they did nothing wrong and that their large salaries were not illegal. Auditors had already determined that Bell was on the brink of bankruptcy and would have to cut services and employees.

"The city had almost no accounting controls—no checks or balances—and the general fund was run like a petty-cash drawer," State Comptroller John Chiang told *USA Today*. Chiang said Rizzo had "total control and discretion" over how city funds were spent, "resulting in a perfect breeding ground for fraudulent, wasteful spending." And for *Lyin' Cheatin' Bastards*.

Randall Tobias (R)
AIDS Czar

Score: 110.0

Resigned in disgrace

Special Award
Hypocrite

IN THE GRAND SCHEME OF THINGS, Randall Tobias didn't do anything *that* bad, but he was a *hypocritical* Bastard, that's for sure.

A Bush favorite, Randy, as he was known, held several senior positions in the State Department. He was the first U.S. global AIDS coordinator, nominated by George W. Bush in 2003. He followed that up with several other assignments, including director of U.S. foreign assistance, administrator of the U.S. Agency for International Development (USAID), and ambassador for the President's Emergency Fund for AIDS relief. But four years after assuming office, the sixty-five-year-old "Global AIDS Czar" was caught up in a prostitution scandal.

In 2007, Deborah Jeane Palfrey, aka the "D.C. Madam," was under federal investigation for running an illegal sex business. Between 10,000 and 15,000 client phone numbers were disclosed during the investigation and Tobias' cell phone number was among them.

Randy said he only used the escort service "to have gals come over to the condo to give me a massage." Of course you did, Randy.

As global AIDS coordinator, Tobias required organizations to take an anti-prostitution oath in order to receive funds from the program. Indeed, the oath's funding restrictions meant that many initiatives focused on sex workers were cut off. According to Think Progress, Brazil lost $40 million for one of its most successful anti-AIDS strategies: persuading sex workers to use condoms. All while Tobias was dialing up hookers in Washington, D.C.

In 2005, Tobias told PBS, "The heart of our prevention programs is what's known as ABC: Abstinence, Be faithful, and the correct and consistent use of Condoms, when appropriate. And it's not 'ABC: Take your pick.' It's abstinence really focused heavily on young people and getting them to understand that the best way to keep from getting infected is to be abstinent and not engage in sexual activity until they are old enough and mature enough and get into a committed relationship, such as a marriage. B is being faithful within that committed relationship."

Apparently, Tobias did not believe A or B (he was married at the time) applied to him. It is not known if he used condoms when he engaged hookers.

Before entering the public sector, Tobias was a heavy hitter in business, holding the top positions at AT&T International and Eli Lily and sitting on the boards of several other Fortune 500 companies. In

Tobias undergoes a public HIV test in Mozambique to help eliminate the stigma of taking the test—a gutsy proposition given his use of hookers. AP Images

fact, Indiana University boasts the Randall L. Tobias Center for Leadership Excellence. Their mission is "inspiring leadership excellence on a national scale."

Their site, however, is not up-to-date: The fact that Tobias resigned in disgrace is not mentioned anywhere.

16

Richard Curtis (R)
State Representative, Washington

Score: 110.0

Special Award
Gay Anti-Gay Legislator

STANDARD OPERATING PROCEDURE for *Lyin' Cheatin' Bastards* is to deny, cover up, and then, if the problem won't go away, blame it on someone else. Richard Curtis turned that strategy on its head. He called the police and claimed he was the victim of extortion by a gay prostitute. A bold move by the Washington state representative who voted against a bill to grant civil rights protections to gays and lesbians and against a bill to create domestic partnerships for same-sex couples.

According to the Spokane, WA, police report, Curtis was hesitant to reveal the details of the incident because, "he spent his career in risk management and he was deciding if the benefits outweighed the risk to his career and his family." He was right to be hesitant. The report reads like an episode from the Marquis de Sade's *The Bedroom Philosophers.*

> ## "If I told you, I'd have to kill you."
>
> —Curtis telling Castagna why he couldn't tell him what he did for a living

Cody Castagna says he met Curtis at the Hollywood Erotic Boutique in Spokane. Before hooking up with Castagna, Curtis changed into women's red stockings and a black sequined lingerie top, and received oral sex from a man with a cane. Then Curtis talked to Castagna, who told him he was short on cash. Curtis told him he could help him out with some money. A few hours later, they were at the Davenport Towers Hotel, where Curtis and Castagna exchanged pleasantries about what they like to do in the sack. Curtis warned Castagna he couldn't tell him his profession: "If I told you, I'd have to kill you."

Curtis couldn't tell him he was a state legislator, but he was OK with donning women's lingerie and offering a man $1,000 to perform unprotected anal sex on him.

Castagna was reluctant to proceed, but was convinced by the $1,000 offer. After performing the sex act, however, Curtis was "too tired" to get the money. Curtis offered up his wallet as collateral, and that's when Castagna realized his date was an elected state representative.

At first, Curtis (right) denied he was gay, but he later resigned. At left is Cody Castagna, the "other man."

Speaking to police later, Curtis claimed "he did not ask to perform bareback sex on the suspect. Bareback sex never took place, nor did he offer the suspect any additional money."

Whether Castagna really tried to blackmail the lawmaker or if Curtis just didn't want to pay up is unclear, but shortly after the incident came to light, Curtis resigned.

Curtis initially told local newspapers he was not gay and that sex was not involved in what he said was an extortion attempt. However, in a statement accompanying his resignation, he wrote, "I sincerely apologize for any pain my actions may have caused. This has been damaging to my family, and I don't want to subject them to any additional pain that might result from carrying out this matter under the scrutiny that comes with holding public office."

In the aftermath following his resignation, Curtis remained quiet, but the media, including Dan Abrams on MSNBC and sex columnist Dan Savage, held Curtis up as yet another example of a gay anti-gay legislator unfrocked.

15

Jim Traficant (D)
Congressman, Ohio

Score: 115.0

Convicted
Served time

Special Award
Tax Evader

Before Rod Blagojevich had ridiculous hair, Jim Traficant (D-OH) had ridiculous hair.

Traficant was elected to the U.S. House of Representatives in 1985 and served for seventeen years. He was famous for wearing out-of-style clothes (bell-bottoms, denim suits, skinny ties), his gravity-defying toupee, and a Star Trek closing to every speech he gave: "Beam me up, Mr. Speaker!"

> **"Beam me up, Mr. Speaker!"**
> —How Traficant ended all his speeches in the House

He clearly marched to the beat of his own drum. Indeed, he voted against his own party so many times he became the first member of the House in more than one hundred years to hold no committee assignments and not one leadership position.

Apparently, he also thought he was above the law—taking bribes, lying on his taxes, and having his aides work on his farm and houseboat.

In 2002, it caught up with him and he was convicted on ten felony counts of bribery, racketeering, and tax evasion. The House voted 420-1 to expel him (the one exception was former U.S. Representative Gary Condit (D-CA)). According to *The Washington Post*, Traficant was only the second House member since the Civil War to get booted for unethical behavior.

Traficant was sentenced to seven years in federal prison and served it all. He spent part of that time in solitary confinement after starting a riot by mouthing off to a correctional officer. While in the clink, Traficant also ran for Congress as an Independent. Alarmingly, he garnered fifteen percent of the vote.

He was released from prison in September 2009 at age sixty-eight. Four days later, 1,200 supporters threw him a welcome home party complete with an Elvis impersonator, a Traficant look-alike contest, and "Welcome Home Jimbo" T-shirts.

Traficant has long claimed his punishment was part of a conspiracy against him. According to a letter attributed to Traficant and posted by several newspapers across the United States, he claims he knows facts about "Waco, Flight 103, Jimmy Hoffa, and the assassination of John F. Kennedy," and "I may yet divulge this information if I can get the proper forum."

When he got out of prison he ran again for office in 2010. He lost to a former aide. We wonder if that aide was in charge of the farm or boat cleanup.

Only Blagojevich has hair that can compete with Traficant's. AP Images

Betty Loren Maltese (I)
President, Cicero, Illinois

Score: 120.0

Convicted
Served time

Special Award
Audacity

IN A CHICAGO SUBURB ONCE RULED by Al Capone, Betty Loren Maltese has become just as notorious. Known as much for her big hair as her big mouth, Loren Maltese was president of Cicero, IL, for almost ten years. During that time, she bilked the town's insurance program out of $12 million. Prosecutors said Loren Maltese and her cohorts—including a former police chief—used Cicero as "a personal piggy bank." She spent the money on a hotel with a golf course in Wisconsin, a horse farm in Indiana, and luxury cars for her friends and associates.

According to the *Chicago Tribune,* the insurance scam was originally put into place by Loren Maltese's husband, Frank, who was a convicted mob bookie and, conveniently, Cicero's town assessor. He and a previous Cicero town president turned over the town's insurance business to a company controlled by the mob. When that town president died, Frank got Betty installed as interim president to keep their insurance racket going.

Loren Maltese had already been heavily involved in running Cicero government and she ended up being elected town president three times—even when she was under federal investigation. Residents weren't bothered by a little corruption.

"We've had cases where organized crime has paid money to public officials to allow organized crime activities to occur," said U.S. Attorney Scott R. Lassar when Loren Maltese was indicted in 2001, along with nine others. "But this is the first time where there has essentially been a looting of a town."

During her trial, her attorney said Loren Maltese was in over her head, especially when it came to financial matters. But the head of the Chicago Crime Commission at the time noted, "Betty wasn't the stereotypical mob wife who went to church and stayed out of the business. She was a powerful and shrewd person."

Not shrewd enough to avoid jail time. Loren Maltese was found guilty in 2003 of racketeering conspiracy and wire and mail fraud. She was sentenced to eight years in prison and ordered to repay $8 million, her share of the money stolen. Loren Maltese's assets were frozen after her sentencing, in hopes of recovering some of that cash. Federal officials had determined she had a gambling problem. They said she spent hundreds of hours gambling over several years, betting millions in casinos in Illinois, Indiana, and Nevada. A federal judge ended up ordering her to prison two months early so she wouldn't blow through what money she had left and owed the government.

No one realized what Betty's campaign poster really meant: That she would take all the money. AP Images

Loren Maltese served seven years in a federal prison in California before getting released into a Nevada halfway house in 2009. She then came back to Chicago and got a job as a hostess at a pizza place. To raise money to help pay her bills, Loren Maltese held a garage sale in 2011, signing autographs and taking pictures with fans.

The *Chicago Sun-Times* reported she had moved to a Chicago suburb in 2012, was doing computer work, and living on a Social Security widow's pension. *Chicago Magazine* reported law enforcement officials were worried she might try to reenter politics. But she says no way.

"There are two things I know for sure: I will never be a virgin again, and I will never get involved in Cicero politics again," she told the magazine. "There are a lot of good people there, but I will never go back. It would be too dangerous." For who?

The 7 Most Audacious

Most *Lyin' Cheatin' Bastards* try to hide what they are doing. This group hid right out in the open.

1. Rita Crundwell (#20)
Stole more than $50 million from the town of Dixon, IL, and bought over 500 horses. The sheer scale of her embezzlement boggles the mind.

2. Betty Loren Maltese (#14)
Stole more than $10 million and bought a hotel with a golf course. How is it that no one notices these things?

3. Bell Council (#18)
Stole over $5 million and it would have been more if they were not caught—they had set up a retirement fund with another $5 million of pilfered money.

4. Edwin Edwards (#8)
Not only admitted he was a *Lyin' Cheatin' Bastard*, claimed he was. His brazenness only added to his fame.

5. Vince Fumo (#4)
Had staff running his farm. Who was taking care of official business? Perhaps there is no official business! Do State Senators actually do anything?

6. Rod Blagojevich (#3)
Tried to sell Obama's Senate seat. Really?

7. Kwame Kilpatrick (#6)
Wrote into a legal agreement that the recipient of a cash settlement could not tell anyone about e-mails that proved he had perjured himself on the stand.

13

Michael Duvall (R)
Assemblyman, California

Score: 125.0

Resigned in disgrace

Special Awards
Stupidity, Caught on Tape

CALIFORNIA ASSEMBLYMAN MICHAEL DUVALL was sitting in a July 8, 2009, Sacramento committee hearing when he used a break in the proceedings to chat with the assemblyman next to him. Duvall did not realize his microphone was on.

Fifteen hours later he resigned in disgrace.

Duvall got caught—on tape—describing in excruciating detail two extramarital affairs he was supposedly having: "She wears little eye-patch underwear ... So, the other day she came here with her underwear, Thursday. And so, we had made love Wednesday, a lot. And so ... she's all, 'I am going up and down the stairs and you're dripping out of me. So messy!' (laughing)."

"So I am getting into spanking her ... Yeah, I like it ... I like spanking her. She goes, 'I know you like spanking me', I said 'Yeah, that's 'cause you're such a bad girl.' (laughing)"

Duvall then provided details that made it possible to identify the woman in question: Heidi DeJong Barsuglia, a thirty-six-year-old lobbyist for Sempra Energy, adding alarming realism to the claim that many lawmakers are in bed with lobbyists. In 2009, Sempra gave Duvall $1,500 in campaign contributions. He was

> ## "So I am getting into spanking her ... Yeah, I like it ... I like spanking her."
> —Duvall caught on tape

Duvall (right) during a council session. He will never go near another microphone again.
AP Images

vice chairman of the Assembly's Committee on Utilities and Commerce.

Of a second affair, Duvall said, "Oh, she is hot. I talked to her yesterday. She goes, 'So are we finished?' I go, 'No, we're not finished.' I go, 'You know about the other one, but she doesn't know about you.' (laughing)"

Whether or not he was actually cheating on his wife (Barsuglia denies having an affair with Duvall), he has earned a place in *Lyin' Cheatin' Bastards* for his hypocritical "family values" platform. Although they regret it now, the Capitol Resource Institute, a leading conservative organization in California, awarded Duvall a 100 percent rating in 2009, noting that, "Assemblyman Duvall has been a consistent trooper for the conservative causes. For the last two years, he has voted time and time again to protect and preserve family values in California."

In his resignation statement, Duvall does not admit to any affairs and claims his only offense "was engaging in inappropriate storytelling." But it doesn't matter. He was either lyin' or he was cheatin', and either way he's a Bastard.

12

Samuel Kent (R)
Federal Judge

Score: 128.5

Impeached
Resigned in disgrace
Convicted
Served time

WHEN THE GAVEL FINALLY CAME down, former federal Judge Samuel Kent was sentenced to thirty-three months in prison for obstruction of justice. Kent was brought down by two former employees who accused him of sexual misconduct.

In testimony before the House Judiciary Committee, Cathy McBroom and Donna Wilkerson recounted years of "unwanted kissing, groping and occasionally furtive sexual touching." The women said they didn't come forward earlier because they were afraid for their jobs. A profile in *Texas Monthly* magazine detailed the years of sexual assault and coercion at the hands of "King Kent." California State Representative Dan Lungren (R-Gold River) called the years Kent served in Galveston, "A judicial reign of terror." Kent admitted to nonconsensual contact with the women, but sexual misconduct charges were dismissed as part of the plea agreement.

Kent tried to work the system. He offered to resign in mid-2010, a move that would have allowed him to receive his $174,000 salary for the first year of his prison term, but the U.S. House of Representatives saw through the ruse and took steps to throw him out. Kent became the fourteenth judge to be impeached by the House (the only one impeached for sexual misconduct). He resigned (via a note from prison) before the Senate could vote. Because the House impeaches (similar to an indictment) and the Senate convicts (similar to a trial), he was not technically removed. But who cares: He's out.

During his impeachment hearings, Kent submitted a written statement in which he blamed his actions on alcoholism, a personality flaw, and having never recovered after losing his first wife to brain cancer. "Perhaps I was attempting to meet an unfilled need for affection," Kent wrote. How groping women would fill this need is not clear.

U.S. Representative Jim Sensenbrenner (R-WI), who had sponsored a resolution to impeach Kent, told the *Houston Chronicle*, "Kent's realization that we would not allow him to take advantage of the system proves that the system works and justice has been served. I hope this process reminds other judges that they are not above the laws they took an oath to uphold. I hope the women Mr. Kent assaulted will find some closure in this man being behind bars and no longer being able to serve on the bench or collect a taxpayer-funded paycheck."

Kent didn't take well to prison. After spending decades sentencing criminals, he couldn't accept his own punishment. Kent submitted a federal court memorandum that he was being treated inhumanely and unfairly, and that he was wrongly excluded from a substance abuse treatment program. No wonder he wanted in on the treatment program—it would have reduced his prison term by as much as a year. In any event, Kent's request was turned down, and he served twenty-nine months of his thirty-three-month term behind bars.

Kent leaves the courthouse after being sentenced to three years in prison.
AP Images

Eliot Spitzer (D)

Governor, New York

Score: 135.0

Resigned in disgrace

Special Awards
Stupidity, Hypocrite

HAVING MADE HIS NAME as a corruption-fighting attorney general, New York Governor Eliot Spitzer made front-page news when he was identified as Client #9 of a prostitution ring.

On March 10, 2008, *The New York Times* reported that Spitzer had patronized a high-priced prostitution service called Emperors Club VIP and met with a $1,000-an-hour call girl going by the name Ashley Alexandra Dupré.

Investigators reported Spitzer paid $80,000 for prostitutes over several years, while he was attorney general and governor. They began looking into the Emperors Club when its bank (HSBC) filed a Suspicious Activity Report (SAR). The bank could not figure out how the company, operating as QAT International, was generating large amounts of cash.

When investigators cross-checked other SARs they came across one from Spitzer's bank (North Fork Bank), that indicated he had sent money to QAT.

He had no one to blame but himself. As later reported in *Rough Justice: The Rise and Fall of Eliot Spitzer* by Peter Elkind, Spitzer called his bank in July 2007 to ask if it was possible "to wire money where it's not evident that it's coming from me." He was trying to hide payments to QAT, a.k.a. the Emperors Club, but it had just the opposite effect: his bank reported the wire and his request for anonymity.

At first, investigators thought Spitzer was hiding bribe money and were no doubt a bit disappointed to learn it was just a bunch of hookers. Nevertheless, when the story broke it was the end of Spitzer's political career.

Threatened with impeachment, Spitzer announced on March 12, 2008, that he would resign his post as governor effective March 17, 2008.

Ashley Alexndra Dupré. No one knows what Spitzer saw in her.

Lucky for him, prosecutors decided not to charge him for his involvement in the sex ring, having found no evidence that he misused public funds. "I appreciate the impartiality and thoroughness of the investigation by the U.S. Attorney's Office, and I acknowledge and accept responsibility for the conduct it disclosed," Spitzer said. In other words, "Phewww! Thank God I had the sense to use my own money!"

Disgraced, but quick to reinvent himself, Spitzer reemerged as a talk show host, a transparent attempt by CNN to cash in on Spitzer's notoriety. (In TV-land, it doesn't matter what you are famous for—only that you are famous.) But it wasn't long before his cohost threw in the towel and his ratings tanked. His show was cancelled in July 2011. While his short-lived program will certainly be forgotten, Spitzer's most enduring legacy may yet be a TV show. *The Good Wife*, a drama at

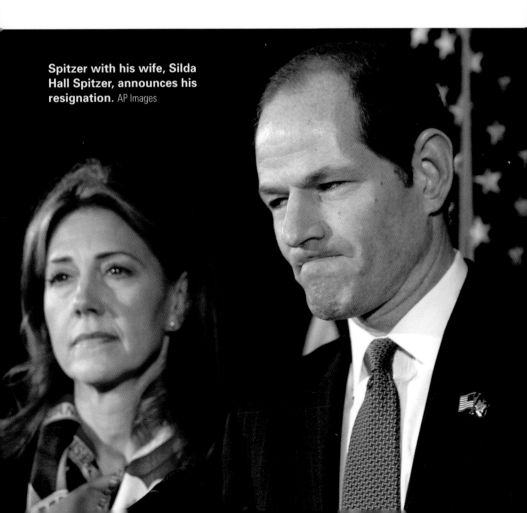

Spitzer with his wife, Silda Hall Spitzer, announces his resignation. AP Images

"Is there way to wire money where it's not evident that it's coming from me?"

—Spitzer asking his bank if there's a way to hide payments to the prostitution ring.

least loosely based on the Spitzer scandal, is one of the most highly rated (and critically acclaimed) shows on television today.

Apparently the show's creators, Robert and Michelle King, were inspired by wives who stand by their men (at least initially) when scandals break—women such as Silda Spitzer and Dina McGreevey (see the handy "Stand by Your Man" sidebar of seven wives in scandal on page 140).

Spitzer's wife, however, does not have the same spunk as her TV counterpart. In *The Good Wife*, Alicia Florrick (played by Julianna Margulies), is furious with her stupid husband. His philandering has forced her to go back to work to support the family and embarrassed them all to no end.

The real Mrs. Spitzer appears to be more forgiving. In Elkind's book, she suggests it was—at least partly—her fault: "The wife is supposed to take care of the sex. This is my failing; I wasn't adequate." A quick survey shows that few women in America agree with her analysis: Most say she should have kicked him out of the house the moment his extracurricular activities came to light.

Clearly, Spitzer gets the Hypocrite Award. You can't fool around with hookers when you are the attorney general. It doesn't look right.

10

Duke Cunningham (R)
Congressman, California

Score: 137.7

Convicted
In prison

IF YOU BELIEVE RANDALL "DUKE" Cunningham (R-CA), he was the inspiration for the movie *Top Gun*. But the former congressman and ex-fighter pilot didn't look much like a hero when he resigned in disgrace after pleading guilty to taking more than $2 million in bribes. After serving twenty years in the Navy and fifteen years in Congress, Cunningham is currently serving eight years and four months in prison. *The San Diego Union-Tribune* and Copley News Service (CNS) shared a Pulitzer Prize for uncovering the conspiracy that is considered to be one of the worst cases of bribery in the history of Congress.

Reporters were originally alerted to Cunningham's misdeeds when he sold his home to defense contractor Mitchell Wade, who in turn sold the home at a $700,000 loss. Cunningham went on to buy a $2.55 million home in Rancho Sante Fe with the proceeds from his sale to Wade. Subsequent reporting from CNS revealed defense contractors had steered campaign donations to Cunningham and lavished him with gifts of cash, antiques, Persian rugs, a Rolls-Royce, and a yacht.

Cunningham was not very good at covering his tracks. At one point, he sent a $16,500 check to the dealer from whom Wade purchased the rugs, with a note claiming he misaddressed the original payment. In a *Vanity Fair* magazine profile, another antiques dealer recalled Cunningham asking her to "remember" $35,000 he gave to Wade in exchange for the luxury purchases. "I never saw it, and believe me, $35,000 in cash I would remember!" the dealer reported.

He moved in Congress under the mantle of a great military hero, often calling into question the patriotism and loyalty of colleagues on the other side of the aisle. An examination of Cunningham's attacks against fellow veteran U.S.

Duke Cunningham breaks down while reading a statement after pleading guilty to bribery. AP Images

Senator John Kerry (D-MA) revealed some of them came on the same days he was cashing $500,000 checks he received as bribes.

The case also highlighted the practice of "earmarking," whereby legislators secretly steer dollars to specific projects. In a column for CNS, George Condon wrote, "By steering contracts vital to the Iraq war effort to cronies, he may have put those troops at greater risk by judging contracts more for what they would do for him than for the military." Ray Smock, the former historian of the House, said, "It does sound like he was playing pretty fast and loose with lives. I don't think there was any question about him being an authentic supporter of the military. But at some point that went sour, and that's the real tragedy."

Even his lawyer, Mark Holscher, didn't think he had a chance. Holscher told a federal judge he recommended a plea after evaluating the U.S. attorney's office's evidence of political corruption, dating to 2000.

When Cunningham entered his guilty plea at a federal courthouse in San Diego in November 2005, he said, "When I announced several months ago that I would not seek reelection, I publicly declared my innocence because I was not strong enough to face the truth. So, I misled my family, staff, friends, colleagues, the public—even myself. For all of this, I am deeply sorry. The truth is—I broke the law, concealed my conduct, and disgraced my high office. I know that I will forfeit my freedom, my reputation, my worldly possessions, and most importantly, the trust of my friends and family. ... In my life, I have known great joy and great sorrow. And now I know great shame."

But prison has changed him—now he thinks he's innocent. In March 2011, he sent a rambling, eight-page declaration to everyone he could think of titled, "The Untold Story of Duke Cunningham," in which he blamed everyone else, rationalized his misdeeds and claimed he only pleaded guilty because he was doped up on sedatives. Fully recovered from his bout with accountability and honesty, he'll be ready to serve again when he gets out.

William Jefferson (D)
Congressman, Louisiana

Score: 140.0

Convicted
In Prison

IT ALL STARTED IN EARLY 2005 when Lori Mody, a Virginia investor, told the FBI she thought something funny was going on. When the FBI investigated, it discovered that a technology company called iGate had paid hundreds of thousands of dollars (and had given millions of shares) to a company called ANJ Group, a company controlled by William Jefferson's wife and children. In return, Congressman Jefferson (D-LA) was helping iGate secure contracts with African governments.

On July 30, 2005, the FBI videotaped Jefferson receiving $100,000 in cash at the Ritz Carlton hotel in Arlington, VA. Jefferson told by-then-FBI informant Mody, who was wearing a wire, that he had to give Nigerian Vice President Atiku Abubakar $500,000 to "motivate" him. Four days later, the FBI raided Jefferson's home and found the money in the freezer.

The FBI created quite a stir when they raided Jefferson's congressional office in May 2006. Many House members—both Democrats and Republicans—felt that congressional offices were off limits. The public did not see it that way: 86 percent of those polled thought the FBI should be allowed to search their offices if they had a warrant to do so (78 percent of Democrats, 94 percent of Republicans).

The issue was so controversial that President Bush stepped in and sealed the files while the debate raged. The judge who issued the search warrant upheld its legality but was overruled by an appellate court. In the end, Jefferson was allowed—under court supervision—to review the files seized and remove those which were privileged.

In spite of the uproar, Jefferson was reelected later that year. But after a federal grand jury indicted him on sixteen charges of corruption in June 2007, he was defeated in the 2008 election.

(Right) Jefferson walks to court during his appeal. He was sentenced to 13 years in prison. AP Images

(Bottom) The police found $90,000 in Jefferson's freezer when they searched his house. FBI photo

Jefferson pleaded not guilty to the charges, at one point implying he was working with the FBI. "The $90,000 was the FBI's money. The FBI gave it to me as part of its plan—part of their plan—that I would give it to the Nigerian vice president, but I did not do that. When all the facts are understood, I trust that I will be vindicated."

Both the CEO of iGate, Vernon Jackson, and Mody's investment advisor, Brett Pfeffer (formerly an aide to Jefferson), testified against Jefferson at his trial and Jefferson was found guilty on eleven of the sixteen counts. Jackson and Pfeffer were sentenced to seven years and eight years, respectively.

Jefferson was sentenced to thirteen years, one of the longest sentences ever handed down to a congressman.

Edwin Edwards (D)
Governor, Louisiana

Score: 142.4

Convicted
Served time

FORMER LOUISIANA GOVERNOR Edwin W. Edwards began his political career with a race for the Crowley, LA, city council in 1954. Nearly fifty years (and three wives) later, he ended it with an eight-year stint in prison.

In May 2000, Edwards and four others were convicted of extorting hundreds of thousands of dollars from businesses applying for riverboat casino licenses. The Louisiana governor began the conspiracy during his last term in office, and continued the shakedown through his law practice after retiring from politics.

According to court documents, Edwards demanded large fees from businesses in return for issuing the licenses. This included a payment of $400,000 from Eddie DeBartolo, the then-owner of the San Francisco 49ers.

Unfortunately for Edwards, the FBI recorded him demanding the money from DeBartolo. The feds also shot video of the former governor receiving said money in his law office—something he should have anticipated. He told the messenger to "make sure that everybody involved is careful about how that's passed out," because he knew the FBI had begun an investigation.

A family man, Edwards got his son involved, too. Stephen Edwards was sentenced to seven years in prison and a $60,000 fine alongside Edwards himself, who received ten years and a fine of $250,000. (It is not clear if *bastarditis* is genetic. More research is needed.)

But the fines were nothing compared to the reported $3 million Edwards and his cronies extorted, and the charges did nothing to diminish Edwards' cult-like status in the state. After all, The Cajun King's constituency expected nothing less. "We all knew he was going to steal," one of his supporters told *The New York Times*. "He told us he was going to do it."

Fifty-one years separate Edwards and his third wife, Trina Grimes Scott.
AP Images

In fact, Edwards' honesty about his dishonesty only contributed to his celebrity. He never lied about his double-dealing, telling newspapers, "Lying is a big part of my job." Edwards didn't even deny accepting questionable contributions from large corporations during his 1971 campaign for governor. "Well," he said, "maybe it was illegal for them to give, but not for me to receive." In 1991, Edwards ran for governor against David Duke, a Ku Klux Klan wizard. Even die-hard Republicans were afraid of what might happen if Duke won. Both sides were so worried, bumper stickers started showing up everywhere that read: Vote for the Crook: It's Important.

Despite his penchant for lying, cheating and stealing, Edwards insisted it wasn't about the money. "I'm just not that into money," he told *The Los Angeles Times* during one of his early scandals. "That's what's so absurd about all of this. Power turns me on, fame turns me on. But not money. It never has."

While that might be true for eighty-four-year-old Edwards, it may not be true of his newest wife. Thirty-two-year-old Trina Grimes Scott, Edwards' third spouse, is fifty-one years his junior. Their courtship began romantically enough, when Grimes Scott began writing letters to Edwards while he was in prison. The mother of two began visiting him soon after their first correspondence, and the happy couple was married in 2011 after Edwards' release. Research has not revealed a previous occupation for Scott Edwards.

Always a gentleman, the lifelong Democrat spoke highly of his new conservative wife at a fundraiser later that year. "I found out a use for Republicans. You sleep with them," Edwards joked. His wife was heard laughing—all the way to the bank.

Dianne Wilkerson (D)
State Senator, Massachusetts

Score: 143.0

Convicted
In prison

Special Awards
Caught on Tape, Tax Evader

THERE ARE MANY PLACES YOU CAN hide bribe money. Former Massachusetts State Senator Dianne Wilkerson (D-2nd Suffolk District) stuffed it in her bra. Unfortunately for her, she was caught on video doing it. The FBI tape shows Wilkerson stuffing ten $100 bills under her sweater at a restaurant near the State House (this is nowhere near the record for cash-stuffed-in-a-bra—$80,000—held by Leslie Johnson, #27).

★ ★ ★ ★ ★

The 7 Female Lyin' Cheatin' Bastards

1. Dianne Wilkerson (#7)

2. Betty Loren Maltese (#14)

3. Rita Crundwell (#20)

4. Leslie Johnson* (#27)

5. Amy Brewer (#38)

6. Amy Koch (#41)

7. Katherine Bryson (#69)

* ranked with her husband

★ ★ ★ ★ ★

The Boston Globe reported it was just one of 150 secret FBI video and audio recordings that implicated Wilkerson. Prosecutors said she took eight cash payments ranging in amounts from $500 to $10,000 from undercover FBI agents between 2007 and 2008.

She later admitted she took $23,500 in bribes and pleaded guilty to attempted extortion charges. Twenty-four other charges were dropped. Prosecutors said she accepted the money in exchange for helping secure a liquor license for a nightclub and pushing legislation for a commercial development in her district.

"Public service is a privilege, and voters and taxpayers expect that elected officials will do what's right for their constituents, not what is financially best for themselves," U.S. Attorney Michael Sullivan said at the time of her arrest.

Wilkerson was the first black woman elected to the Massachusetts State Senate and was considered a rising star. She served for sixteen years before she was forced to resign after her arrest. But it wasn't the first time she had been in trouble with the law. Back in 1997, she was convicted of failing to file federal taxes. "She has a long history of acting as if she was above the law," Assistant U.S. Attorney John McNeil told the judge at Wilkerson's first court appearance on the bribery charges.

At her sentencing hearing in 2011, the judge said she had imposed her own "Wilkerson tax" on the community by accepting the bribes. She pleaded for mercy, telling the court the bribes didn't affect her work for the district.

"If it was possible to do something criminal without being criminal, that would be me," she said. But, of course, that is not possible. The judge sentenced her to three and a half years in prison. She's scheduled to be released in 2014.

Wilkerson on her way to the courthouse during her trial. AP Images

Kwame Kilpatrick (D)
Mayor, Detroit, Michigan

Score: 156.3

Convicted
Served time
Facing more charges

Special Award
Audacity

6

ON JAN. 1, 2002, KWAME Kilpatrick became Detroit's youngest mayor at age thirty-one. It was pretty much downhill from there.

Not only did he have an affair with his Chief of Staff, Christine Beatty (he was married at the time), but he lied about it under oath. Eventually that caught up with him when, in 2008, reporters from the *Detroit Free Press* went through 14,000 text messages the two had sent each other. Amid many city business texts were many personal texts that contained graphic sexual content and that clearly showed they had conspired to fire Deputy Police Chief Gary Brown.

Kilpatrick's attorneys had tried to keep the text messages a secret for years. When the city settled with Brown in 2007, they made the settlement contingent on Brown agreeing never to reveal their existence. Kilpatrick's lawyers claimed the messages were personal and private—even though a directive signed by Kilpatrick himself said that electronic communications on city equipment were not to be "considered personal or private." Making a farce out of it, the mayor's office argued at one point that the policy only applied to city-owned equipment and the text messages were exempt because they were sent on leased equipment.

In any event, it all came out and on March 24, 2008, Kilpatrick was charged with perjury, misconduct, and obstruction of justice. Additional charges were added pertaining to an incident in which Kilpatrick had shoved a police officer trying to serve a subpoena to an associate. In September, he pleaded guilty to two counts of obstruction of justice and no contest to the assault charge. As part of the deal, he had to resign as mayor, pay $1 million in restitution to the city of Detroit, serve four months in prison, surrender his license to practice law, and agree not to run for public office for five years.

But that was not the end of it. In 2010, he failed to make a required restitution payment and was rearrested for violating terms of his parole. He was sentenced to one and a half to five years. He was released on parole again on Aug. 2, 2011. Nor does the story end there. In December 2010, Kilpatrick was indicted on thirty-eight new charges related to fraudulent contracts. His next trial is scheduled for September 2012.

Kilpatrick is handcuffed and taken away for parole violation. AP Images

Larry Langford (D)

Mayor, Birmingham, Alabama

Score: 235.2

Convicted
In prison

Special Award
Tax Evader

BIRMINGHAM, AL, MAYOR LARRY LANGFORD didn't seem to grasp the situation. He had just been found guilty on sixty counts of bribery, wire fraud, tax evasion, and money laundering. He faced a possible sentence of 805 years.

Outside the courtroom, he told reporters, "All this trial did was interrupt my Bible study classes for two weeks." Fifteen years would be more accurate.

Langford was quite the clothes horse and multiple counts were racked up for accepting luxury items that included a cashmere cardigan, a watch, jewelry, and numerous purchases at Ermenegildo Zegna, Salvatore Ferragamo, and Remon's, a popular Birmingham "gentleman's clothier." He was also found guilty of filing false tax returns and of mail fraud—for having his designer clothes sent to him special delivery.

He had a long career as a respected public official, and his attorneys tried to blame his crimes on childhood issues. "Larry Langford came from Loveman Village (a public housing project in Birmingham)," Glennon Threatt said during closing arguments. "Perhaps something from his childhood led him to overvalue the collection of material objects." Perhaps. But many politicians have grown up poor and have gone on to do great things, and just as many trust-fund babies have been caught lyin', cheatin', and stealin'.

Alabama lawmakers were divided between their opinion of Langford as a good-hearted man and their desire to be tough on government corruption.

"He's a good man," said State Representative John Rogers (D-52nd District). "He's got flaws. We've all got flaws. Sometimes when you've got flaws people prey on your weakness. I think it sends a lesson to all public officials to be very, very careful."

State Senator Scott Beason (R-17th District) took a harder line against Langford. "I'm pleased. We've been hearing about these kinds of things for years," Beason said. "I think it's a step in the right direction. Elected officials need to understand if they are involved in corruption they are eventually going to (get) caught."

There must be something in the water in Alabama. As of 2009, Langford was the fifth former Jefferson County commissioner to face public corruption charges. The people of

Langford and his wife, Melva, speak to reporters during jury selection. AP Images

Birmingham might want to be more particular about their elected officials before they go broke. According to *The Birmingham News*, the county's debt, including sewer, school and other bonds, rose by about $1 billion under Langford. At the time of Langford's conviction, the county was facing bankruptcy.

Langford's coconspirators in the bribery and bond scheme, Bill Blount and Al LaPierre, received relatively light sentences (fifty-two months and forty-eight months, respectively), but Langford was hit harder for his corruption and sentenced to fifteen years in prison. Adding to his pain, he will serve it in an orange jumpsuit.

4

Vince Fumo (D)
State Senator, Pennsylvania

Score: 241.8

Special Awards
Audacity, Tax Evader

"THAT'S THE ROLE OF A LEADER, to take care of people who can't take care of themselves. A leader also has a responsibility to tell those people not to milk the system." That's a quote from Vince Fumo's website.

The sixty-nine-year-old Fumo did not quite live up to those ideals during his thirty-year reign in the Pennsylvania State Senate. He abused his position as a leader, defrauding the state and two nonprofits out of more than $2 million and using his staff to charter yachts, work on his farm, and spy on political opponents and an ex-wife.

On Feb. 6, 2007, a federal grand jury named Fumo in a 137-count indictment. Charges included mail fraud, wire fraud, conspiracy, obstruction of justice, and filing a false tax return. Now he's serving a five-year prison term.

The 200-plus-page indictment makes for an interesting read, because it includes colorful e-mails sent by Fumo to his staff. Details of their official duties are laid out such as paying Fumo's personal bills, acting as "project manager" of the refurbishment of his mansion, wrapping and shipping 150 Vincent J. Fumo bobble heads, and fixing leaks. The e-mail Fumo sent regarding this issue was titled: "LEAKS!!!!!!!!!!!!!!!! FUCK-FUCK-FUCK!!!!!!!!!!!!!"

The multi-millionaire owned four homes and sat on the board of the Independence Seaport Museum. Investigation revealed that Fumo had commandeered yachts from the museum for years. According to the *Philadelphia Inquirer*, those pleasure cruises cost the museum $115,000.

The *Inquirer* calculated that in all, Fumo's crimes cost taxpayers, the nonprofits he stole from, and the maritime museum $4 million.

He certainly didn't need to steal money. Fumo was a director—and largest individual shareholder—of a local bank his grandfather founded, which he sold for a personal gain of $15 million. Additionally, he was paid $1 million per year by a law firm he consulted for, according to the indictment.

About one year after charges were brought against him, Fumo announced he was dropping his bid for reelection due to the stress of the charges. Fumo didn't see the problem with his actions and claimed his behavior was really a senatorial norm in Pennsylvania. When that didn't work, he claimed drugs made him do it, saying an addiction "directly contributed [to] my criminality."

Fumo leaves the courthouse after being sentenced to fifty-five months in prison for corruption. AP Images

After four years of investigation and a five-month trial, Fumo was convicted on all 137 counts of corruption in 2009. Prosecutors wanted a seventeen- to twenty-two-year sentence for the crooked politician, but Fumo walked away with just fifty-five months.

They appealed the sentence, and both the prosecutors and the defense expected a double-digit jump in jail time—but the same judge, U.S. District Judge Ronald Buckwalter, only tacked on six additional months to Fumo's stay in federal prison. Buckwalter said keeping the then-sixty-eight-year-old Fumo in jail for fifteen years, like the prosecution requested, would be a death sentence.

After decades of abuses, Fumo got just sixty-one months in the clink, $2.3 million in restitution, and ten hours per week of community service when he gets out.

A perfect example of a Fumo-official e-mail:

"We need to do the following ASAP:

1 - Set up the Run in barn for the horses
2 - Buy hay and feed, etc.
3 - Buy buckets and other supplies for feeding and watering the horses
4 - Buy 2 saddles, bridles and whatever else we need for the horses as well.
5 - Get busy with the fencing ASAP

Anything else you can think of?"

E-mails from Prison

Fumo wrote a number of e-mails from prison, lamenting his fate and how unfair the world had treated him. In them he calls his 2009 conviction on all 137 counts "a travesty of justice."

"What do they want from me, my very life? My blood? A pound of my flesh? To them this is a draconian game! A joke! Sport! To me it is real life and suffering for me and my entire family."

"Who did I kill? Who did I rape? Who did I cause irreversible harm to? Who are my real 'victims'? On a scale of the good I did versus the evil I stand convicted of, is not the scale at least balanced, if not tilted in my overwhelming favor? Am I to suffer endlessly for my 'first nonviolent' offense against society?"

"I miss decent food. I miss movies. I miss my kids. . . . I miss cooking and I miss fixing things. I miss helping people too. And for what????? What in the name of God did I do to deserve this?"

3

Rod Blagojevich (D)
Governor, Illinois

Score: 257.0

Convicted
In prison

Special Awards
Audacity, Caught on Tape

FORMER ILLINOIS GOVERNOR ROD Blagojevich was arrested on federal corruption charges on Dec. 9, 2008. Investigators claimed he was trying to "sell" President Barack Obama's vacated Illinois Senate seat and extort the owners of the Tribune Company (Blagojevich was allegedly trying to force the newspaper to fire editors critical of his administration).

On Jan. 9, 2009, the Illinois House of Representatives voted to impeach Blagojevich by a 114-1 vote. "Blago" (as he is often called because his last name is hard to pronounce), then went on a number of TV shows including *Good Morning America, The Today Show,* and *The View,* as well as programs on MSNBC, Fox, and CNN, declaring his innocence and claiming he would be vindicated. That, however, did not happen. On Jan. 29, he was convicted and removed from office by a unanimous 59-0 vote in the Illinois State Senate. In a separate motion, the Senate also voted unanimously to bar Blagojevich from office in the state of Illinois.

Initially, Blago fared pretty well on the legal front (impeachment being a political, not criminal, action). At his first corruption trial in August 2010, he was found guilty on only one of twenty-four charges (lying to the FBI). The jury hung on the other charges. But his troubles were not over because the prosecution immediately announced it would seek another trial.

"I've got this thing and it's fucking golden. I'm not just giving it up for fucking nothing."
—FBI recording of Blagojevich talking about Obama's vacated Senate seat

202

Trying to stay busy while waiting for his next court date, Blago asked the judge for permission to fly to Costa Rica to participate in the reality show *I'm a Celebrity...Get Me out of Here!*, but his request was turned down (bizarrely, his wife went in his place). Undeterred, he appeared on *Celebrity Apprentice*, but Donald Trump fired him in the fourth episode.

The charges were reduced to twenty at Blagojevich's retrial, and on June 27, 2011, he was found guilty of seventeen charges, including all charges pertaining to the

Blagojevich and his wife, Patti, speak to reporters after Blago's fourteen-year prison sentence is announced. AP Images

Senate seat, as well as extortion relating to state funds being directed toward a children's hospital and racetrack. At his sentencing on Dec. 7, 2011, Blago apologized, saying he was "unbelievably sorry," but it didn't work. U.S. District Court Judge James Zagel said, "The jury didn't believe you and neither do I." Blago was sentenced to fourteen years in jail, one of the longest sentences ever handed down to a U.S. politician.

Blago was elected governor in 2003, defeating the unfortunately named Republican Attorney General Jim Ryan. The previous governor, George Ryan (#31) (no relation), was in prison for corruption, and some voters reportedly confused the two. Blago won fifty-two percent of the vote.

When he won the election, Blago declared that Illinois had "voted for change," but that is not what Illinois got. Blago would become the second governor in a row to go to prison on corruption charges.

While in office, his vanity manifested itself in several ways. In 2004, shortly after becoming governor, he had thirty-two signs put up at toll plazas with his name on them at a cost of $480,000. (His name has since been removed.) On a more mundane level, Blagojevich made his aides carry a hairbrush for him at all times that he referred to as "the football," a reference, presumably, to the "nuclear football," the launch codes always within reach of the president.

He got along with few people. At one point in 2008, Blago said he was afraid that House Democrats would gain more seats because then he would face more opposition.

Never a popular governor, Blago sunk to new lows due to his legal problems. A poll in October 2008 (before his arrest), showed an unprecedented zero percent of Illinois voters rated Blagojevich as excellent. Indeed, Blagojevich ranked as "Least Popular Governor" in the nation, according to *Rasmussen Reports by the Numbers*. But he had not hit bottom. Before his arrest in 2008, his overall approval ratings were in the low twenties; after his arrest in December (but while he was still governor), his approval rating plummeted to seven percent, quite possibly a record.

2

Neil Goldschmidt (D)
Governor, Oregon

Score: 1,025.0

Confessed child molester

FORMER OREGON GOVERNOR NEIL Goldschmidt got away with rape. By keeping his relationship with a fourteen-year-old girl a secret until the statute of limitations expired, he avoided being charged with third-degree rape (a felony punishable by up to five years in prison), and being labeled a sex offender for the rest of his life.

On May 6, 2004, Goldschmidt admitted to having a sexual relationship with the girl and entering into a financial settlement with her in 1994. Trying to imply his confession was a matter of conscience, Goldschmidt said, "I'm just living with this personal hell. The lie has gone on too long." But the truth is he only owned up to his crimes because the *Willamette Week* had broken the story. In fact, *Willamette Week* reporter Nigel Jaquiss won the 2005 Pulitzer Prize for the story.

In his statements and interviews, Goldschmidt continually referred to his relationship with the teenager as "an affair." But you can't have an "affair" with a fourteen-year-old in Oregon—sex with anyone under the age of sixteen is rape.

"You can't say something that is illegal is an 'affair,'" University of Oregon child psychologist Elizabeth Stormshak told *Willamette Week*. "I can't think of a way that it would be anything other than molestation."

While Goldschmidt claims the relationship lasted only a few months in the 1970s while he was mayor of Portland, his victim told a different story to a columnist from *The Oregonian*. She said the sexual relationship continued through his career as mayor, his time as U.S. secretary of transportation, and his term as Oregon's governor.

According to the victim, the sexual relationship began at the girl's mother's birthday party, when the mayor coerced her into performing oral sex. It continued

Workers remove the portrait of Goldschmidt from the Senate Hall. AP Images

"You can't say something that is illegal is an 'affair.' I can't think of a way that it would be anything other than molestation."

—University of Oregon child psychologist
Elizabeth Stormshak

with the mayor picking her up from school or coming over to her house when her mother wasn't home and having sex with her.

Shortly before his resignation, *Willamette Week* published the results of a two-month investigation into Goldschmidt's relationship with the teenage girl. During the investigation, more than a dozen people claimed they knew about the relationship and court documents revealed monthly payments to Goldschmidt's victim. Indeed, one of the most disturbing aspects of the story is that several prominent people knew about the relationship and did not report it, including Multnomah County Sheriff Bernie Giusto (who announced his early retirement in 2008 after a state police board recommended he be removed for numerous incidents including his knowledge of Goldschmidt's relationship with the teenager).

The girl dropped out of high school, fell into alcohol and drugs, and attempted suicide several times. His victim asked to remain anonymous, but she wanted to share her story to help protect other victims of abuse and "to stop keeping the secrets." She died in a hospice in early 2011.

Even Goldschmidt acknowledged the heinousness of his crimes. At the time of his resignation he said, "if people work hard enough [investigating other politicians], I think you'll find indiscretions. But nothing as ugly as this."

Phil Giordano (R)

Mayor, Waterbury, Connecticut

Score: 1,422.0

Convicted child molester
In prison

THERE'S A SPECIAL PLACE IN HELL for people who abuse children and Philip Giordano is on his way there—but first he has to serve out his thirty-seven-year prison term.

The former mayor of Waterbury, CT, was arrested in July 2001 when, during an investigation into municipal corruption, the FBI found something far more disturbing. In a wiretapped conversation, Giordano—husband and father of three—was caught arranging sex with a crack-addicted prostitute, Guitana Jones.

Tragically, it gets worse. Turns out he wasn't just interested in Jones. He was also interested in her daughter and niece, who were ages eight and ten at the time. Giordano routinely abused the girls, a pattern that started in 2000. Jones, who'd had a longstanding relationship with Giordano, brought her daughter and niece to him for sex. Allegedly, the acts sometimes occurred in his office.

Federal prosecutors brought an eighteen-count indictment against Giordano, which included using an interstate facility to entice a minor to engage in sexual activity and conspiracy to commit that offense. In September 2001, Giordano was also charged with violating the girls' civil rights. Those charges carried a maximum sentence of life in prison and a $250,000 fine and were added to the original charges.

Giordano pleaded "not guilty" and defiantly took the case to trial, forcing the two young girls to testify about what he did to them and what he forced them to do to him. That strategy backfired and Giordano was sentenced to thirty-seven years in prison. Giordano's lawyer pleaded with the judge for a more lenient sentence, citing Giordano's former military service, the impact his incarceration would have on his family and, incredibly, his "unusual susceptibility to abuse" (i.e., child rapists don't generally do well in prison).

Senior U.S. District Judge Alan H. Nevas was not moved and berated Giordano for his abhorrent conduct. "You destroyed these girls emotionally and psychologically," Nevas said. "You preyed upon them and you destroyed their innocence to satisfy your own sexual desires." Nevas also told Giordano that this was the worst case he'd seen in his eighteen years on the bench. "Your guidelines initially provided for a life sentence, and I can tell you, Mr. Giordano, I would have had no hesitation in

Artist's sketch of Giordano (in the foreground) listening as the prosecutor questions Guitana Jones, the prostitute who testified she brought her preteen daughter and niece to his office to have sex with him. AP Images

The 7 Longest Prison Sentences

1. Philip Giordano (#1)
   37 years

2. Larry Langford (#5)
   15 years

3. Rod Blagojevich (#3)
   14 years

4. William Jefferson (#9)
   13 years

5 Edwin Edwards (#8)
   10 years

6. Joseph Ganim (#19)
   9 years

7. Duke Cunningham (#10)
   8 years

sentencing you to life for what you've done," Nevas told Giordano at his sentencing. Unfortunately, Nevas was unable to give Giordano a life sentence because Giordano had cooperated with the investigation.

Giordano said nothing at his sentencing, never admitting wrongdoing or apologizing to the girls whose lives he ruined. He also never apologized to his sister, mother, or wife, who all sat in the audience at his trial.

Three years into his sentence, the former mayor sent a letter to Waterbury asking for $61,000 he said he was owed for unused personal days, sick days, and vacation time. He didn't get it. Giordano also tried to appeal his conviction several times but to no effect. Jones was sentenced to ten years in prison in 2003.

The former Waterbury mayor is currently serving his sentence at an Illinois prison, and, with any luck, getting what he deserves. He'll be nearly seventy years old when he is released, and hopefully will spend his last years dying a slow, lonely, and painful death.

POOR
JUDGMENT

Poor Judgment

Seven public officials are included in this special section. They are not Bastards, but they have exhibited what can only be called "poor judgment."

In no particular order...

Carmen Kontur-Gronquist (I)
Mayor, Arlington, Oregon
Recalled

ONE SMALL-TOWN MAYOR couldn't put out the fire on her red-hot scandal and ended up stripped not only of her clothes, but her office.

Carmen Kontur-Gronquist was the mayor of Arlington, OR, a city of 586 people. Hoping to stir up some romance for the single mom, a relative created a MySpace account for the mayor and posted some racy photos of Kontur-Gronquist taken at the fire station.

Appearing on ABC's *20/20*, Kontur-Gronquist said the photos were going to be used for a women's fitness contest sponsored by *Sports Illustrated* (if the contest was "Buffest Mayor in America," she'd have won hands down). Kontur-Gronquist added she had permission from the fire chief to pose on the town's now-famous engine. She was working at the fire station as an executive secretary at the time.

Indeed, the photos were taken a year before she was elected mayor. She says she saw no reason to remove them from her MySpace page after taking office. Her reasoning? It didn't say Arlington on her profile, nor that she was the mayor, just that she lived in the United States.

In true small-town fashion, when word spread about the photos, someone printed them up and handed them out. Kontur-Gronquist was on vacation, so it was her eighteen-year-old daughter who had to break the news to her. It can't be easy for a senior in high school to see pictures showing her late-thirties mother looking in better shape than most of her high school friends.

"I immediately called each one of the council members. I did not apologize for the photo, but I did apologize for putting them in that position if they felt uncomfortable," Kontur-Gronquist told *The Today Show*. "At that point, I thought the situation was done and resolved."

But it was not. According to *The Oregonian*, it only takes forty-one names to launch a recall in Arlington, and that's exactly what happened. Just weeks after

Kontur-Gronquist took these photos and posted them on her MySpace page. Not surprisingly, they were soon printed off and circulating around town.

photos of the mayor posing in her underwear were circulated, the recall was on the ballot. In a painfully close vote of 142-139, the town's first female mayor became the town's first former female mayor. (News later surfaced about a lack of ballot box security and then forty-two-year-old Kontur-Gronquist contemplated asking for a recount, but ultimately vacated her spot.)

KEPR-TV, the CBS news affiliate in the area, said most Arlington residents admitted the recall was really about Kontur-Gronquist's views on the local golf course and water allocation, but her enemies used the photos to polarize the community.

She told *The Today Show* that thousands of people requested signed copies of the photos that sparked the scandal, so she began selling them on eBay—a more lucrative venture than serving as the Arlington mayor, which pays nothing. Kontur-Gronquist, also the town's former lifeguard, declared she would donate a portion of the money to the local ambulance service.

Clearly, Carmen Kontur-Gronquist is not really a *Lyin' Cheatin' Bastard*. Nevertheless, she was recalled from office (ostensibly) over a "sex scandal," and is therefore included here in our special section, "Poor Judgment."

6

Eric Brewer (D)
Mayor, East Cleveland
Lost reelection

FORMER EAST CLEVELAND, OH, MAYOR Eric Brewer now offers an important piece of campaign advice: If you're a man, don't let anyone take pictures of you dressed as a woman while you're running for office. No matter what assurances you get, the photos will be leaked and you'll end up losing the election.

Then fifty-five-year-old Brewer suffered this fate in the fall of 2009, when he was running for his second term as mayor. The photos first appeared on WKYC-TV a week before election day, showing Brewer in women's lingerie in various poses. In a strange counter-offensive, Brewer held a news conference the next day and blasted the media for not getting his comment on the photos before publishing them ... but did not confirm or deny that the photos were of him.

He did not admit the photos were of him until after he lost the election, at which point he made it worse—he did an exclusive interview for the national tabloid show *Inside Edition*.

"That is me in those pictures," he told the interviewer. When asked how he ended up in women's clothes, Brewer said a girlfriend had suggested he put them on and then took photos. "Once in her home ... once in my apartment ... and the pictures are personal," Brewer added, in case that was not obvious to viewers.

The interviewer told Brewer, "No offense, but you weren't the best-looking woman."

"To the lady I was with, I looked great," Brewer replied. "We had a good time."

But good times always come to an end. He blamed the photos for his election loss. "I myself heard someone say that they were voting for the mayor who wore pants, and one lady said that she did not want to vote for a mayor who would compete with her for wearing her panties," Brewer said.

He called for a criminal investigation into the leak, accusing his opponent Gary Norton and members of the city's police department of releasing the compromising photos. He said the pictures were stolen from his personal computer. Norton and the police department denied any involvement.

Brewer quit politics completely after the scandal. According to the *Cleveland Plain Dealer*, he now owns a small restaurant that serves heart healthy food and lives a private life.

"He has an eccentric and outgoing personality. He always has an interesting story to tell," said a neighboring shop owner. Never truer words.

Although he doesn't look too bad in women's clothes, Brewer should have known better than to take such pictures during an election.

David Vitter (R)
Senator, Louisiana
Still in office

WE'VE ALL BEEN BOMBARDED during the dinner hour with sales calls, requests for donations, and political pleas, but U.S. Senator David Vitter (R-LA) found his name on a different call list in July 2007. The Republican lawmaker's phone number was found on the "D.C. Madam's" rolodex. (He was not the only politician on the list, see Randall Tobias #17.)

When *Hustler* magazine contacted the senator's office to ask about it, he didn't even try to insult voters with a lie. He immediately issued a public apology for his "very serious sin," and his honesty probably allowed him to retain his Senate seat.

Deborah Jean Palfrey (the D.C. Madam herself) didn't buy Vitter's high-road approach. While Palfrey was battling federal prostitution charges, she reminded *Time* magazine that prostitution is illegal for both parties of the transaction. "Why am I the only person being prosecuted? Senator Vitter should be prosecuted [if he broke the law]," Palfrey said. (Palfrey was later found dead in her jail cell, an apparent suicide.)

While the Madam had a good point, sometimes a Bastard can admit to being a Bastard, but manage to worm his way out of charges. Vitter managed to avoid losing his seat or facing charges by not addressing any details of his sins in his so-called confession. He avoided any mention of services rendered by the escort agency, how often he used the service, or any other details beyond admitting that he had committed a "very serious sin."

In regards to Vitter's marriage, he said it had survived his sins. "Several years ago, I asked for and received forgiveness from God and my wife in confession and marriage counseling. Out of respect for my family, I will keep my discussion of the matter there with God and them," Vitter said. "But I certainly offer my deep and sincere apologies to all I have disappointed and let down in any way."

Vitter does seem to be a good sort of guy. Jeanette Maier, the Madam of a high-priced brothel in New Orleans that was shut down in 2002, agrees. She told New Orleans TV news station WDSU that Vitter had been her client since the 1990s and he was "one of the nicest and most honorable men I've ever met."

Maier has no doubt met many men throughout her years as a madam and is probably a skilled judge of character. The voters of Louisiana seemed to agree with her and reelected Vitter in 2010.

Vitter's wife Wendy was not too happy to discover his phone number was in the D.C. Madam's rolodex. AP Images

Greg Davis
Mayor, Southaven, Mississippi
Still in office

WHILE WE CONGRATULATE SOUTHAVEN, MS, Mayor Greg Davis on coming out of the closet, he has exercised very poor judgment.

After the state auditor's office started investigating receipts submitted by Davis for entertainment and recruiting expenses, Davis was forced to reveal personal details he'd tried to keep secret. "While I have performed my job as mayor, in my opinion, as a very conservative, progressive individual—and still continue to be a very conservative individual—I think that it is important that I discuss the struggles I have had over the last few years when I came to the realization that I am gay."

Davis' receipts, submitted in 2011, include thousands of dollars at a Mississippi chophouse, thousands at liquor stores, and a particularly intriguing charge of $67 at Priape, one of Canada's leading gay sex shops. What can one buy for $67 at Priape? According to the shop's website, three Wolf Leather Masks, one Latex Brief, or nine packages of Magnum condoms. He told reporters he doesn't remember what he purchased.

Sex toys aside, Mississippi state auditors have demanded Davis repay $170,000 of improper charges—a reasonable request, given Mississippi has slashed budgets for most state agencies.

As of March 2011, Davis has repaid $96,000 of the questionable charges, but the game is not over: Duplicate invoices submitted to both the Southaven Chamber of Commerce and the city of Southaven have emerged.

Davis told *The Commercial Appeal* (a Memphis newspaper), "There has never been any intentional double billing of any type or any kind." Davis added, "... I would not do anything to jeopardize my family name or the job performance that we have done over the last fifteen years. Unfortunately, there are those that want to take numbers and twist and turn them, but the hardcore facts are there.

Anybody can look them up. And we [are] confident as we work through the process with the state auditor, hopefully, he will see the same thing we do."

When those "hardcore" facts were checked, *The Commercial Appeal* found twenty-six invoices submitted to the chamber between July and September 2010 that matched the dates, name of business, and amount on invoices submitted to the city.

While Davis waits to find out how much money he has to pay back to the city, he's been staying busy. He remains in office as Southaven's mayor, but he turned himself in to law enforcement officials on March 27 on charges he unlawfully passed a school bus in a private vehicle that displayed police-type lights. The mayor claimed he was acting as the city's chief law enforcement official and was pursuing another vehicle.

In 2008, Davis ran (unsuccessfully) for Congress on a "conservative, family-values" platform. Too bad he lost. Outed gay conservative, embezzler, phony traffic cop—he would have fit right in.

Davis campaigning with Vice President Dick Cheney. AP Images

Eric Massa (D)
Congressman, New York
Resigned

FORMER U.S. REPRESENTATIVE Eric Massa (D-NY) wasn't in office even one full term before he resigned amid allegations of sexually harassing young male staffers.

It was not the first time Massa had faced allegations of inappropriate behavior. When he was serving in the Navy during Operation Desert Shield, two of his junior officers, Tom Maxfield and Stuart Borsch, came forward with strikingly similar reports. Both claimed they awoke during the middle of the night to find their boxer shorts pulled down and Massa groping them. Maxfield told *The Washington Post* that when he woke up, Massa "scooted back to his own bunk ... feigning sleep." Borsch also told the paper, "I was awakened when a senior officer, Massa, seemed to be groping me. I believe he may have been drinking." Angry words ensued. "I shouted at him and he left."

> **"Not only did I grope him, I tickled him until he couldn't breathe."**
>
> —Massa tells Glen Beck what really happened

What happened on the ocean might have stayed on the ocean if it hadn't continued on land. When Massa arrived in Washington, D.C., and moved into a townhouse with several young, male staffers, stories started flying about groping, tickle parties, and sexually suggestive conversations. It stopped being funny when a staff member filed a complaint and the House Ethics Committee launched an investigation.

On March 3, 2010, Massa announced he would not seek reelection because of his health. He resigned two days later, citing both his health and the harassment

Eric Massa resigned when he was accused of harassing young male staffers. AP Images

charges. Four days after that, on March 9, he went on Glenn Beck's TV show to tell America the real reason he was leaving.

After first portraying his "groping" as nothing more than horseplay (telling Beck, "Not only did I grope him, I tickled him until he couldn't breathe."), he claimed he was railroaded by his own party because he would not toe the line on issues like the budget or health care reform.

Beck prompted Massa for specifics, but got none. By the end of the show, all Beck could say was, "America, I've got to shoot straight with you. I think I've wasted your time. And I apologize for that."

Hearing Massa cite his opposition to health care reform as his reason for resigning, White House Press Secretary Robert Gibbs characterized Massa's claims as "crazy."

"On Wednesday, he was having a recurrence of cancer," Gibbs said during an appearance on ABC's *Good Morning America*. "On Thursday, he was guilty of using salty language. On Friday, we learned he's before the Ethics Committee to be investigated on charges of sexual harassment."

Since Massa left office in March 2010, he has avoided the spotlight. No word on whether the tickle parties continue at his home in New York.

John Doolittle (R)
Congressman, California
Now a lobbyist

JOHN T. DOOLITTLE'S (R-CA) NAME appeared so often next to other *Lyin'
Cheatin' Bastards* and convicted felons it's surprising he wasn't charged with any
crimes. Nevertheless, he wins a spot on our *Poor Judgment* list.

The Citizens for Responsibility & Ethics in Washington (CREW) certainly
didn't like what he was doing and named Doolittle to "CREW's Most Corrupt
Report 2006: Beyond DeLay," saying, "Rep. Doolittle's ethics issues stem from
his wife's relationship to his campaign and political action committees, as well as
campaign contributions and personal financial benefits he accepted from those
who sought his legislative assistance." Doolittle was also named in the 2007 and
2008 reports.

Doolittle's Northern Virginia home was raided by the FBI in 2007, and the
Justice Department investigated payments his wife received from convicted felon
Jack Abramoff. Doolittle was also connected to the 2005 conspiracy led by former
Congressman Duke Cunningham (#10).

Doolittle helped steer millions of dollars of defense money to a company called
Perfect Wave, owned by Brent Wilkes. Doolittle claimed he did so based on the
merits of the technology and written support from the military. The *San Diego
Union-Tribune*, however, reported that the funds were not requested by the military but stuck in by Doolittle's committee after the fact, and that the only record
of military support was a letter written by a low level program manager two years
after Doolittle started earmarking funds for Perfect Wave.

In the end no charges were filed although Doolittle was forced by Republican
leaders to resign from the House Appropriations Committee and ultimately retire
instead of seeking a 10th term. "It was not my initial intent to retire, and I fully

expected and planned to run again right up until very recently," said Doolittle in a written statement. "[My wife and I] were ready for a change after spending almost our entire married lives with me in public service."

He hasn't completely left the political arena—now he's a lobbyist. He certainly knows how to play that game.

Doolittle, pictured here at the press conference announcing his retirement, grimaces at a reporter's question.
AP Images

Sam Adams (D)
Mayor, Portland, Oregon
Still in office

VISIT THE MAYOR'S PAGE ON THE Portland, OR, city website, and you'll find Mayor Sam Adams' Facebook, Twitter, and LinkedIn profiles. Adams is certainly plugged into his young constituency—but maybe too much so when he had a relationship with legislative intern Beau Breedlove.

Accusations against Adams (an openly gay man) came out while he was serving as city commissioner and campaigning for mayor. Adams denied the charges of a sexual relationship with the then-seventeen-year-old Breedlove, but days before his 2009 inauguration he admitted there was truth to the rumors.

Even though *The Oregonian*, the local gay publication *Just Out*, and the local police union called for his resignation, Adams refused to step down. Attorney General John Kroger undertook a five-month investigation into Adams' relationship with Breedlove, but concluded there was "insufficient evidence to charge Mayor Adams with a criminal offense."

Kroger said his investigation considered a number of possibilities, including:

1. Did Adams have sexual intercourse with Breedlove before Breedlove was eighteen?
2. Did Adams have sexual contact of a lesser nature with Breedlove before Breedlove was eighteen (which in Oregon is still a violation of the law)?
3. Did Adams hire a former reporter in an effort to get her to stop pursuing an investigation into this matter?
4. Did Adams use government resources to cover up the story about him and Breedlove?
5. Did Adams lie about his relationship with Breedlove when Adams was fundraising for his mayoral campaign?

Although no charges were filed, Adams was criticized for his handling of the affair.

Sam Adams admitted his mistakes and apologized. AP Images

Portland City Commissioner Randy Leonard, a former friend of Adams, spoke to *Time* magazine about Adams. "The part that bothers me is that I defended Sam back in 2007 more so than anybody else." When Adams admitted he asked Breedlove to lie about their relationship, Leonard said, "I was troubled that he called Beau and asked him to lie... Why would he ask [Breedlove] to lie about a consensual relationship between adults?"

The real question was: When did the relationship begin? In Oregon, sexual contact of any kind with someone younger than eighteen is illegal. Both men claimed they did not have sex until shortly after Breedlove turned eighteen, but their stories differ as to when they started kissing. Breedlove told investigators, "They embraced each other body to body and engaged in a long, mutual kiss on the lips," before he was eighteen. The incident reportedly took place in a City Hall bathroom, but Adams claims they didn't kiss.

While the investigative report let Adams off the hook, he issued a statement saying, "I made mistakes in my personal life," and "I want to reiterate that I am sorry." He told reporters from *Willamette Week*, "I've obviously made bad judgments, about lying to you and others about whether or not I had a sexual relationship with Beau after he was an adult. I have apologized for that and my apologies are sincere."

The people of Portland seem to have accepted Adams' apology. After the attorney general declined to charge Adams, some voters started a campaign to recall the mayor, but two attempts by a volunteer group failed to get enough signatures to put a recall vote on the ballot.

SCORING
TABLES

Scoring Tables

Each Bastard has been scored according to a complex, highly scientific system that accurately calculates their "bastardness-ness."

Details of the Scoring System are given in the Introduction.

★ ★ ★ LYIN' CHEATIN' BASTARDS ★ ★ ★

	Prison Sentence	Convictions	Impeached	Removed / Terminated	Resigned Disgrace	Cheating on Spouse	Dollars Stolen
Mike Easley	-	1.0	-	-	-	-	-
Roland Burris	-	-	-	-	-	-	-
Robert Watson	-	1.0	-	-	-	-	-
John Rowland	10.0	1.0	-	-	-	-	0.1
Don Sherwood	-	-	-	-	-	25.0	-
Arnold Schwarzenegger	-	-	-	-	-	25.0	-
Jim Gibbons	-	-	-	-	-	25.0	-
John Edwards	-	-	-	-	-	25.0	-
Katherine Bryson	-	-	-	-	-	25.0	-
Roy Ashburn	-	1.0	-	-	-	-	-
Daniel Gordon	1.7	2.0	-	-	-	-	-
Paul Patton	-	1.0	-	-	-	25.0	-
Eddie Perez	30.0	5.0	-	-	-	-	-
Marion Barry	-	-	-	-	-	-	-
Charlie Rangel	-	-	-	-	-	-	-
David Wu	-	-	-	-	50.0	-	-
Jim West	-	-	-	-	-	-	-
Thomas Porteous	-	-	25.0	25.0	-	-	-
Chip Pickering	-	-	-	-	-	25.0	-
Tim Mahoney	-	-	-	-	-	25.0	-
Hank Johnson	-	-	-	-	-	-	-
James Holley	-	-	-	-	-	-	-
Thad Viers	-	1.0	-	-	50.0	-	-
Larry Craig	-	1.0	-	-	-	-	-
Claude Allen	-	1.0	-	-	50.0	-	-
Sharpe James	22.5	5.0	-	-	-	25.0	-

Ethics Violations	Censured	Recalled	Hookers	Special Awards	Stupidity Adjustment	Drugs or Alcohol	Molesting Minors	Total Score
-	-	-	-	-	-	-	-	1.0
-	10.0	-	-	-	-	-	-	10.0
-	-	-	-	-	-	10.0	-	11.0
-	-	-	-	-	-	-	-	11.1
-	-	-	-	-	-	-	-	25.0
-	-	-	-	-	-	-	-	25.0
-	-	-	-	-	-	-	-	25.0
-	-	-	-	-	-	-	-	25.0
-	-	-	-	-	-	-	-	25.0
-	-	-	-	25.0	-	-	-	26.0
-	-	-	-	25.0	-	-	-	28.7
4.0	-	-	-	-	-	-	-	30.0
-	-	-	-	-	-	-	-	35.0
-	10.0	-	-	25.0	-	-	-	35.0
11.0	10.0	-	-	25.0	-	-	-	46.0
-	-	-	-	-	-	-	-	50.0
-	-	25.0	-	25.0	-	-	-	50.0
-	-	-	-	-	-	-	-	50.0
-	-	-	-	25.0	-	-	-	50.0
-	-	-	-	25.0	-	-	-	50.0
-	-	-	-	25.0	25.0	-	-	50.0
-	-	50.0	-	-	-	-	-	50.0
-	-	-	-	-	-	-	-	51.0
-	-	-	-	50.0	-	-	-	51.0
-	-	-	-	-	-	-	-	51.0
-	-	-	-	-	-	-	-	52.5

	Prison Sentence	Convictions	Impeached	Removed / Terminated	Resigned Disgrace	Cheating on Spouse	Dollars Stolen
Bill Campbell	25.0	3.0	-	-	-	-	-
Vincent Cianci, Jr	53.3	1.0	-	-	-	-	-
Tom Anderson	50.0	7.0	-	-	-	-	-
Philip Hinkle	-	-	-	-	-	25.0	-
Vito Fossella	0.1	1.0	-	-	-	25.0	-
Bruce Barclay	-	10.0	-	-	50.0	-	-
Peter Cammarano	20.0	1.0	-	-	50.0	-	-
Paul Stanley	-	-	-	-	50.0	25.0	-
Paul Morrsion	-	-	-	-	50.0	25.0	-
Jim McGreevey	-	-	-	-	50.0	25.0	-
Amy Koch	-	-	-	-	50.0	25.0	-
Mark Foley	-	-	-	-	50.0	-	-
John Ensign	-	-	-	-	50.0	25.0	-
Amy Brewer	-	-	-	-	50.0	-	-
Bob Levy	-	1.0	-	-	50.0	-	-
Bob Ney	25.0	2.0	-	-	50.0	-	-
John Lake	50.0	3.0	-	-	-	-	-
Lewis Libby	25.0	4.0	-	-	50.0	-	-
Kyle Foggo	30.8	1.0	-	-	50.0	-	-
Tom DeLay	80.0	2.0	-	-	-	-	-
George Ryan	65.0	18.0	-	-	-	-	-
Eddie Shrock	-	-	-	-	-	25.0	-
Bob Ryan	-	-	-	-	-	25.0	-
Chris Myers	-	-	-	-	50.0	25.0	-
Jack & Leslie Johnson	82.5	3.0	-	-	-	-	0.2
Mark Sanford	-	-	-	-	-	25.0	-

Ethics Violations	Censured	Recalled	Hookers	Special Awards	Stupidity Adjustment	Drugs or Alcohol	Molesting Minors	Total Score
-	-	-	-	25.0	-	-	-	53.0
-	-	-	-	-	-	-	-	54.3
-	-	-	-	-	-	-	-	57.0
-	-	-	10.0	25.0	-	-	-	60.0
-	-	-	-	-	25.0	10.0	-	61.1
-	-	-	10.0	-	-	-	-	70.0
-	-	-	-	-	-	-	-	71.0
-	-	-	-	-	-	-	-	75.0
-	-	-	-	-	-	-	-	75.0
-	-	-	-	-	-	-	-	75.0
-	-	-	-	-	-	-	-	75.0
-	-	-	-	25.0	-	-	-	75.0
-	-	-	-	-	-	-	-	75.0
-	-	-	-	25.0	-	-	-	75.0
-	-	-	-	25.0	-	-	-	76.0
-	-	-	-	-	-	-	-	77.0
-	-	-	-	-	25.0	-	-	78.0
-	-	-	-	-	-	-	-	79.0
-	-	-	-	-	-	-	-	81.8
-	-	-	-	-	-	-	-	82.0
-	-	-	-	-	-	-	-	83.0
-	-	-	10.0	50.0	-	-	-	85.0
-	-	25.0	-	25.0	-	10.0	-	85.0
-	-	-	10.0	-	-	-	-	85.0
-	-	-	-	-	-	-	-	85.7
37.0	10.0	-	-	25.0	-	-	-	97.0

233

	Prison Sentence	Convictions	Impeached	Removed / Terminated	Resigned Disgrace	Cheating on Spouse	Dollars Stolen
Anthony Weiner	-	-	-	-	50.0	25.0	-
Mark Souder	-	-	-	-	50.0	25.0	-
Chris Lee	-	-	-	-	50.0	25.0	-
Bob Allen	-	1.0	-	-	50.0	-	-
Marc Dann	-	-	25.0	-	50.0	25.0	-
Rita Crundwell	-	-	-	25.0	-	-	53.0
Joseph Ganim	90.0	16.0	-	-	-	-	0.5
Bell Council	-	-	-	-	50.0	-	6.7
Randall Tobias	-	-	-	-	50.0	25.0	-
Richard Curtis	-	-	-	-	50.0	25.0	-
James Traficant	70.0	10.0	-	-	-	-	-
Betty Loren Maltese	80.0	3.0	-	-	-	-	12.0
Michael Duvall	-	-	-	-	50.0	25.0	-
Samuel Kent	27.5	1.0	25.0	-	50.0	25.0	-
Eliot Spitzer	-	-	-	-	50.0	25.0	-
Randall Cunningham	83.3	2.0	-	-	50.0	-	2.4
William Jefferson	130.0	10.0	-	-	-	-	-
Edwin Edwards	100.0	17.0	-	-	-	-	0.4
Diane Wilkerson	35.0	8.0	-	-	50.0	-	-
Kwame Kilpatrick	53.3	3.0	-	-	50.0	25.0	-
Larry Langford	150.0	60.0	-	-	-	-	0.2
Vince Fumo	50.8	137.0	-	-	-	-	4.0
Rod Blagojevich	140.0	17.0	25.0	25.0	-	-	-
Neil Goldschmidt	-	-	-	-	-	25.0	-
Phil Giordano	370.0	17.0	-	-	-	25.0	-

Ethics Violations	Censured	Recalled	Hookers	Special Awards	Stupidity Adjustment	Drugs or Alcohol	Molesting Minors	Total Score
-	-	-	-	-	25.0	-	-	100.0
-	-	-	-	25.0	-	-	-	100.0
-	-	-	-	-	25.0	-	-	100.0
-	-	-	-	50.0	-	-	-	101.0
2.0	-	-	-	-	-	-	-	102.0
-	-	-	-	25.0	-	-	-	103.0
-	-	-	-	-	-	-	-	106.5
-	-	25.0	-	25.0	-	-	-	106.7
-	-	-	10.0	25.0	-	-	-	110.0
-	-	-	10.0	25.0	-	-	-	110.0
-	10.0	-	-	25.0	-	-	-	115.0
-	-	-	-	25.0	-	-	-	120.0
-	-	-	-	25.0	25.0	-	-	125.0
-	-	-	-	-	-	-	-	128.5
-	-	-	10.0	25.0	25.0	-	-	135.0
-	-	-	-	-	-	-	-	137.7
-	-	-	-	-	-	-	-	140.0
-	-	-	-	25.0	-	-	-	142.4
-	-	-	-	50.0	-	-	-	143.0
-	-	-	-	25.0	-	-	-	156.3
-	-	-	-	25.0	-	-	-	235.2
-	-	-	-	50.0	-	-	-	241.8
-	-	-	-	50.0	-	-	-	257.0
-	-	-	-	-	-	-	1,000.0	1,025.0
-	-	-	10.0	-	-	-	1,000.0	1,422.0

SOURCES

★ ★ ★ **SOURCES** ★ ★ ★

Introduction

Baumeister, Roy. "Is There Anything Good About Men?" Oxford University Press. 2010.

Ghitis, Frida. "Are Men Stupid?" *CNN.com.* 23 Apr. 2012. Web. 23 Aug. 2012.

Moore, Frazier. "Roger Ailes: I Hired Sarah Palin Because She Was 'Hot and Got Ratings'." *Huffington Post.* 5 Oct. 2011. Web. 12 Aug. 2012.

Stolberg, Sheryl. "When It Comes to Scandal, Girls Won't Be Boys." *New York Times.* 11 June 2011. Web. 23 Aug. 2012.

Wasniewski, Matthew, Editor. Women in Congress, 1917-2006. House Committee on House Administration, Office of the Clerk. Washington, D.C. 2006

"1992 Census of Governments." *U.S. Department of Commerce, Economics and Statistics Administration, Bureau of the Census.* census.gov. June 1995. Web. 3 Aug. 2012.

"CREW'S Most Corrupt Alumni List." *CREW (Citizens for the Responsibility and Ethics in Washington).* crewsmostcorrupt.org. 2011. Web. 3 Aug. 2012.

"Table 1: Apportionment Population and Number of Representatives, by State." 2010 U.S. Census. *U.S. Department of Commerce, Economics and Statistics Administration, Bureau of the Census.* N.d. Web. 12 Aug. 2012.

77. Mike Easley

Curliss, Andrew J. "Sources Say Easley Has Agreed to a Plea Deal." *newsobserver.com.* 20 Nov. 2010. Web. 30 Apr. 2012.

Curliss, Andrew J., and Dan Kane. "Easley Convicted of Felony; State, Federal Probes End." *newsobserver.com.* 6 Apr. 2011. Web. 30 Apr. 2012.

Locke, Mandy, and Rob Christensen. "How Mike Easley Went From Political Star to Convicted Felon." *mcclatchydc. com.* 28 Nov. 2010. Web. 30 Apr. 2012.

"Lots of Discounts but No Charges." *newsobserver.com.* 24 Nov. 2010. Web. 30 Apr. 2012.

76. Roland Burris

Condon, Stephanie. "Roland Burris Admonished by Senate Ethics Panel, but No Punishment." *CBS News.* 20 Nov. 2009. Web. 31 Mar. 2012.

Cowan, Richard, and Thomas Ferraro. "Democrat Roland Burris Blocked From Senate." *Reuters.* 6 Jan. 2009. Web. 31 Mar. 2012.

Hulse, Carle, and David Stout. "Burris, Blocked From Taking Seat, Gains New Support." *New York Times.* 6 Jan. 2009. Web. 31 Mar. 2012.

Steinberg, Neil. "An Update on Roland Burris? It'll Cost You." *Chicago Sun-Times.* 28 Mar. 2012. Web. 21 Mar. 2012.

Sweet, Lynn. "Burris Farewell Speech: Lack of Blacks in Senate 'Troubling'." *Chicago Sun-Times.* 18 Nov. 2010. Web. 31 Mar. 2012.

"Ethics Panel Investigating Burris, Senator Says." *CNN.com.* Feb. 18, 2009. Web. 31 Mar. 2012.

"Ex-Sen. Roland Burris Said He Did Nothing Wrong." *Associated Press.* The News-Gazette. 25 Feb. 2012. Web. 31 Mar. 2012.

75. Robert A Watson

Armental, Maria. "South Kingstown Police: Rep. Watson Slurred, Cursed, Said, 'You Got Your Guy'." *Providence Journal.* 23 Jan. 2012. Web. May 2012.

Jordan, Jennifer D. "Rep. Watson Arrested in South Kingstown, Charged with Possessing Marijuana." *Providence Journal.* 22 Jan. 2012. Web. May 2012.

McNamara, Elizabeth. "State Rep. Bob Watson In Treatment In Florida." *East Greenwich Patch.* 10 Feb. 2012. Web. May 2012

---. "Watson Pleads No Contest To Marijuana Possession Charge." *East Greenwich Patch.* 1 Mar. 2012. Web. May 2012.

Richmond, Trevor. South Kingstown Police Department *Arrest Report #12-63-AR.* South Kingstown: South Kingstown Police Dept., 21 Jan. 2012.

Sardelli, Melissa. "Rep's Controversial Remarks Under Fire." *WPRI-TV.com.* 11 Feb. 2011. Web. May 2012.

"Poll: Should Rep. Bob Watson Resign?" *Middletown Patch*. 24 Jan. 2012. Web. May 2012.

"Rep. Returns to State House After Rehab." *WPRI-TV.com*. 6 Mar. 2012. Web. May 2012.

"RI Lawmaker Arrested for Pot Back from Treatment." *Boston.com*. 6 Mar. 2012. Web May 2012.

"Robert Watson Faces Drug Charges After Being Stopped At Police Checkpoint." *Huffington Post*. 24 Apr. 2011. Web. May 2012.

74. John Rowland

Apuzzo, Matt, and John Christoffersen. "Former Gov. Rowland Gets a Year in Prison for Graft." *Associated Press*. USA TODAY. 18 Mar. 2005. Web. Mar. 2012.

Bayles, Fred. "Scandal-Plagued Conn. Governor to Resign." *USA TODAY*. 21 June 2004. Web. Apr. 2012.

Cowan, Alison Leigh. "Connecticut Official and State Contractor Are Each Sentenced to 30 Months in Prison." *New York Times*. 26 Apr. 2006. Web. Mar. 2012.

Hutchinson, Bill. "Gifts Scandal Topples Gov. Rowland of Conn." *NYDailyNews.com*. 22 June 2004. Web. Mar. 2012.

Mehren, Elizabeth. "Freebie Scandal Ends in Guilty Plea." *Los Angeles Times*. 24 Dec. 2004. Web. Mar. 2012.

Rowland, John G. "John G. Rowland." *jgrowland.com*. Web. Mar. 2012.

Stowe, Stacey. "Rowland Home After Serving 10 Months in Corruption Case." *New York Times*. 14 Feb. 2006. Web. Mar. 2012.

"Embattled Conn. Governor Resigns." *Associated Press*. MSNBC.com. 21 June 2004. Web. Mar. 2012.

"Ex-Connecticut Governor to Spend a Year in Prison." *Associated Press*. MSNBC.com. 19 Mar. 2005. Web. Mar. 2012.

"Guilty Plea for Ex-Conn. Governor." *Associated Press*. cbsnews.com. 11 Feb. 2009. Web. Mar. 2012.

73. Don Sherwood

Lee, Kristen A. "The 10th District in Pennsylvania." *New York Times*. N.d. Web. 24 Apr. 2012.

Mauriello, Tracie. "Congressman's Indiscretion Endangers GOP Seat." *post-gazette.com*. 16 Mar. 2012. Web. 24 Apr. 2012.

Rubinkam, Michael. "GOP Rep. Don Sherwood Paid Mistress $500K To Keep Quiet about Abuse Allegations." *Associated Press*. Mother Jones. 2 Nov. 2006. Web. 24 Apr. 2012.

---. "Pa. Congressman's Affair Threatens Seat." *Associated Press*. boston.com. 28 Sept. 2006. Web. 24 Apr. 2012.

Vogel, Kenneth P., and Ryan Grim. "Ex-Rep Sherwood Challenging Settlement to Ex-Mistress." *Politico*. 23 Jan. 2007. Web. 24 Apr. 2012.

"Congressman Apologizes for Affair in TV Ad." *Associated Press*. nbcnews.com. 4 Oct. 2006. Web. 24 Apr. 2012.

72. Arnold Schwarzenegger

Allen, Nick. "Has Arnold Schwarzenegger's Love-Child Scandal Terminated His Career for Good?" *The Telegraph*. 21 May 2011. Web. 19 Feb. 2012.

Barabak, Mark Z., and Victoria Kim. "Schwarzenegger Fathered a Child with Longtime Member of Household Staff." *Los Angeles Times*. 17 May 2011. Web. 19 Feb. 2012.

Dillon, Nancy. "Maria Shriver Proceeding with Divorce." *NYDailyNews.com*. 6 Jan. 2012. Web. 19 Feb. 2012.

Fisher, Luchina, David Wright, and Kevin Dolak. "Mother of Arnold Schwarzenegger's Love Child Revealed." *ABC Nightline*. 18 May 2011. Web. 19 Feb. 2012.

Hughes, Sarah Anne. "Arnold Schwarzenegger: A History of Accusations and Denials." *Washington Post*. 17 May 2011. Web. 19 Feb. 2012.

Lewis, Michael. "California and Bust." *Vanity Fair*. Nov. 2011. Web. 19 Feb. 2012.

Palmeri, Christopher, and Ronald Grover. "Schwarzenegger Love Child Admission Hurts Political Clout, Not Film Appeal." *Bloomberg*. 17 May 2011. Web. 19 Feb. 2012.

Weiss, Piper. "A Brief History of Arnold Schwarzenegger's Sex Scandals." *Shine from Yahoo*. 17 May 2011. Web. 19 Feb. 2012.

"Mildred Baena, the Housekeeper Who Had a Child with Arnold Schwarzenegger Speaks Out for the First Time." *HELLO!* 14 June 2011. Web. 19 Feb. 2012.

"Mother of Schwarzenegger Child Reportedly Identified." *MSNBC.com*. 18 May 2011. Web. 19 Feb. 2012.

71. Jim Gibbons

Chereb, Sandra. "Nevada Governor Affair Allegations: Jim Gibbons Accused By Wife Of Affair With Former Playboy Model." *Associated Press.* The Huffington Post. 6 Apr. 2009. Web. 24 June 2012.

Coolican, J. Patrick. "Jim Gibbons First Governor of Nevada to Lose a Primary Race." *Las Vegas Sun.* 9 June 2010. Web. 24 June 2012.

Coolican, J. Patrick, and David McGrath Schwartz. "Gibbons Portrayed as Absentee Governor While State in Crisis." *Las Vegas Sun.* 16 May 2010. Web. 24 June 2012.

Friess, Steven. "Divorce Turns Ugly for Nevada's Governor." *New York Times.* 30 May 2008. Web. 24 June 2012.

Knapp, George. "I-Team: Governor Jim Gibbons Under Oath." *KLAS-TV.* 22 Feb. 2010. Web. 24 June 2012.

Malcolm, Andrew. "Nevada's Gov. Jim Gibbons Gets Testy About His, um, Traveling Companion." *Los Angeles Times.* 25 Feb. 2010. Web. 24 June 2012.

McGrath Schwartz, David. "Governor's Textual Misconduct." *Las Vegas Sun.* 12 June 2008. Web. 24 June 2012.

---. "Turbulent Four Years Coming to an End for Gov. Jim Gibbons." *Las Vegas Sun.* 31 Dec. 2010. Web. 24 June 2012.

Vogel, Ed. "Gibbons Denies Affair With Woman." *Las Vegas Review-Journal.* 28 May 2008. Web. 24 June 2012.

"Gov. Gibbons, First Lady, Reach Divorce Settlement." *Las Vegas Sun.* 28 Dec. 2009. Web. 24 June 2012.

70. John Edwards

Edwards, Elizabeth. Blog. *Daily KOS.* 20 Nov. 2006. Web. 20 July 2012.

Franke-Ruta, Garance. "John Edwards Admits Paternity." *Washington Post.* 21 Jan. 2010. Web. 17 July 2012.

Gerstein, Josh. "Justice Dept. Won't Retry John Edwards." *Politico.* 13 June 2012. Web. 20 July 2012.

Hunter, Rielle. "What Really Happened." Benbella Books, 2012. Print.

Stein, Sam. "Scrubbed: Edwards Filmmaker's Deleted Website Raises Questions." *Huffington Post.* 8 Aug. 2008. Web. 20 July 2012.

Young, Andrew. *The Politician: An Insiders Account of John Edward's Pursuit of the Presidency and the Scandal that Brought Him Down.* Thomas Dunne Books, 2010. Print.

"John Edwards Love Child Scandal." *National Enquirer.* 19 Dec. 2007. Web. 17 July 2012.

69. Katherine Bryson

Eddington, Mark. "GOP's Bryson Pulls Her Candidacy in Orem Race." *The Salt Lake Tribune.* 17 Mar. 2004. Web. 24 Apr. 2012.

Haddock, Sharon. "Bryson Disputes Wife's Comment About Gun Threat." *Deseret News.* 30 Jan. 2004. Web. 24 Apr. 2012.

---. "Bryson Divorce Case a Web of Controversy." *Deseret News.* 31 Jan. 2004. Web. 24 Apr. 2012.

---. "Commissioner Asks for Probe of Bryson." *Deseret News.* 19 Oct. 2004. Web. 24 Apr. 2012.

---. "Doors Shut on Bryson Case." *Deseret News.* 7 Oct. 2004. Web. 24 Apr. 2012.

Hyde, Jesse. "Bitter Bryson Saga Nears Final Chapter." *Deseret News.* 9 Feb. 2005. Web. 24 Apr. 2012.

---. "Kay Bryson Won't Be Charged." *Deseret News.* 30 Nov. 2004. Web. 24 Apr. 2012.

Mullen, Holly. "A Tale of Two Marriages: One Ends in Love, the Other in Hatred." *The Salt Lake Tribune.* 3 Oct. 2004. Web. 24 Apr. 2012.

Warburton, Nicole. "Bryson Divorce Fight Gets Messier." *The Salt Lake City Tribune.* 30 Sept. 2004. Web. 24 Apr. 2012.

Warburton, Nicole, and Matt Canham. "Police Probe Bryson Claim." *The Salt Lake Tribune.* 6 Oct. 2004. Web. 24 Apr. 2012.

Warner, Laura. "Bryson Says No to Race for 5th Term." *Deseret News.* 18 Mar. 2004. Web. 24 Apr. 2012.

68. Roy Ashburn

Bedell, Christine. "Q&A: Roy Ashburn on His Supervisor Run, Life Since the Legislature." *The Bakersfield Californian.* 20 Feb. 2012. Web. 31 May 2012.

Bedell, Christine, and Gretchen Wenner. "Roy Ashburn: 'I Am Gay'." *The Bakersfield Californian.* 8 Mar. 2010. Web. 31 May 2012.

Elliott, Justin. "FLASHBACK: CA Sen. Spotted At Gay Clubs Fought Gay Marriage For 'The Future Of Our Children'." *Talking Points Memo.* 5 Mar. 2010. Web. 31 May 2012.

Henry, Lois. "Lois Henry: Ashburn Dodges Gay Question." *The Bakersfield Californian*. 4 Mar. 2010. Web. 31 May 2012.

Jenner, Mike. "Mike Jenner: Relevance Guides Our Coverage." *The Bakersfield Californian*. 6 Mar. 2010. Web. 31 May 2012.

McGreevy, Patrick. "State Sen. Roy Ashburn Sentenced to Two Days in Jail." *Los Angeles Times*. 14 Apr. 2010. Web. 31 May 2012.

67. Daniel Gordon

Marcelo, Philip. "U.S. Marines Affirm Official R.I. Rep. Gordon Military Record." *Providence Journal*. 6 Oct. 2011. Web. 14 Apr. 2012.

McGee, Sandy. "Rep. Dan Gordon Says 'Self-Medicating With Alcohol,' Military Trauma Led to Arrests." *Portsmouth Patch*. 20 Sept. 2011. Web. 14 Apr. 2012.

Sanderson, Matthew. "Rep. Gordon's 2008 Massachusetts Charges Dismissed in Court." *Tiverton-Little Compton Patch*. 17 Oct. 2011. Web. 29 Apr. 2012.

White, Tim. "RI Rep. Gordon Jailed 3 Times in Mass." *WPRI.com Eyewitness News*. 19 Sept. 2011. Web. 14 Apr. 2012.

"Lawmaker's Gulf War Claims, Records Don't Match." *CBS News*. 24 Sept. 2011. Web. 29 Apr. 2012.

"RI Lawmaker Released on $1,000 Bail; Long History of Crimes Committed in Massachusetts." *The New England Post*. N.d. Web. 14 Apr. 2012.

"Tiverton Rep. Dan Gordon Arrested on 2008 Mass. Warrant." *Associated Press*. 18 Sept. 2011. Web. 14 Apr. 2012.

66. Paul Patton

Brammer, Jack. "Tina Connor, 41, Ex-Mistress of KY Governor Paul Patton, Indicted for Mail Fraud." *Lexington Herald-Leader*. 10 July 2003. Web. Apr. 2012

Breed, Allen G. "Patton Trying to Salvage Legacy After Sex Scandal." *Associated Press*. Bowling Green Daily News. 11 Feb. 2003. Web. Apr. 2012.

Clines, Francis X. "Kentucky Governor Admits 'Inappropriate Relationship'." *New York Times*. 21 Sept. 2002. Web. Apr. 2012.

Duncan, JJ. "Governor Paul Patton Gets Dumped, Closes Home for Elderly." *Zimbio.com*. 26 May 2009. Web. Apr. 2012.

"Kentucky Governor Paul E. Patton." *National Governor's Association*. National Governor's Association. 2011. Web. Apr. 2012.

"Tina Conner Loses Appeal in Patton Case." *The Cincinnati Enquirer*. 17 Apr. 2004. Web. Apr. 2012.

65. Eddie Perez

Bailey, Jr., Everton. "Eddie Perez, Connecticut Mayor, Found Guilty On Charges Of Corruption, Bribery, Larceny by Extortion." *HuffingtonPost*. 18 June 2010. Web. 25 May 2012.

Browning, Lynnley. "Hartford Mayor Arrested for Second Time This Year." *New York Times*. 2 Sept. 2009. Web. 25 May 2012.

---. "Mayor of Hartford Is Accused of Taking Bribe in a Municipal Corruption Plot." *New York Times*. 27 Jan. 2009. Web. 25 Apr. 2012.

Keating, Christopher. "Hartford Mayor Eddie Perez To Serve Three Years in Prison: "The City Has Suffered. My Family Has Suffered. I Have Suffered." *Hartford Courant*. 14 Sept. 2010. Web. 25 May 2012.

Kovner, Josh. "Mayor Eddie A. Perez Found Guilty on Five of Six Charges." *Hartford Courant*. 18 June 2010. Web. 25 May 2012.

Pazniokas, Mark. "Keeping a High Profile Under a Cloud." *New York Times*. 17 Apr. 2009. Web. 25 May 2012.

Winter, Michael. "Hartford Mayor Eddie Perez Resigns After Corruption Conviction." *USA TODAY*. 20 June 2010. Web. 25 May 2012.

"Ex-Hartford Mayor Wants Conviction Overturned." *Associated Press*. wtnh.com. 9 Jan. 2012. Web. 25 May 2012.

"Hartford Mayor Quits Under Fire." *Associated Press*. New York Times. 25 June 2010. Web. 25 May 2012.

64. Marion Barry

Bingham, Amy. "Former D.C. Mayor Marion Barry Says Asians' 'Dirty Shops…Ought To Go'." *ABC News*. 5 Apr. 2012. Web. 9 May 2012.

---. "Marion Barry Says 'Dirty [Asian] Shops' Comment Was 'Not Racial'." *ABC News*. 23 Apr. 2012. Web. 9 May 2012.

Blinder, Alan. "Marion Barry 'Sick Of' Media After His Latest Blast." *The Washington Examiner*. 24 Apr. 2012. Web. 9 May 2012.

DeBonis, Mike. "Marion Barry on Arrest: Friend Donna Watts 'Betrayed' Me." *Washington City Paper*. 5 July 2009. Web. 9 May 2012.

Nuckols, Ben. "Marion Barry Gears Up For Another Campaign: 'They Can't Touch Me Politically'." *Huffington Post*. 5 Jan. 2012. Web. 9 May 2012.

Potter, Matthew. "Marion Barry the Latest to Get Investigated for No-bid Contract." *CBS News*. 7 Apr. 2010. Web. 20 May 2012.

"D.C.'s Marion Barry Arrested Again." *CNN.com*. 5 July 2009. Web. 9 May 2012.

"Former DC Mayor Barry's Car Booted Over Tickets." *Associated Press*. 1 Mar. 2011. Web. 9 May 2012.

"Marion Barry Taxes: IRS Files Federal Tax Lien Against Former Mayor." *Huffington Post*. 15 Dec. 2011. Web. 9 May 2012.

63. Charles Rangel

Allen, Jonathan, and John Bresnahan. "Charles Rangel to Democrats: Drop Me if You Must." *Politico*. 28 July 2010. Web. 16 Mar. 2012.

Attkisson, Sharyl. "Is Rangel's 'Monument to Me' Worth It?" *CBS Evening News*. 26 May 2009. Web. 16 Mar. 2012.

Condon, Stephanie. "Ethics Committee: 13 Charges Against Charlie Rangel." *cbsnews.com*. 29 July 2010. Web. 16 Mar. 2012.

Kane, Paul, and Ben Pershing. "Despite Charges, Rep. Charles Rangel Says He Won't Resign." *Washington Post*. 11 Aug. 2010. Web. 16 Mar. 2012.

Karoliszyn, Henrick, and Kathleen Lucadamo. "Rep. Charles Rangel Says It Would be Unpatriotic of Him to Resign Amid Ethics Scandal." *NYDailyNews.com*. 24 July 2010. Web. 16 Mar. 2012.

Khan, Huma. "Embattled Rep. Charles Rangel Censured: 'There's No Evidence'." *ABC World News with Diane Sawyer*. 2 Dec. 2010. Web. 16 Mar. 2012.

Kocieniewski, David. "House Panel Finds Rangel Guilty." *New York Times*. 16 Nov. 2010. Web. 16 Mar. 2012.

Margasak, Larry. "Charles Rangel Censured: House Votes to Censure Longtime Congressman." *HuffingtonPost*. 3 Dec. 2010. Web. 16 Mar. 2012.

Palmer, Anna, and John Bresnahan. "What Censure? Charles Rangel's Back." *Politico*. 16 Nov. 2011. Web. 16 Mar. 2012.

Soltis, Andy. "How The Post Broke the Rangel Scandals." *New York Post*. 30 July 2010. Web. 16 Mar. 2012.

"Charles Rangel: Dates of a Scandal." *Wall Street Journal*. 3 Dec. 2010. Web. 16 Mar. 2012.

"Rangel Censured by House for Ethics Violations." *FoxNews.com*. 2 Dec. 2010. Web. 16 Mar. 2012.

"Scandal: Charlie Rangel." *Propublica*. 25 Feb. 2010. Web. 16 Mar. 2010.

62. David Wu

Camina, Catalina. "Oregon Lawmaker David Wu Quits House Amid Sex Scandal." *USA TODAY*. 28 July 2011. Web. 21 Apr. 2012.

Cartier, Curtis. "David Wu, Oregon Congressman, Wears Fuzzy Tiger Suit, Does Crazy Stuff." *Seattle Weekly*. 21 Feb. 2011. Web. 21 Apr. 2012.

Condon, Stephanie. "David Wu Announces Resignation Amid Sex Scandal." *CBS News*. 26 July 2011. Web. 21 Apr. 2012.

Pope, Charles, Janie Har, and Beth Slovic. "Sources: Young Woman Accuses Oregon Rep. David Wu of Aggressive, Unwanted Sexual Encounter." *The Oregonian*. 22 July 2011. Web. 21 Apr. 2012.

Tehsuckdotnet. "Rep. David Wu (D-Oregon) - "Klingons in the White House"." *YouTube*. N.d. Web. 21 Apr. 2012.

"Allegation of Assault on Woman in 1970s in College Shadow U.S. Rep. David Wu." *The Oregonian*. 12 Oct. 2004. Web. 21 Apr. 2012.

"Congressman Blames Erratic Behavior on Drugs." *CBS News*. 23 Feb. 2011. Web. 21 Apr. 2012.

61. Jim West

Duncan, J.J. "Mayor James West, AKA Cobra82 on Gay.com." *Zimbio*. 20 May 20 2009. Web. 17 July 2012.

McGann, Chris, and Kathy Mulady. "Gay Sex Scandal Rocks Spokane." *Seattle Post-Intelligencer*. 5 May 2005. Web. 17 July 2012.

Steele, Karen Dorn. "West's Public Policy Conflicts with Private Life." *The Spokesman-Review*. 5 May 2005. Web. 17 July 2012.

"Interview with James West on 'The Today Show'." Transcript from 31 May 2005. *Spokesman-Review*. Web. 17 July 2012.

"Voters Recall Mayor Jim West." *Spokesman-Review*. 6 Dec. 2005. Web. 17 July 2012.

60. Thomas Porteus

Broach, Drew. "Judge Porteus' Old Friends Snared by Scandal." *The Times-Picayune*. 29 Nov. 2009. Web. 17 July 2012.

Evans, Ben. "Judge G. Thomas Porteus Faces Impeachment Trial in Congress." *Huffington Post*. 13 Sept. 2010. Web. 17 July 2012.

Litvan, Laura. "Louisiana Judge is Removed From Bench for Corruption in Rare Senate Action." *Bloomberg News*. 8 Dec. 2010. Web. 17 July 2012.

Steinhauer, Jennifer. "Senate, for Just the 8th Time, Votes to Oust a Federal Judge." *New York Times*. 8 Dec. 2010. Web. 17 July 2012.

"Articles of Impeachment Against United States District Court Judge G. Thomas Porteus, Jr." Works of the United States Government. 14 July 2011. Web. 17 July 2012.

59. Chip Pickering

Blumenthal, Max. "The Secret GOP Sex Diary." *The Daily Beast*. 23 July 2009. Web. 20 June 2012.

Boyer, Peter J. "Frat House for Jesus." *The New Yorker*. 13 Sept. 2010. Web. 20 June 2012.

Bresnahan, John. "Chip Pickering's Wife Sues Alleged Mistress." *Politico*. 16 July 2009. Web. 20 June 2012.

Mark, David. "Pickering Removes Himself From Senate Consideration." *Politico*. cbsnews.com. 26 June 2009. Web. 20 June 2012.

Minor, Bill. "Will the Truth Really Set You Free?" *desototimestribune.com*. 29 July 2009. Web. 20 June 2012.

Mooney, Alexander. "A Third 'C Street' Republican Embroiled in Sex Scandal." *CNN.com*. 17 July 2009. Web. 20 June 2012.

Mott, Ronni. "Wife Says Pickering's Affair Ended Career, Two Marriages." *Jackson Free Press*. 16 July 2009. Web. 20 June 2012.

Wagster Pettus, Emily. "Chip Pickering's Wife Claims He Had Affair." *Huffington Post*. 16 July 2009. Web. 20 June 2012.

"Ex-Rep. Pickering's Wife Says He Cheated." *Associated Press*. cbsnews.com. 3 June 2010. Web. 20 June 2012.

58. Tim Mahoney

Dettman, Christina. "Court Hearing Held for DUI Case of Former Rep. Tim Mahoney." *NBC News Channel 5*. 17 Jan. 2012. Web. 25 Apr. 2012.

Florin, Hector. "Mahoney's Florida District Has Sex-Scandal Deja Vu." *Time*. 16 Oct. 2008. Web. 25 Apr. 2012.

Gaskell, Stephanie. "West Palm Beach Congressman Tim Mahoney Allegedly Fired Volunteer Patricia Allen After Affair." *NYDailyNews.com*. 13 Oct. 2008. Web. 25 Apr. 2012.

Lambiet, Jose. "Former U.S. Rep Tim Mahoney Divorced." *The Palm Beach Post*. 14 Jan. 2010. Web. 25 Apr. 2012.

Roldan, Cynthia. "Former Congressman Tim Mahoney Charged with DUI." *The Palm Beach Post*. 14 Nov. 2011. Web. 25 Apr. 2012.

---. "Judge Allows DUI Lawyer for Ex-Lawmaker Mahoney to Interview Police." *The Palm Beach Post*. 14 Nov. 2011. Web. 25 Apr. 2012.

Schwartz, Emma, Rhonda Schwartz, and Vic Walter. "Congressman's $121,000 Payoff to Alleged Mistress." *ABC News*. 13 Oct. 2008. Web. 25 Apr. 2012.

---. "Did Mahoney Help Second Alleged Mistress Win Federal Grant?" *ABC News*. 15 Oct. 2008. Web. 25 Apr. 2012.

Schwartz, Emma, and Vic Walter. "Congressman Mahoney Admits to Multiple Affairs." *ABC News*. 17 Oct. 2008. Web. 25 Apr. 2012.

Thrush, Glenn, and Josh Kraushaar. "Mahoney Tied to $121K Sex Scandal." *Politico*. 13 Oct. 2008. Web. 25 Apr. 2012.

Urbina, Ian. "Sex Scandal Shakes Race for Congress in Florida." *New York Times*. 13 Oct. 2008. Web. 25 Apr. 2012.

"Florida Congressman Facing Sex Scandal." *Associated Press*. Los Angeles Times. 14 Oct. 2008. Web. 25 Apr. 2012.

"Former US Congressman Tim Mahoney Charged with DUI." *Associated Press*. CBS4 Miami. 6 Aug. 2011. Web. 25 Apr. 2012.

57. Hank Johnson

Condon, Stephanie. "Hank Johnson Worries Guam Could 'Capsize' After Marine Buildup." *CBS News.com*. 1 Apr. 2010. Web. Feb. 2012.

Harden, Blaine. "On Guam, Planned Marine Base Raises Anger, Infrastructure Concerns." *Washington Post*. 22 Mar. 2010. Web. Feb. 2012.

psvanbeek. "3-25-2010_Hank_Johnson_Guam_Tip_Over.wmv." *YouTube*. 31 Mar. 2010. Web. Feb. 2012.

Randall, Pete. "Hank Johnson (D-Fulcrum) Explains His Comments About Guam & U.S. Marines." *Peach Pundit*. Tanalach Media, LLC. 1 Apr. 2010. Web. Feb. 2012.

56. James Holley

Dougherty, Kerry. "Mayor Holley Really Ought to Think Before He Doesn't Speak Up." *The Virginia-Pilot*. 27 July 2008. Web. May 2012.

Foster, Dave. "Voters Recall Portsmouth Mayor James Holley." *The Virginian-Pilot*. 14 July 2010. Web. May 2012.

Hoyer, Meghan. "Highlighting Portsmouth's Positives Has Worked for a Leader Who Once Was Recalled." *The Virginian-Pilot*. 13 Apr. 2008. Web. May 2012.

Mallonee, MaryKay. "Mayor Holley's Assistant Breaks Silence." *WAVY-TV 10*. 8 July 2010. Web. May 2012.

McCaffery, Jen. "Portsmouth Mayor James W. Holley Wins Re-election." *The Virginian-Pilot*. 6 May 2008. Web. May 2012.

McCammon, Ross. "Hizzoner." *Esquire*. 16 Jan. 2007. Web. 27 July 2012.

Russell, Lia. "Portsmouth's First Citizen Forged Local Civil Rights ." *The Virginian-Pilot*. 20 Apr. 2008. Web. May 2012.

Stokes, Lorraine A. "Dear Citizens of Portsmouth and the General Public." *wavy.com*. 2 July 2010. Web. May 2012.

"Officials Link a Virginia Mayor to Hate Mail." *New York Times*, 14 July 1987. Web. May 2012.

"Portsmouth Mayor Among America's Best Dressed." *WVEC.com*. 13 Aug. 2007. Web. May 2012.

55. Thad Viers

Smith, Gina. "Viers Steps Down in Face of Harassment Charge." *The State*. 21 Mar. 2012. Web. 30 Mar. 2012.

Taylor, Ashley. "Thad Viers Speaks Exclusively with WMBF News." *WMBF News*. 23 Mar. 2012. Web. 30 Mar. 2012.

"Former State Rep. Viers Indicted on Stalking Charges." *Associated Press*. 23 Mar. 2012. Web. 30 Mar. 2012.

54. Larry Craig

Akers, May Ann. "Larry Craig: Still Not Gay." *Washington Post*. 28 Aug. 2007. Web. 17 July 2012.

Karsnia, Sgt. Dave. Minneapolis-St. Paul International Airport Police Department. "Lewd Conduct. 07002008."Minneapolis-St. Paul: Minneapolis-St. Paul International Airport Police Dept., 6 June 2007. Web. 17 July 2012.

Court Order. State of Minnesota, County of Hennepin, Fourth Judicial District.

"Defendant's Motion to Withdraw a Pleas is hereby Denied." 7 Oct. 2007. Web. 17 July 2012.

"Craig: I Did Nothing 'Inappropriate' in Airport Bathroom." *CNN.com*. 28 Aug. 2007. Web. 17 July 2012.

"U.S. Senator Gets Flushed." *The Smoking Gun*. 28 Aug. 2007. Web. 17 July 2012.

53. Claude Allen

Chmela, Holli. "Ex-Bush Aide Admits Shoplifting and Is Fined." *New York Times*. 5 Aug. 2006. Web. 14 Apr. 2012.

Jones, Leigh. "Former Bush Adviser Stripped of Law License." *Reuters*. 8 Sept. 2011. Web. 14 Apr. 2012.

Londono, Ernesto, and Michael A. Fletcher. "Former Top Bush Aide Accused of Md. Thefts." *Washington Post*. 11 Mar. 2006. Web. 14 Apr. 2012.

Shteir, Rachel. "Former Bush Aide Charged in Felony Theft." *Slate*. 10 Mar. 2006. Web. 14 Apr. 2012.

Spain, William. "Bush Adviser Loses Law License Over Shoplifting." *Wall Street Journal*. 9 Sept. 2011. Web. 14 Apr. 2012.

Weigel, Jenniffer. "Getting a Rush Out of Sneaky Theft." *Chicago Tribune*. 22 July 2011. Web. 14 Apr. 2012.

52. Sharpe James

Feuer, Alan, and Nate Schweber. "Former Newark Mayor Is Sentenced to 27 Months." *New York Times*. 30 July 2008. Web. 19 May 2012.

Honan, Edith. "Former Newark Mayor Indicted on Federal Charges." *Reuters*. 12 July 2007. Web. 19 May 2012.

Jones, Richard G. "Affair Is Cited at Fraud Trial of Ex-Mayor of Newark." *New York Times*. 4 Mar. 2008. Web. 19 May 2012.

Office of the Attorney General. *Former Newark Mayor Sharpe James Indicted; Allegedly Traveled, Spent Lavishly on Newark Credit Cards, and Engaged in Fraudulent Land "Flipping" with Companion*. New Jersey: Office of the Attorney General. 12 July 2007. Web. 19 May 2012.

"Court Reverses Sharpe James' Conviction." *Associated Press*. CBS 2 New York. 16 Sept. 2010. Web. 19. May 2012.

"Former Newark, N.J., Mayor Sharpe James Sentenced to 2 Years, 3 Months in Federal Prison." *Associated Press*. Fox News. 29 July 2008. Web. 19 May 2012.

51. Bill Campbell

Cook, Rhonda, and Bill Rankin. "Former Atlanta Mayor Bill Campbell Goes Free Friday." *ajc.com*. 23 Oct. 2008. Web. 23 June 2012.

Dewan, Shaila. "Ex-Mayor of Atlanta Enrolled in Prison Drug Program After Denial of Problem." *New York Times*. 5 Mar. 2008. Web. 23 June 2012.

Goodman, Brenda. "A Longer Prison Term for a Former Mayor." *New York Times*. 8 Mar. 2008. Web. 23 June 2012.

Rankin, Bill. "Stakes, Drama High as Trial of Ex-Atlanta Mayor Begins." *ajc.com*. 16 Jan. 2006. Web. 23 June 2012.

Suggs, Ernie. "Ex-Atlanta Mayor Bill Campbell Resurfaces." *ajc.com*. 4 May 2011. Web. 23 June 2012.

Torpy, Bill, Jeffry Scott, and Beth Warren. "The Bill Campbell Verdict: Split Decision: Ex-Mayor Cleared of Public Corruption." *ajc.com*. 11 Mar. 2006. Web. 23 June 2012.

Whitt, Richard, and Alan Judd. "Campbell Indicted." *ajc.com*. 31 Aug. 2004. Web. 23 June 2012.

"Atlanta's Former Mayor Sentenced to Prison." *CNN.com*. 13 June 2006. Web. 23 June 2012.

"Ex-Atlanta Mayor Gets Prison for Tax Evasion." *Associated Press*. nbcnews.com. 13 June 2006. Web. 23 June 2012.

50. Vincent Cianci, Jr.

Ball, Molly. "Cianci Book: 'I'm No Angel'." *Politico*. 20 Dec. 2010. Web. 22 Apr. 2012.

Barry, Dan. "Now Free to Speak His Mind, an Ex-Mayor Is Doing So." *New York Times*. 28 Apr. 2008. Web. 22 Apr. 2012.

---. "Providence Mayor Is Guilty of Corruption." *New York Times*. 25 June 2002. Web. 22 Apr. 2012.

---. "Providence Politics Play Out in Courtroom Drama." *New York Times*. 7 May 2002. Web. 22 Apr. 2012.

Belluck, Pam. "A Sentence for Corruption Ends an Era in Providence." *New York Times*. 7 Sept. 2002. Web. 22 Apr. 2012.

Cianci, Jr, Vincent A. "Buddy." "Vincent A. "Buddy" Cianci, Jr." *buddycianci.com*. N.d. Web. 22 Apr. 2012.

Keating, Christopher. "Jury Ponders Plunder Dome Case." *Hartford Courant*. 12 June 2002. Web. 22 Apr. 2012.

Mehren, Elizabeth. "Another Shoe Drops for Mayor 'Buddy'." *Los Angeles Times*. 4 Apr. 2001. Web. 22 Apr. 2012.

---. "Closing Arguments in Mayor's Trial." *Los Angeles Times*. 12 June 2002. Web. 22 Apr. 2012.

---. "Providence Mayor Gets Prison Sentence for Corruption." *Los Angeles Times*. 7 Sept. 2002. Web. 22 Apr. 2012.

Mehren, Elizabeth, and Karen Tumulty. "He's Still Their Buddy: Despite His Felony Conviction, Voters Sent Cianci Back to Providence City Hall." *Los Angeles Times*. 18 Jan. 1991. Web. 22 Apr. 2012.

Zezima, Katie. "Providence Journal; Colorful Ex-Mayor Is Missing His Own Comeback." *New York Times*. 10 Aug. 2003. Web. 22 Apr. 2012.

49. Tom Anderson

Cockerham, Sean. "Convicted Alaska Lawmaker Released to Halfway House." *The Anchorage Daily News*. 2 Feb. 2011. Web. 17 Mar. 2012.

Doogan, Sean. "The Redemption of Tom Anderson." *KTVA-11 Alaska*. 3 Feb. 2012. Web. 17 Mar. 2012.

U.S. Department of Justice. *"Alaska State Senator Pleads Guilty to Public Corruption Charges."* Alaska: Department of Justice, 19 Dec. 2008. Web. 17 Mar. 2012.

"Early Release for Former Rep. Anderson." *Associated Press.* KTUU-Alaska. 2 Feb. 2011. Web. 17 Mar. 2012.

"Grand jury indicts Alaska lawmaker on extortion, 6 more counts." *The Associated Press.* The Anchorage Daily News. 21 Dec. 2007. Web. 17 Mar. 2012.

"Team." *Optima Public Relations.* Seattle Design Group, N.d. Web. 17 Mar. 2012.

48. Phillip Hinkle

Campbell, Alex. "E-mail Rendezvous Entangles State Rep. Phillip Hinkle." *Indianapolis Star.* 12 Aug. 2011. Web. 21 May 2012.

---. "Hinkle: I Paid Young Man." *Indianapolis Star.* 23 Aug. 2011. Web. 21 May 2012.

---. "Hinkle: I Paid Young Man $80 for Encounter." *Indianapolis Star.* 24 Aug. 2011. Web. 21 May 2012.

Rayfield, Jillian. "IN GOPer: I Just Talked about Baseball with the Young Man I Solicited on Craigslist." *TPMMuckracker.* 25 Aug. 2011. Web. 21 May 2012.

Tully, Matthew. "Tully: 'Don't Know' What I Was Thinking, Hinkle Says." *Indianapolis Star.* 23 Aug. 2011. Web. 21 May 2012.

47. Vito Fossella

Barron, James. "Fossella Admits He Had an Extramarital Affair." *New York Times.* 9 May 2008. Web. Apr. 2012.

Bresnahan, John. "Vito Fossella Is Long Gone, but FEC Still Hasn't Forgotten." *Politico.com.* 18 Mar. 2011. Web. Apr. 2012.

Hick, Jonathon P. "Signs Fossella May Run Again Unnerve GOP." *New York Times.* 19 May 2008. Web. Apr. 2012.

Meek, James Gordon. "Former Rep. Vito Fossella Enters Alexandria Detention Center to Serve DUI Conviction." *NY Daily News.* 17 Apr. 2009. Web. Apr. 2012.

---. "Staten Island Rep. Vito Fossella Sentenced 5 Days for Drunken Driving." *NY Daily News.* 8 Dec. 2008. Web. Apr. 2012.

"Congressman Vito Fossella Convicted of Drunken Driving." *FOX News.com.* 17 Oct. 2008. Web. Apr. 2012.

"Vito Fossella Cries On House Floor After Drunk Driving, Adultery Revelations." *Huffington Post.* 16 May 2008. Web. Apr. 2012.

"Vito Fossella Lied to Other Woman; Wife Considers Dumping Him." *NY Daily News.* 10 May 2008. Web. Apr. 2012.

"Where Are They Now? Some Sex Scandal Pols Vanish, Others Get a Second Chance." *FoxNews.com.* 17 June 2009. Web. Apr. 2012.

46. Bruce Barclay

Creason, Naomi, Alex Roarty, and John Hilton. "Secret Sex Network Target of Barclay Investigation." *The Sentinel.* 9 Apr. 2008. Web. 17 July 2012.

Miller, Dan. "Bruce Barclay, Former Cumberland County Official, Escapes Jail Time on Computer, Prostitution Charges." *The Patriot News.* 30 Dec. 2012. Web. 2 July 2012.

---. "Bruce Barclay Would Be Found Guilty of Hiring Prostitutes, Lawyer Says." *The Patriot News.* 23 Nov. 2010. Web. 2 July 2012.

Shapiro, Lila. "All is Local: Sex and Lots and Lots of Videotape," *TPM Muckraker.* 13 Apr. 2008. Web. 2 July 2012.

Stauffer, Heather. "Barclay Cleared on Rape Charges." *The Sentinel.* 11 Apr. 2008. Web. 17 July 2012.

45. Peter Cammarano

Carroll, Timothy J. "The Meteoric Fall of Peter Cammarano." *Hudson Reporter.* 2 Aug. 2009. Web. 11 May 2012.

Halbfinger, David. "44 Charged by U.S. in New Jersey Corruption Sweep." *New York Times.* 23 July 2009. Web. 11 May 2012.

Sherman, Ted. "Former Hoboken Mayor Peter Cammarano Gets 2 Years in Prison for Taking Bribes." *The Star Ledger.* NJ.com. 5 Aug. 2010. Web. 11 May 2012.

"Ex-Hoboken Mayor Gets 2 Years in Corruption Case." *NBC 4 New York.* 5 Aug. 2010. Web. 11 May 2012.

"Ex-Hoboken Mayor Peter Cammarano Released From Prison." *Associated Press.* CBS 2 New York. 15 Sept. 2011. Web. 11 May 2012.

"Hoboken Mayor Arrested Just 3 Weeks Into Term." *Associated Press.* 25 July 2009. Web. 11 May 2012.

44. Paul Stanley

Schelzig, Erik. "Paul Stanley, Tennessee State Senator, Quits After Affair With 22-Year-Old Intern." *Huffington Post.* 28 July 2009. Web. 27 May 2012.

Weinger, Mackenzie. "Life After the Fall: 4 Sex Scandal Pols." *Politico.com.* 21 May 2012. Web. 27 May 2012.

43. Paul Morrison

Carpenter, Tim. "More Details Disclosed in Morrison Affair." *cjonline.com.* 16 Dec. 2007. Web. 22 May 2012.

---. "Morrison Resigning Amid Sex Scandal." *cjonline.com.* 15 Dec. 2007. Web. 22 May 2012.

---. "Sebelius Discusses Morrison's Downfall, A.G. Replacement." *cjonline.com.* 22 Dec. 2007. Web. 22 May 2012.

---. "Sex Scandal Rocks A.G." *cjonline.com.* 9 Dec. 2007. Web. 22 May 2012.

Hanna, John. "Sex Scandal Rocks Kansas AG's Office." *Associated Press.* USA TODAY. 10 Dec. 2007. Web. 22 May 2012.

"Kansas AG Resigns After Admitting Affair." *Associated Press.* USA TODAY. 14 Dec. 2007. Web. 22 May 2012.

42. Jim McGreevey

Handwerker, Haim, and Yossi Melman. "Israeli Denies He Was NJ Governor's Lover." *Haaretz.* 15 Aug. 2004. Web. 16 June 2012.

Hassel, John, and Jeff Whelan. "McGreevey Quits, Admits Gay Affair." *Star-Ledger.* NJ.com. 13 Aug. 2004. Web. 16 June 2012.

Kocieniewski, David. "An Adviser to McGreevey Resigns." *New York Times.* 15 Aug. 2002. Web. 16 June 2012.

Rennie, Kevin. "Another Resignation." *Hartford Courant.* 22 Aug. 2004. Web. 16 June 2012.

Vitello, Paul. "Out of Politics and Closet, McGreevey Pursues Dream to Join Clergy." *New York Times.* 16 May 2011. Web. 16 June 2012.

"Ex-N.J. Gov. McGreevey Now Teaches Ethics." *CBS News.* 11 Feb. 2009. Web. 16 June 2012.

"Former N.J. Gov. McGreevey is Denied Bid for Priesthood." *Star-Ledger.* NJ.com. 25 Apr. 2011. Web. 16 June 2012.

"New Jersey Governor Quits, Comes Out As Gay." *CNN.com.* 13 Aug. 2004. Web. 16 June 2012.

41. Amy Koch

Demko, Paul. "Senate Majority Leader Amy Koch Resigns Post, Will Not Seek Reelection." *Politics in Minnesota.* 15 Dec. 2011. Web. 29 July 2012.

Grow, Doug. "Latest Amy Koch Developments Complicate GOP Plans Across the Board." *minnpost.com.* 16 Dec. 2011. Web. 29 July 2012.

Helgeson, Baird. "Amy Koch: 'I Won't Be Running Again'." *Star Tribune.* 23 Jan. 2012. Web. 27 June 2012.

---. "Sen. Amy Koch: Back Up After 'Punch to the Face'." *Star Tribune.* 21 Jan. 2012. Web. 27 June 2012.

Johnson, Luke. "Amy Koch Affair: Michael Brodkorb, Fired Minnesota GOP Staffer, Threatens To Expose More Affairs." *Huffington Post.* 15 Mar. 2012. Web. 27 June 2012.

Scheck, Tom. "Minn. GOP Left Shaky After Sen. Koch Steps Down." *MPR news.* 16 Dec. 2011. Web. 27 June 2012.

Scheck, Tom, and Catharine Richert. "Former Top Koch Staffer Raised Concerns About Her Conduct Months Ago." *MPR news.* 21 Dec. 2011. Web. 27 June 2012.

Stassen-Berger, Rachel E. "Brodkorb Warns Senate He Plans to Sue for $500,000." *Star Tribune.* 6 Apr. 2012. Web. 27 June 2012.

---. "Sen. Koch Quit Over 'Inappropriate' Relationship." *Star Tribune.* 17 Dec. 2011. Web. 27 June 2012.

"Sources: Sen. Amy Koch Resigned After Allegations." *WCCO-TV.* 16 Dec. 2011. Web. 27 June 2012.

40. Mark Foley

Babington, Charles, and Jonathan Weisman. "FBI to Examine Foley's E-Mails." *Washington Post.* 2 Oct. 2006. Web. 21 Feb. 2012.

Bash, Dana. "Congressman Quits After Messages to Teens Found." *CNN.com.* 29 Sept. 2006. Web. 21 Feb. 2012.

Epstein, Edward. "Foley Report Rips GOP House Leaders but Panelists Find No Ethics Violations in Scandal over Pages." *Chronicle Washington Bureau.* 9 Dec. 2006. Web. 21 Feb. 2012.

Lunsford, Jessica. "House Passes Stricter Sex Offender Bill." *Associated Press.* 15 Sept. 2005. Web. 21 Feb. 2012.

Ross, Brian. "Foley's IM Exchange With Underage Page." *ABC News.* 29 Sept. 2006. Web. 21 Feb. 2012.

"Attorney: Clergyman Molested Foley as Teen." *CNN.com.* 3 Oct. 2006. Web. 21 Feb. 2012.

"Denied Access to Critical Data, FDLE Concludes Investigation Into Former Congressman Foley." *Florida Department of Law Enforcement.* 19 Sept. 2008. Web. 21 Feb. 2012.

"Ex-House Clerk Testifies in Foley Probe." *Associated Press.* 19 Oct. 2006. Web. 21 Feb. 2012.

"Former Congressman Mark Foley Begins Talk Radio Career in West Palm Beach." *PRWeb.com.* 7 Sept. 2009. Web. 21 Feb. 2012.

"GOP House Leaders Call For Criminal Investigation of Foley." *CNN.com.* 1 Oct. 2006. Web. 21 Feb. 2012.

39. John Ensign

Cilliza, Chris, and Paul Kane. "Nevada Sen. John Ensign to Resign." *Washington Post.* 21 Apr. 2011. Web. 29 Apr. 2012.

Creed, Ryan. "Sen. John Ensign Announces Resignation From US Senate." *ABC News.* 21 Apr. 2011. Web. 29 Apr. 2012.

Montopoli, Brian. "GOP Senator John Ensign Admits Affair." *CBS News.* 26 June 2009. Web. 29 Apr. 2012.

Myers, Laura. "Ensign's Former Mistress Speaks in Ethics Report." *The Las-Vegas Review Journal.* 13 May 2011. Web. 29 Apr. 2012.

Tapper, Jake, and Matthew Jaffe. "John Ensign's Sordid Tale: Ethics Committee Report Alleges Senator Broke Law." *ABC News.* 13 May 2011. Web. 29 Apr. 2012.

Walter, Amy. "Sen. John Ensign to Resign Early Amid Ethics Investigation." *ABC News.* 22 Apr. 2011. Web. 29 Apr. 2012.

Yost, Pete. "Doug Hampton Indicted In Lobbying Case." *Associated Press.* Huffington Post. 24 Mar. 2011. Web. 29 Apr. 2012.

"Ensign Accuser Doug Hampton Arraigned on Lobbying Charges." *Politico.* 4 Apr. 2011. Web. 29 Apr. 2012.

"'The Rachel Maddow Show' for Thursday, May 12th, 2011." *NBC News.* 13 May 2011. Web. 29 Apr. 2012.

"Tom Coburn Helped Cover Up John Ensign Affair: Senate Ethics Report." *Huffington Post.* 12 May 2011. Web. 29 Apr. 2012.

38. Amy Brewer

Baker, Jennifer. "Milford Cop Suspended for Sex with Mayor." *Cincinnati.com.* 13 May 2010. Web. 31 May 2012.

Bradley, Eric. "Milford Mayor Resigns Over Sex With On-Duty Cop." *Cincinnati.com.* 18 May 2010. Web. 31 May 2012.

City of Milford, Ohio. City of Milford. N.d. Web. 31 May 2012.

Frontier Days Milford, Ohio. Milford Chamber of Commerce. N.d. Web. 31 May 2012.

"Milford, Ohio Community Resume." *City of Milford, Ohio.* City of Milford. N.d. Web. 31 May 2012.

37. Bob Levy

Jones, Richard G. "Atlantic City's Latest Problem: Mayor is Missing." *New York Times.* 6 Oct. 2007. Web. 15 June 2012.

Kennedy, Helen. "Politics Dicey in Atlantic City After the Mayor Goes Missing." *New York Daily News.* 5 Oct. 2007. Web. 15 June 2012.

Larini, Rudy. "Ex-Atlantic City Mayor Gets Probation for Embellishing War Record." *NJ.com.* 25 July 2008. Web. 15 June 2012.

Mulvihill, Geoff. "Ex-Mayor Who Lied About Army Record to Face Judge." *Associated Press.* USA TODAY. 25 July 2008. Web. 15 June 2012.

Parry, Wayne. "Former NJ Mayor Gets Probation in War Lies Case." *Associated Press.* USA TODAY. 25 July 2008. Web. 15 June 2012.

"Atlantic City Mayor Pleads Guilty to Cheating Veterans Department." *CNN.com.* 1 Nov. 2007. Web. 15 June 2012.

"Lawyer Says Missing Mayor Under Investigation, Has Resigned." *CNN.com.* 10 Oct. 2007. Web. 15 June 2012.

36. Bob Ney

Eaton, Sabrina. "Former Ohio Congressman Bob Ney Featured in Documentary About Jack Abramoff Scandal." *Cleveland Plain Dealer.* 5 Jan. 2010. Web. Feb. 2012.

Shenon, Philip. "Bob Ney, Guilty but Still at Capitol." *New York Times.* 19 Oct. 2006. Web. Feb. 2012.

---. "Congressman Pleads Guilty but Won't Resign for Now." *New York Times.* 14 Oct. 2006. Web. Feb. 2012.

---. "Ney Is Sentenced to 2½ Years in Abramoff Case." *New York Times.* 20 Jan. 2007. Web. Feb. 2012.

"National Briefing | Washington: Congressman Resigns Over Scandal." *New York Times.* 4 Nov. 2006. Web. Feb. 2012.

35. John Lake

Office of the Attorney General. "*Mayor of Carneys Point Indicted in Attempt to Bribe Political Opponent to Drop Out of Committee Race.*" New Jersey: Office of the Attorney General. 21 Nov. 2006. Web. 15 June 2012.

Six, Jim. "Ex-Carneys Point Mayor Found Guilty of Corruption." *South Jersey Media Group.* NJ.com. 7 Dec. 2007. Web. 15 June 2012.

---. "Former Carneys Point Mayor Sentenced to Three Years in Prison." *South Jersey Media Group.* NJ.com. 15 Apr. 2008. Web. 15 June 2012.

"Appeals Court Increases Sentence to 5 Years for Ex-Carneys Point Mayor John 'Mack' Lake in Bribery Case." *NJ.com.* 27. July 2009. Web. 15 June 2012.

"Former Mayor Convicted of Trying to Bribe Opponent." *Associated Press.* 7 Dec. 2007. Web. 15 June 2012.

34. Lewis 'Scooter' Libby

Pallasch, Adam M. "Dick Cheney: 'Scooter' Libby Didn't Deserve Prosecution by Patrick Fitzgerald." *Chicago Sun-Times.* 19 Sept. 2011. Web. 26 Mar. 2012.

Schmitt, Eric. "Public Lives; Cheney Aide Will Eat Horse Guts Before He'll Spill Beans." *New York Times.* 30 Apr. 2001. Web. 26 Mar. 2012.

Seidman, Joel. "Plame Was 'Covert' Agent at Time of Name Leak." *NBC News.* 29 May 2007. Web. 26 Mar. 2012.

"Bush Commutes Libby's Prison Sentence." *CNN.com.* 2 July 2007. Web. 26 Mar. 2012.

"Jurors Convict Libby on Four of Five Charges." *NBC News.* 6 Mar. 2007. Web. 26 Mar. 2012.

"Key Players in the CIA Leak Investigation." *Washington Post.* 3 July 2007. Web. 26 Mar. 2012.

"Lewis Libby's Complete Grand Jury Testimony." *NPR.* 9 Feb. 2007. Web. 26 Mar. 2012.

"Publisher To Reissue I. Lewis Libby's Novel." *USA TODAY.* 9 Nov. 2005. Web. 26 Mar. 2012.

33. Kyle Foggo

Barakat, Matthew. "Feds: Misconduct by CIA's Foggo Spanned Decades." *Associated Press.* 25 Feb. 2009. Web. 30 May 2012.

Esposito, Richard, and Brian Ross. "Foggo Out at CIA." *ABC News.* 8 Mar. 2006. Web. 30 May 2012.

Esposito, Richard, Brian Ross, and Rhonda Schwartz. "Exclusive: Top CIA Official Under Investigation." *ABC News.* 3 Mar. 2006. Web. 30 May 2012.

Rood, Justin. "Feds: Ex-CIA Official Pushed Agency to Hire Mistress." *ABC News.* 21 May 2008. Web. 30 May 2012.

"Kyle 'Dusty' Foggo." *New York Times.* 13 Aug. 2009. Web. 30 May 2012.

32. Tom DeLay

Allen, Mike, and Josh Gerstein. "DeLay 'Knew This Day Would Come'." *Politico.com.* 16 Aug. 2010. Web. 25 Apr. 2012.

Dubose, Lou. "Broken Hammer?" *Salon.com.* 08 Apr. 2005. Web. 25 Apr. 2012.

Markels, Alex. "Tom DeLay: How the 'Hammer' Got Nailed." *NPR.* 06 Dec. 2005. Web. 25 Apr. 2012.

Mittelstadt, Michelle. "DeLay Unleashes Conservative Call to Arms." *Houston Chronicle.* 21 Mar. 2007. Web. 25 Apr. 2012.

Smith, R. Jeffrey. "Tom DeLay, Former U.S. House Leader, Sentenced to 3 Years in Prison." *Washington Post.* 10 Jan. 2011. Web. 25 Apr. 2012.

Whitman, Jake. "DeLay: Indicting Me Is Like the Holocaust." *ABC News.* 09 Apr. 2007. Web. 25 Apr. 2012.

"Tom DeLay." *New York Times.* 10 Jan. 2011. Web. 25 Apr. 2012.

"Tom DeLay Dancing With The Stars VIDEO: Dances The Cha Cha With Cheryl Burke." *Huffington Post.* 21 Nov. 2009. Web. 25 Apr. 2012.

31. George Ryan

Davey, Monica. "Former Gov. Ryan of Illinois is Indicted on Graft Charges." *New York Times.* 18 Dec. 2003. Web. 19 Apr. 2012.

Einhorn, Catrin. "Ex-Gov. Ryan of Illinois Reports to Prison." *New York Times*. 8 Nov. 2007. Web. 19 Apr. 2012.

O'Connor, Matt, and Rudolph Bush. "A Christmas Card Defense." *Chicago Tribune*. 3 Feb. 2006. Web. 19 Apr. 2012.

Schaper, David. "Former Illinois Gov. George Ryan Heading to Prison." *NPR*. 6 Nov. 2007. Web. 19 Apr. 2012.

Zorn, Eric. "George Ryan's Day of Infamy." *Chicago Tribune*. 3 Feb. 2006. Web. 10 Feb. 2012.

"Ex-Governor Convicted of Racketeering." *Associated Press*. msnbc.com. 17 Apr. 2006. Web. 19 Apr. 2012.

"George Ryan Arrives at Prison Camp."*WLS-TV*. 7 Nov. 2007. Web. 19 Apr. 2012.

"Operation Safe Road." *Illinois Issues*. June 2006. Web. 19 Apr. 2012.

30. Ed Schrock

Byrne, John. "Rep. Schrock Resigns After 'Gay Phone Sex Call' Surfaces on Web." *The Raw Story*. 31 Aug. 2004. Web. Mar. 2012.

D., Michael. "Update: Schrock Audio Released." *Daily Kos*. 30 Aug. 2004. Web. Mar. 2012.

Shear, Michael D., and Chris L. Jenkins. "Va. Legislator Ends Bid for 3rd Term." *Washington Post*. 31 Aug. 2004. Web. Mar. 2012.

"Schrock, Edward." *Biographical Directory of the United States Congress*. N.d. Web. Mar. 2012.

29. Bob Ryan

Benson, Dan. "Former Sheboygan Mayor Bob Ryan Pleads Not Guilty to Sex Assault Charges." *Sheboygan Press*. 7 May 2012. Web. May 2012.

Davidian, Geoff. "Bob Ryan, Sheboygan Mayor, Escapes First Round Of Recall in Wisconsin." *Reuters*. Huffington Post. 18 Jan. 2012. Web. May 2012.

George, Michael, and Mick Trevey. "Sheboygan Mayor Admits Relapse." *NBC 4 WTMJ*. Web. May 2012.

Hutchinson, Courtney. "Sheboygan Mayor Bob Ryan Blames Alcoholism for Public Bender and Bar Brawl." *ABC News*. 1 Aug. 2011. Web. May 2012

Litke, Eric. "Sheboygan Mayor Bob Ryan Sexual Harassment Suit: City, Former HR Director Angela Payne Settle for $310K." *Sheboygan Press*. 7 May 2012. Web. May 2012.

Williams, Justin. "Former Sheboygan Mayor Bob Ryan Charged with Sexual Assault." *FOX 6 Milwaukee*. 9 Apr. 2012. Web. May 2012.

"Van Akkeran Hopes to 'Move (Sheboygan) Forward' After Beating Ryan." *Associated Press*. NBC 4 WTMJ. 22 Feb 2012. Web. May 2012.

28. Christopher Myers

Araiza, Karen. "Medford Mayor Resigns Amid Sex Scandal Allegations." *nbcphiladelphia.com*. 6 Dec. 2011. Web. 16 May 2012.

Camilli, Danielle. "Website Alleges Mayor Paid for Sex." *phillyburbs.com*. 21 Oct. 2011. Web. 16 May 2012.

Coppock, Kristen. "Chris Myers Resigns." *phillyburbs.com*. 6 Dec. 2011. Web. 16 May 2012.

---. "Company Mum on Status on Medford Mayor." *phillyburbs.com*. 11 Nov. 2011. Web. 16 May 2012.

---. "Medford Mayor Mum on Website." *phillyburbs.com*. 3 Nov. 2011. Web. 16 May 2012.

---. "Some Residents Want Myers Out." *phillyburbs.com*. 16 Nov. 2011. Web. 16 May 2012.

---. "Township Manager: Medford Mayor Hasn't Resigned." *phillyburbs.com*. 27 Oct. 2011. Web. 16 May 2012.

DiUlio, Nick. "The Sad Case of the Blue Undies." *New Jersey Monthly*. 3 Nov. 2011. Web. 16 May 2012.

Madden, David. "Medford, NJ Mayor Resigns Amid Sex Scandal Allegations." *CBS Philly*. 6 Dec. 2011. Web. 16 May 2012.

"Chris Myers, New Jersey Mayor, Resigns After Alleged Encounter With Male Escort." *Associated Press*. Huffington Post. 5 Dec. 2011. Web. 16 May 2012.

"Knucklehead of the Week: Medford Mayor Chris Myers." *nj.com*. 30 Oct. 2011. Web. 16 May 2011.

27. Jack and Leslie Johnson

Castaneda, Ruben, and Miranda S. Spivack. "Jack Johnson Pleads Guilty." *Washington Post*. 17 May 2011. Web. 12 May 2012.

---. "Leslie Johnson Pleads Guilty." *Washington Post*. 30 June 2011. Web. 12 May 2012.

Fard, Maggie Fazeli, and Cheryl W. Thompson. "Live Coverage: Jack Johnson Sentenced to More Than 7 Years in Prison." *Washington Post*. 6 Dec. 2011. Web. 12 May 2012.

Noble, Andrea. "Leslie Johnson Resigns From P.G. County Council." *The Washington Times*. 5 July 2011. Web. 12 May 2012.

Schwartzman, Paul, Ruben Castaneda, and Cheryl W. Thompson. "Jack Johnson, Prince George's County Executive, and His Wife, Leslie, Arrested." *Washington Post*. 13 Nov. 2010. Web. 12 May 2012.

Thompson, Cheryl W., and Mary Pat Flaherty. "Prosecutors Seek Tough Sentence for Jack Johnson in Corruption Case." *Washington Post*. 21 Nov. 2011. Web. 12 May 2012.

Trull, Armando. "Former PG County Exec Jack Johnson Sentenced to 7 Years." *wamu.org*. 6 Dec. 2011. Web. 12 May 2012.

"Former Prince George's County Executive Jack Johnson Sentenced to Over Seven Years in Federal Prison for Federal Extortion and Bribery." *fbi.gov*. Federal Bureau of Investigation. 6 Dec. 2011. Web. 12 May 2012.

"Jack Johnson Begins Serving Prison Term." *wjla.com*. 18 Feb. 2012. Web. 12 May 2012.

"Jack Johnson Timeline: Events Leading up to Tuesday's Sentencing." *wjla.com*. 6 Dec. 2011. Web. 12 May 2012.

"Jack, Leslie Johnson Phone Call Released." *wtop.com*. 15 Nov. 2011. Web. 12 May 2012.

"Leslie Johnson Reports to Prison." *nbcwashington.com*. 10 Mar. 2012. Web. 12 May 2012.

"Leslie Johnson Sentenced To Prison For Role In Husband's Corruption." *CBS Baltimore*. 9 Dec. 2011. Web. 12 May 2012.

26. Mark Sanford

Brown, Robbie. "Mysteries Remain After Governor Admits Affair." *New York Times*. 24 June 2009. Web. 17 July 2012.

Dewan, Shaila. "Gov. Sanford Faces 37 Ethics Charges." *New York Times*. 23 Nov. 2009. Web. 17 July 2012.

McCann, Josh. "Sanford Welcomed Monday by Friendly Crowd on Hilton Head Island." *Island Packet*. 4 Jan. 2010. Web. 17 July 2012.

Padgett, Tim. "Sanford's Sex Scandal: Assessing the Damage." *Time*. 25 June 2009. Web. 17 July 2012.

Stein, Sam. "Sanford Was Harsh Critic of Clinton Affair, Called President a Rascal." *Huffington Post*. 25 July 2009. Web. 17 July 2012.

"Exclusive: Read E-mails Between Sanford, Woman." *The State*. 25 June 2009. Web. 17 July 2012.

25. Anthony Weiner

Cuomo, Chris, Chris Vlasto, and Devin Dwyer. "Rep. Anthony Weiner: 'The Picture Was of Me and I Sent It'." *ABC News*. 6 June 2011. Web. 11 Apr. 2012.

Fahrenthold, David A., and Paul Kane. "Rep. Anthony Weiner Resigns." *Washington Post*. 16 June 2011. Web. 11 Apr. 2012.

Glynn, Casey. "Former Porn Star Ginger Lee Says Anthony Weiner Asked Her to Lie." *CBS News*. 15 June 2011. Web. 11 Apr. 2012.

Hernandez, Raymond. "Weiner Resigns in Chaotic Final Scene." *New York Times*. 16 June 2011. Web. 29 Apr. 2012.

Kim, Michelle. "A Timeline of Weiner's Sexting Scandal." *NBC 4 New York*. 17 June 2011. Web. 11 Apr. 2012.

24. Mark Souder

Belz, Emily. "Lessons From a Broken Man." *World Magazine*. 19 June 2010. Web. 22 June 2012.

Choe, Jaywon. "Disgraced Rep. Souder Says Loneliness Played a Role in Affair." *CBS News*. 17 June 2010. Web. 22 June 2012.

Hechtkopf, Kevin. "Mark Souder Resigns Because of Affair with Staffer." *CBS News*. 18 May 2010. Web. 22 June 2012.

Pergram, Chad, and Steve Brown. "Indiana Rep. Mark Souder Resigns After Affair with Staffer." *Fox News*. 18 May 2010. Web. 22 June 2012.

Smith, Sylvia A. "Souder Discusses Affair, Relationships Damaged and Decision to Leave Office." *Fort Wayne Journal Gazette*. 24 May. 2010. Web. 22 June 2012.

Weigel, David. "What Does Mark Souder's Resignation Mean For Abstinence Education?" *Washington Post*. 18 May 2010. Web. 22 June 2012.

"Ex-Ind. Rep. Mark Souder Hospitalized." *Associated Press*. WISH-TV.com. 03 Apr. 2012. Web. 22. June 2012.

23. Chris Lee

Hoot, Fred. "GOP Representative Christopher Lee Sets World Record for Fastest Resignation After Exposure." *Liberal Fair*. CosmoFair Network. 10 Feb. 2011. Web. Mar. 2012.

Jaffe, Matthew. "Congressman Chris Lee Resigns After Shirtless Photo Posted on Internet." *ABC News*. 9 Feb. 2011. Web. Mar. 2012.

O'Conor, Maureen. "Married GOP Congressman Sent Sexy Pictures to Craigslist Babe." *Gawker*. 9 Feb. 2011. Web. Mar. 2012

Schouten, Fredreka. "GOP Rep. Chris Lee Resigns over Shirtless Photo on Web." *USA TODAY*. 10 Feb. 2011. Web. Mar. 2012.

Stern, Remy. "The Craigslist Congressman and the Crossdressing Prostitute." *Gawker*. 25 Feb. 2011. Web. Mar. 2012.

Zremski, Jerry. "Lee Faces Two More Flirtation Allegations." *Buffalo News.com*. 26 Feb. 2011. Web. Mar. 2012.

"Chris Lee, Craigslist Ex-Congressman, Reportedly Trolled Site For Transgender Women." *Huffington Post*, 25 Feb. 2011. Web. Mar. 2012.

22. Bob Allen

Sherman, Christopher. "Allen Insists He's Innocent, Will Not Quit." *Orlando Sentinel*. 13 July 2007. Web. Mar. 2012.

"Florida Rep. Illicit Sex Excuse." *CNN.com*. YouTube.com. 8 Aug. 2007. Web. Mar. 2012.

"Florida State Rep. Bob Allen Resigns Amidst Sex Conviction." *Edgeboston.com*. 20 Nov. 2007. Web. Mar. 2012.

"Rep. Bob Allen Found Guilty of Soliciting Prostitution." *WFTV.com*. 9 Nov. 2007. Web. Mar. 2012.

"Taped Evidence Released in Case Against Arrested Legislator." *WFTV.com*. 3 Aug. 2007. Web. Mar. 2012.

21. Marc Dann

Ewinger, James. "Former Attorney General Marc Dann Fights for His Law License." *Cleveland Plain Dealer*. 3 Nov. 2011. Web. 27 May 2012.

Fields, Reginald. "Marc Dann Fined $1,000 and Reprimanded for Campaign Violations." *Cleveland Plain Dealer*. 19 Mar. 2009. Web. 27 May 2012.

Jindra, Christine. "Marc Dann Admits to Affair with Staff Member." *Cleveland Plain Dealer*. 2 May 2008. Web. 27 May 2012.

Johnson, Alan. "Second Dann Aide Suspended in Probe." *The Columbus Dispatch*. 16 Apr. 2008. Web. 27 May 2012.

Jones, Ashby. "Marc Dann Resigns as Ohio Attorney General". *Wall Street Journal*. 14 May 2008. Web. 27 May 2012.

Kuehner, John C. "Dann Should Resign: A Plain Dealer Editorial." *Cleveland Plain Dealer*. 3 May 2008. Web. 27 May 2012.

Siegel, Jim. "House Dems Seek Dann's Impeachment." *The Columbus Dispatch*. 13 May 2008. Web. 27 May 2012.

Weinger, Mackenzie. "Life After The Fall: 4 Sex Scandal Pols." *Politico.com*. 21 May 2012. Web. 27 May 2012.

"Editorial: Dann Should Go." *The Columbus Dispatch*. 4 May 2008. Web. 27 May 2012.

"Ohio Official Balks at Quitting." *New York Times*. 6 May 2008. Web. 27 May 2012

20. Rita Crundwell

Driscoll, Sean F. "Ex-Dixon Comptroller's 400 Horses to Be Sold." *Rockford Register Star*. 15 June 2012. Web. June 2012.

Kim, Susanna. "How Comptroller of Small Illinois City Stole $30 Million over 6 Years." *ABC News*. 18 Apr. 2012. Web. June 2012.

Jenco, Melissa. "Former Dixon Comptroller Pleads Not Guilty to Taking $53M." *Chicago Tribune*. 7 May 2012. Web. June 2012.

Jenco, Melissa, and Andy Grimm. "Feds Say Dixon Thefts Worse Than Believed: $53M--Ex-Comptroller Indicted in Theft of City Funds over 22 Years." *Chicago Tribune*. 2 May 2012. Web. June 2012.

Ray, Robert. "Rita Crundwell: Dixon, Illinois Comptroller Pleads Not Guilty To Stealing $53 Million." *Huffington Post*. 7 May 2012. Web. June 2012.

Schaper, David. "Alleged $30M Theft By Comptroller Stuns Ill. City." *NPR*. 19 Apr. 2012. Web. June 2012.

United States Attorney, Northern District of Illinois. "Federal Indictment Charges Former Dixon Comptroller Rita Crundwell With Engaging in $53 Million Fraud Since 1990." *justice.gov*. 1 May 2012. Web. June 2012.

"Dixon Comptroller Fired After Alleged $30M Theft." *ABC 7 NEWS*. 23 Apr. 2012. Web. June 2012.

United States of America v. Rita A. Crundwell. 12 CR 50027. Unites States District Court, Northern District of Illinois, Western Division. Dec. 2011.

19. Joseph Ganim

Caito, Nick. "Former Mayor Joseph Ganim A Free Man." *Hartford Courant*. 19 July 2010. Web. 17 May 2012.

Mahony, Edmund H. "Grand Jury Amends Ganim Indictment." *Hartford Courant*. 28 Mar. 2002. Web. 17 May 2012.

---. "Joe Ganim Is Back (And Feds Are Watching)." *Hartford Courant*. 12 Nov. 2011. Web. 17 May 2012.

Mayko, Michael P. "Ganim Released From Prison, Enters Hartford Halfway House." *Connecticut Post*. 22 Jan. 2010. Web. 17 May 2012.

Zielbauer, Paul. "Bridgeport Mayor Convicted on 16 Charges of Corruption." *New York Times*. 20 Mar. 2003. Web. 17 May 2012.

---. "Bridgeport Mayor Indicted on Corruption Charges." *New York Times*. 1 Nov. 2001. Web. 17 May 2012.

"Mayor Resigns After Corruption Conviction." *Los Angeles Times*. 29 Mar. 2003. Web. 17 May 2012.

18. Bell Council

Gottlieb, Jeff. "336 Voters Opened Bell's Wallet." *Los Angeles Times*. 23 July 2010. Web. 29 July 2012.

---. "Bell's Auditors Should Have Spotted Most of the Alleged Corruption, State Controller Finds." *Los Angeles Times*. 21 Dec. 2010. Web. 26 June 2012.

---. "Former Bell Officials' Pensions Reduced Even Further." *Los Angeles Times*. 18 June 2012. Web. 26 June 2012.

---. "Six Former Bell Council Members Lose Appeal." *Los Angeles Times*. 31 Dec. 2011. Web. 26 June 2012.

Gottlieb, Jeff, and Ruben Vives. "Bell's Finances So Bad City Could Have Trouble Providing Basic Services, Audit Concludes." *Los Angeles Times*. 6 Jan. 2011. Web. 26 June 2012.

---. "Is a City Manager Worth $800,000?" *Los Angeles Times*. 15 July 2010. Web. 26 June 2012.

Gottlieb, Jeff, Ruben Vives, and Jack Leonard. "Bell Leaders Hauled Off in Cuffs." *Los Angeles Times*. 22 Sept. 2010. Web. 26 June 2012.

Knoll, Corina. "In Closing Arguments, Prosecution Accuses Bell's Robert Rizzo of Stealing More Than $5 million." *Los Angeles Times*. 10 Mar. 2011. Web. 26 June 2012.

Leonard, Jack. "Prosecutors Detail Steps Bell Leaders Allegedly Took to Hide High Salaries." *Los Angeles Times*. 23 Sept. 2010. Web. 26 June 2012.

Leonard, Jack, Jeff Gottlieb, Ruben Vives, and Richard Winton. "Rizzo Faces 53 Counts; Bell Was 'Corruption on Steroids,' DA Cooley Says." *Los Angeles Times*. 21 Sept. 2010. Web. 26 June 2012.

Leonard, Jack, Ruben Vives, and Richard Winton. "Bell Officials Arrested as Prosecutors Are Set to File Criminal Charges." *Los Angeles Times*. 21 Sept. 2010. Web. 26 June 2012.

Medina, Jennifer. "As Officials Face Corruption Charges, California City Struggles to Move On." *New York Times*. 21 Nov. 2010. Web. 29 July 2012.

Rogers, John. "Bell Votes to Recall Council Members by Over 95%." *Associated Press*. The Huffington Post. 9 Mar. 2011. Web. 26 June 2012.

Suter, Leanne, John North, and Subha Ravindhran. "Bell Leaders Cut Pay by 90%, Remain in Posts." *KABC-TV*. 26 July 2010. Web. 26 June 2012.

Welch, William M. "Bell, Calif., Residents Cheer Arrest of Officials." *USA TODAY*. 23 Sept. 2010. Web. 26 June 2012.

Winton, Richard. "3 Accused Bell Officials Want Cash-Strapped City to Pay Their Legal Bills." *Los Angeles Times*. 10 Jan. 2011. Web. 26 June 2012.

"Judge Rules Bell City Council Corruption Case Will Go Forward." *Associated Press*. CBS Los Angeles. 1 Dec. 2011. Web. 26 June 2012.

"Secret Robert Rizzo Fund Contained $4.5 Million." *Associated Press*. The Huffington Post. 26 Apr. 2011. Web. 26 June 2012.

17. Randall Tobias

Chapman, Sandra. "'DC Madam' Scandal Ensnares Tobias." *WTHR.com*. N.d. Web. Mar. 2012.

Kessler, Glenn. "Rice Deputy Quits After Query Over Escort Service." *Washington Post*. 28 Apr. 2007. Web. Mar. 2012.

Montes, Sue Anne Pressley. "Escort-Service Scandal Set to Ignite D.C. Explosion." *The Seattle Times*. 29 Apr. 2007. Web. Mar. 2012.

Rood, Justin. "Dial 'D' for Divorce." *ABC News*. 16 Mar. 2009. Web Mar. 2012.

Ross, Brian, and Justin Rood. "Senior Official Linked to Escort Service Resigns." *ABC News*. 27 Apr. 2007. Web. Mar. 2012.

Sekoff, Roy. "Randall Tobias: Another GOP Hypocrite Bites the Dust." *Huffington Post*. 28 Apr. 2007. Web. Mar. 2012.

"ABC's Ross: DC Madam's List Includes White House & Pentagon Officials, Prominent Lawyers." *ThinkProgress.com*. 28 Apr. 2007. Web. Mar. 2012.

"Official Caught Using Escort Service Demanded Anti-Prostitution 'Loyalty Oaths'." *ThinkProgress.com*. 28 Apr. 2007. Web. Mar. 2012.

"State Department Official Resigns Over 'D.C. Madam'." *CNN.com*. 27 Apr. 2007. Web. Mar. 2012.

16. Richard Curtis

Savage, Dan. "Richard Curtis Goes National." *The Stranger*. 31 Oct. 2007. Web. 30 Apr. 2012.

"'Live with Dan Abrams' for Oct. 31." *MSNBC.com*. 1 Nov. 2007. Web. 30 Apr. 2012.

"Spokane Police Department Additional Report." *Spokesman Review*. 28 Oct. 2007. Web. 30 Apr. 2012.

"Wash. Legislator Resigns Amid Gay Sex Scandal." *Associated Press*. 31 Oct. 2007. Web. 30 Apr. 2012.

15. Jim Traficant

Dwyer, Devin. "Ex-Con Jim Traficant Seeks Reelection to House as Independent." *ABC News*. 4 May 2010. Web. June 2012.

Firth, Robert J. *Scoundrels*. eBookIt.com, 2011. Web. June 2012.

Montopoli, Brian. "Jim Traficant: I'm Going to Run For Congress." *CBS News*. 30 Dec. 2009. Web. June 2012.

Rodgers, Bill. "White Nationalists, Conspiracy Theorists Join Traficant's Cause." *Tribune Chronicle*. 30 Aug. 2009. Web. June 2012.

Russell, Nicole. "Beam Me Up, Jimbo." *The American Spectator*. 2 Sept. 2009. Web. June 2012.

Whittington, Mark. "Jim Traficant Is Free from Jail." *Yahoo!* 2 Sept. 2009. Web. June 2012.

"The 2002 Elections: Midwest; Ohio." *New York Times*. 7 Nov. 2002. Web. June 2012.

"Beam Him Out, Voters." *The Post and Courier*. 6 May 2010. Web. June 2012.

"Exclusive: Traficant – I Was a Target…I Must Have Been Doing Something Right." *FoxNews.com*. 11 Sept. 2009. Web. June 2012.

"Traficant Arrives at Federal Prison." *CNN.com*. 5 Aug. 2002. Web. June 2012.

"Traficant Case Gives Glimpse of Corrupt Legal Process." *Law and Ethics Reform*. N.d. Web. June 2012.

14. Betty Loren-Maltese

Fountain, John W. "3 Officials Charged with Corruption in Al Capone's Old Fief." *New York Times*. 16 June 2001. Web. 20 Apr. 2012.

---. "Top Official in Cicero, Ill., Gets 8 Years in Fund Theft." *New York Times*. 10 Jan. 2003. Web. 20 Apr. 2012.

---. "Town President Is Convicted In Scheme to Steal $12 Million." *New York Times*. 24 Aug. 2002. Web. 20 Apr. 2012.

Gregory, Ted. "Betty Loren-Maltese Now a Lot Closer to Cicero." *Chicago Tribune*. 15 Feb. 2010. Web. 20 Apr. 2012.

Grossman, Ron. "Rise to Power, Cicero-Style." *Chicago Tribune*. 24 Aug. 2002. Web. 20 Apr. 2012.

Kavanagh, Anne. "Trauma Queen." *Chicago Magazine*. Mar. 2008. Web. 20 Apr. 2012.

Rodriguez, Alex, and Andrew Zajac. "Feds Trace How Cicero Plot Began." *Chicago Tribune*. 17 June 2001. Web. 20 Apr. 2012.

Ruzich, Joseph. "Betty Loren-Maltese Scheduled to Arrive in Chicago on Monday." *Chicago Tribune*. 14 Feb. 2010. Web. 20 Apr. 2012.

---. "Betty Loren-Maltese Takes Job as Hostess at Pizzeria." *Chicago Tribune*. 7 Apr. 2010. Web. 20 Apr. 2012.

---. "Betty Loren-Maltese's House Auctioned for $87,000." *Chicago Tribune*. 28 July 2011. Web. 20 Apr. 2012.

---. "Betty Loren-Maltese Unloads Personal Belongings at Garage Sale." *Chicago Tribune*. 3 Sept. 2011. Web. 20 Apr. 2012.

Sneed, Michael. "Betty Loren-Maltese, Daughter Reunite." *Chicago Sun-Times*. 1 Apr. 2012. Web. 20 Apr. 2012.

Zorn, Eric. "Betty Loren-Maltese's New Job." *Chicago Tribune*. 8 Apr. 2010. Web. 20 Apr. 2012.

"Judge Orders Loren-Maltese to Prison Early." *Chicago Tribune*. 22 Jan. 2003. Web. 20 Apr. 2012.

"Loren-Maltese's Assets Frozen." *Chicago Tribune*. 18 Jan. 2003. Web. 20 Apr. 2012.

13. Michael Duvall

Moxley, R. Scott. "OC Assemblyman In Bed With Lobbyist...No, Literally In Bed." *OC Weekly Blogs*. OC Weekly. 8 Sept. 2009. Web. 26 July 2012.

Williams, Juliet. "Heidi DeJong Barsuglia Denies Mike Duvall Affair: Energy Lobbyist Reinstated After Recorded Sex Talk." *Huffington Post*. 2 Nov. 2009. Web. Feb. 2012.

Woo, Stu. "Open Mic Gives California Assembly a Lot to Talk About." *Wall Street Journal*. 9 Sept. 2009. Web. Feb. 2012.

"Calif. Lawmaker in Sex Scandal Denies Affairs." *Boston.com*. 11 Sept. 2009. Web. Feb. 2012.

"Calif. Pol Quits After 'Spanking' Boasts." *CBS News*. 3 June 2010. Web. Feb. 2012.

"Sempra Energy Under Fire in Lobbyist Sex Scandal." *CBS 8 San Diego*. 18 Sept. 2009. Web. Feb. 2012.

12. Samuel Kent

Cook, Theresa, and Gina Sunseri. "Federal Judge Indicted in Sex Abuse Case." *ABC News*. 29 Aug. 2008. Web. 30 Apr. 2012.

Hollandsworth, Skip. "Perversion of Justice." *Texas Monthly*. Dec. 2009. Web. 30 Apr. 2012.

Olsen, Lise. "Disgraced Ex-Judge Kent Out of Prison, Confined to Cabin." *Houston Chronicle*. 30 July 2011. Web. 30 Apr. 2012.

---. "Former Federal Judge Kent Calls Prison Unfair, 'Cruel'." *Houston Chronicle*. 3 Aug. 2011. Web. 30 Apr. 2012.

Powell, Stewart M. "U.S. House Learns of Samuel Kent's 'Judicial Reign of Terror'." *Houston Chronicle*. 3 June 2009. Web. 30 Apr. 2012.

11. Eliot Spitzer

Elkind, Peter. *Rough Justice: The Rise and Fall of Eliot Spitzer*. New York: Penguin Books, 2010. Print.

Hakim, Danny, and William Rashbaum. "Spitzer is Linked to Prostitution Ring." *New York Times*. 10 Mar. 2008. Web. 17 July 2012.

Kovaleski, Serge, and Ian Urbina. "For an Aspiring Singer, a Harsher Spotlight." *New York Times*. 13 Mar. 2008 Web. 17 July 2012.

Masters, Brooke. "Review of Peter Elkind's Rough Justice: The Rise and Fall of Eliot Spitzer'." *Washington Post*. 25 Apr. 2010. Web. 17 July 2012.

Stelter, Brian. "CNN Cancels 'In the Arena' With Eliot Spitzer." *New York Times*. 6 July 2011. Web. 17 July 2012.

"Spitzer as Client 9: Read Text Messages from Spitzer to Prostitute." *Huffington Post*. 28 Mar. 2008. Web. 17 July 2012.

10. Randall Cunningham

Babcock, Charles, and Jeff Weisman. "Congressman Admits Taking Bribes, Resigns." *Washington Post*. 29 Nov. 2005. Web. 27 Mar. 2012.

Bachrach, Judy. "Washington Babylon." *Vanity Fair*. Aug. 2006. Web. 27 Mar. 2012.

Cantlupe, Joe, and Marcus Stern. "FBI Looking at Sale of Cunningham Home." *Union-Tribune*. 17 June 2005. Web. 27 Mar. 2012.

Condon, George. "Congressman's Betrayal of Troops Called Greatest Sin." *Union-Tribune*. 1 Dec. 2005. Web. 27 Mar. 2012.

Maass, Dave. "'The Untold Story of Duke Cunningham'." *San Diego City Beat*. 6 Apr. 2011. 27 Mar. 2012.

McDonald, Jeff. "U-T, Copley News Win Pulitzer Prize." *Union-Tribune*. 18 Apr. 2006. Web. 27 Mar. 2012.

Soto, Onell R. "'Overwhelming Case' Forced Cunningham to Accept Deal." *Union-Tribune*. 30 Nov. 2005. Web. 27 Mar. 2012.

"Congressman Resigns After Bribery Plea." *CNN.com*. 28 Nov. 2005. Web. 27 Mar. 2012

9. William Jefferson

Barakat, Matthew. "La. Congressman Pleads Not Guilty to Bribery." *Associated Press*. 9 June 2007. Web. 17 July 2012.

---. "William Jefferson, Ex-Congressman, Gets 13 Years In Freezer Cash Case." *Huffington Post.* 13 Nov. 2009. Web. 17 July 2012.

The United States Department of Justice. "Former Congressman William J. Jefferson Convicted of Bribery, Racketeering, Money Laundering, and Other Related Charges." *justice.gov.* 5 Aug. 2009. Web. 6 July 2012.

"Louisiana Democrat Wins House Runoff, Despite Bribery Scandal." *Associated Press.* 10 Dec. 2006. Web. 17 July 2012.

"Poll: Americans Support Searches."*ABC News.* 1 June 2006. Web. 17 July 2012.

8. Edwin Edwards

Brazil, Eric. "FBI Video Shows Casino Cash." *SF Gate.* 16 Mar. 2000. Web. 21 Feb. 2012.

Dietz, David, and Howard Arceneaux. "DeBartolo Guilty of Felony / $1 Million Fine, 2 Years of Probation." *SF Gate.* 7 Oct. 1998. Web. 21 Feb. 2012.

Robertson, Campbell. "Well-Known Felon Still Draws a Crowd, but Louisiana Has Moved On." *New York Times.* 23 Oct. 2011. Web. 21 Feb. 2012.

Stumbo, Bella. "Edwards Faces Trial : Cajun King's Crown Slips in Louisiana." *Los Angeles Times.* 14 Aug. 1985. Web. 21 Feb. 2012.

"2001: Former Gov. Edwin Edwards Is Convicted of Extortion." *The Times-Picayune.* NOLA.com. Web. 13 Jan. 2012. Web. 21 Feb. 2012.

"Ex-Governor Is Convicted." *Amarillo Globe-News.* 10 May 2000. Web. 21 Feb. 2012.

"Ex-La. Gov, 83, Marries 32-year-old Prison Pen Pal." *Associated Press.* USA TODAY. 29 July 2011. Web. 21 Feb. 2012.

"Former Louisiana Governor Released From Prison." *CNN.com.* 13 Jan. 2011. Web. 21 Feb. 2012.

7. Dianne Wilkerson

The Federal Bureau of Investigation. "Former Massachusetts State Senator Dianne Wilkerson Pleads Guilty to Extortion." *fbi.gov.* 3 June 2010. Web. 18 Apr. 2012.

McPhee, Michele. "Mass. Pol Accused of Stuffing Bra With Bribes." *ABC News.* 28 Oct. 2008. Web. 18 Apr. 2012.

Saltzman, Jonathan. "Wilkerson Sentenced to 3 1/2 Years in Corruption Case." *boston.com.* 6 Jan. 2011. Web. 18 Apr. 2012.

Saltzman, Jonathan, and Travis Anderson. "Wilkerson Admits She Took $23,500." *boston.com.* 4 June 2010. Web. 18 Apr. 2012.

Sweet, Laurel J. "Conviction Upheld for Shamed Ex. Sen. Dianne Wilkerson." *BostonHerald.com.* 5 Apr. 2012. Web. 18 Apr. 2012.

Walker, Adrian. "Onetime Rising Star Falls Hard." *boston.com.* 4 June 2010. Web. 18 Apr. 2012.

"FBI: Photos Show Massachusetts Lawmaker Stuffing Bribes in Bra." *Associated Press.* FoxNews.com. 28 Oct. 2008. Web. 18 Apr. 2012.

"Former Massachusetts Sen. Dianne Wilkerson, Scheduled to Report to Prison, Says 2 Black Ministers Collaborated Against Her." *Associated Press.* masslive.com. 11 Mar. 2011. Web. 18 Apr. 2012.

"U.S. Appeals Court Dismisses Dianne Wilkerson Appeal." *Associated Press.* masslive.com. 5 Apr. 2012. Web. 18 Apr. 2012.

6. Kwame Kilpatrick

Elrick, M.L., Jim Schaefer, Ben Schmitt, and Joe Swickard. "Kilpatrick Admits Guilt, Resigns Office." *Detroit Free Press.* 5 Sept. 2008. Web. 4 July 2012.

Elrick, M.L. "Kwame Kilpatrick Inspires Law Banning Use of Campaign Funds to Pay Attorneys." *Detroit Free Press.* 4 July 2012. Web. 5 July 2012.

Gallagher, John. "Free Press Wins Pulitzer For Coverage of Mayoral Scandal." *Detroit Free Press.* 20 Apr. 2009. Web. 4 July 2012. "'Kilpatrick Enterprise' Faces September 2012 Federal Trial in Detroit Corruption Case." *Associated Press.* 14 Apr. 2011. Web. 5 July 2012.

5. Larry Langford

Hubbard, Russell. "Larry Langford: 'Calm Inside' As Verdicts Halt Career." *The Birmingham News.* 29 Oct. 2009. Web. 3 July 2012. Morton, Jason. "Larry Langford Gets 15 Years." *Tuscaloosa News.* 6 Mar. 2010. Web. 3 July 2012.

"Larry Langford Found Guilty on All 60 Counts -- Updated." *The Birmingham News*. 28 Oct. 2009. Web. 3 July 2012.

4. Vince Fumo
Dale, MaryClaire "Feds: Vince Fumo's E-mails Hint at Revenge." *NBC10 Philadelphia*. 18 Oct. 2011. Web. June 2012.

---. "Vince Fumo Aide Ordered to Pay $800,000." *NBC10 Philadelphia*. 16 Nov. 2011. Web. June 2012.

Davies, Dave. "Did Vince Rip Us Off Because He Was High?" *Newsworks.org*. 9 Nov. 2011. Web. June 2012.

McCoy, Craig R. "Fumo's Defense Releases More E-mails." *Philly.com*. 5 Nov. 2011. Web. June 2012.

"Biography." *State Senator Vincent J. Fumo*. 2000. Web. June 2012.

"Fmr. Senator Vince Fumo Gets 6 More Months in Prison." *Associated Press*. NBC10 Philadelphia. 10 Nov. 2011. Web. June 2012.

United States of America v. Vincent J. Fumo. 06-319. United States District Court for the Eastern District of Pennsylvania. 6 Feb. 2007.

3. Rod Blagojevich
Davey, Monica. "Two Sides of a Troubled Governor, Sinking Deeper." *New York Times*. 14 Dec. 2008. Web. 17 July 2012.

Long, Ray, and Rick Pearson. "Impeached Illinois Gov. Rod Blagojevich Has Been Removed from Office." *Chicago Tribune*. 30 Jan. 2009. Web. 17 July 2012.

Mendell, David. "The Less Theatrical Blagojevich Trial." *The New Yorker*. 27 June 2011. Web. 17 July 2012.

Samuel, Peter. "Blago Signs Being Covered up on Illinois Tollway." *Toll Road News*. 30 Jan. 2009. Web. 17 July 2012.

Scherer, Michael. "Governor Gone Wild: The Blagojevich Scandal." *Time*. 11 Dec. 2008. Web. 17 July 2012.

Wisniewski, Mary, and Janan Hanna. "Ex-Illinois Governor Blagojevich Guilty of Corruption." *Reuters*. 27 June 2011. Web. 17 July 2012.

"Blago Approval Rating at 7 Percent." *Politico*. 11 Dec. 2008. Web. 17 July 2012.

"Blagojevich Guilty on One Count: Mistrial on 23 Others." *MSNBC*.com. 17 Aug. 2010. Web. 17 July 2012.

2. Neil Goldschmidt
Boulé, Margie. "Neil Goldschmidt's Sex-Abuse Victim Tells of the Relationship that Damaged Her Life." *The Oregonian*. 31 Jan. 2011. Web. 13 May 2012.

Esteve, Harry, and Gail Kinsey Hill. "Facing Exposure, Neil Goldschmidt Admits Sexual Relationship with 14-Year-Old Girl While He Was Mayor of Portland." *The Oregonian*. 7 May 2004. Web. 13 May 2012.

Jaquiss, Nigel. "The Goldschmidt Resignation." *Willamette Week*. 5 May 2004. Web. 13 May 2012.

1. Phil Giordano
Cowan, Alison Leigh. "Jurors Selected in Trial of Ex-Mayor of Waterbury." *New York Times*. 5 Mar. 2003. Web. 30 May 2012.

Holtz, Jeff. "The Week; Imprisoned Ex-Mayor Seeks Waterbury Pay." *New York Times*. 27 Aug. 2006. Web. 30 May 2012.

Mahony, Edmund H. "Former Construction Executive Who Spurred Giordano Investigation Sentenced." *Hartford Courant*. 23 Apr. 2010. Web. 30 May 2012.

Scarponi, Diane. "Conn. Mayor Arrested on Child Sex Charges." *ABC News*. 27 July 2001. Web. 30 May 2012.

Stowe, Stacey. "Waterbury Corruption Case Is Moving Forward Again." *New York Times*. 10 Mar. 2005. Web. 30 May 2012.

Tuohy, Lynne. "A Payback for Nightmares." *Hartford Courant*. 14 June 2003. Web. 30 May 2012.

"Ex-Waterbury Mayor Phillip Giordano Seeks Records on His Child-Sex Victim." *Associated Press*. New Haven Register. 11 Dec. 2011. Web. 30 May 2012.

"Mayor Arrested on Sexually Related Charges Involving Child." *CNN.com*. 26 July 2001. Web. 30 May 2012.

"Prosecutors Responding to Former Waterbury Mayor Giordano's Latest Appeal." *Associated Press*. New Haven Register. 6 June 2011. Web. 30 May 2012.

"Waterbury Mayor Faces Civil Rights Charges Too." *Los Angeles Times*. 21 Sept. 2001. Web. 30 May 2012.

Poor Judgment

7. Carmen Kontur-Gronquist

Celizic, Mike. "Ousted Mayor Makes No Apologies for Lingerie Photos." *TODAY Show*. 3 Mar. 2008. Web. Mar. 2012.

Connelly, Chris. "Public Inferno Over Mayor's Not-So-Private Photos Results in Recall." *ABC 20/20*. 27 Feb. 2008. Web. Mar. 2012.

Shahbazi, Rudabeh. "Ousted Arlington Mayor Fights Back." *KEPR-TV*. 7 Nov. 2008. Web. Mar. 2012.

"Arlington Mayor Recalled in Close Vote." *KATU.com*. 26 Feb. 2008. Web. Mar. 2012

"Ore. Mayor in MySpace Flap Faces Recall." *USA TODAY*. 30 Jan. 2008. Web. Mar. 2012.

"Voters Recall Oregon Mayor Who Posed on Fire Truck in Underwear." *FOX News.com*. 26 Feb. 2008. Web. Mar. 2012.

6. Eric Brewer

Blay, Zandie. "Frisky Fashion: East Cleveland Mayor (Allegedly) Drags Out His Lingerie Collection." *HuffingtonPost*. 29 Sept. 2009. Web. 27 May 2012.

Caniglia, John. "East Cleveland Mayor Eric Brewer Admits to Being in Racy Photos." *cleveland.com*. 6 Oct. 2009. Web. 27 May 2012.

---. "East Cleveland Mayor Eric Brewer Tells TV Show He Was the Man in Racy Lingerie Photos." *cleveland.com*. 6 Oct. 2009. Web. 17 May 2012.

Donaldson, Stan. "Controversial Ex-East Cleveland Mayor Eric Brewer: Whatever Happened to?" *cleveland.com*. 2 Oct. 2011. Web. 27 May 2012.

Guillen, Joe. "East Cleveland Mayor Eric Brewer Blames TV station, Opponent in Photo Flap." *cleveland.com*. 24 Sept. 2009. Web. 27 May 2012.

McCormick, Eugene. "East Cleveland Mayor Eric Brewer Responds to Sexually Explicit Photo Scandal." *clevelandleader.com*. 24 Sept. 2009. Web. 27 May 2012.

"Blame Game: East Cleveland Mayoral Candidate Says He Didn't Release Flamboyant Photos." *woio.com*. 25 Sept. 2009. Web. 27 May 2012.

"East Cleveland Mayor Admits Exclusively to 'Inside Edition' It's Him in Those Drag Photos." *InsideEdition.com*. 6 Oct. 2009. Web. 27 May 2012.

"East Cleveland's Mayor Discusses Photos." *wtam.com*. 24 Sept. 2009. Web. 27 May 2012.

"It's Me: East Cleveland Mayor Eric Brewer Admits to Dressing in Drag." *woio.com*. 7 Oct. 2009. Web. 27 May 2012.

5. David Vitter

Gray, Madison, and James S. Snyder. "Top 10 Political Sex Scandals." *Time*. 8 June 2011. Web. 3 July 2012.

Nossiter, Adam. "A Senator's Moral High Ground Gets a Little Shaky." *New York Times*. 11 July 2007. Web. 3 July 2012.

Zagorin, Adam. "Did Senator Vitter Get Hustled?" *Time*. 10 July 2007. Web. 3 July 2012. "David Vitter." *New York Times*. 2 Nov. 2011. Web. 3 July 2012

4. Greg Davis

Jones, Yolanda. "Court Date Set for Southaven Mayor Davis." *The Commercial Appeal*. 29 Mar. 2012. Web. 31 Mar. 2012.

---. "State Auditor's Letter Chastised Southaven Aldermen." *The Commercial Appeal*. 23 Mar. 2012. Web. 31 Mar. 2012.

---. "Southaven Mayor Greg Davis' Expense Receipts Prompt Frank Revelation." *The Commercial Appeal*. 16 Dec. 2011. Web. 31 Mar. 2012.

Jones, Yolanda, and Marc Perrusquia. "Southaven Mayor Greg Davis Sought Reimbursement from City, Chamber for Same Charges, Records Show." *The Commercial Appeal*. 4 Mar. 2012. Web. 31 Mar. 2012.

Towle, Andy. "GOP 'Family Values' Mayor Greg Davis of Southaven, MS Forced Out of Closet by Receipts from Gay Sex Shop." *Towleroad.com*. 16 Dec. 2011. Web. 31 Mar. 2012.

"Gov. Bryant Revises His Proposed State Budget." *Mississippi Business Journal*. 28 Mar. 2012. Web. 31 Mar. 2012.

Priape.com. N.p. N.d. Web. 31 Mar. 2012.

3. Eric Massa

Haygood, Will, Carol Leonnig, and Ben Pershing. "Eric Massa: Who Is the Man Behind the Hard Stare?" *Washington Post.* 16 Mar. 2010. Web. 22 June 2012.

Hernandez, Raymond. "Ex-Congressman Describes Tickle Fights With Aides." *New York Times.* 9 Mar. 2010. Web. 22 June 2012. "Massa Seeks to Divert Attention from Harassment Allegations." *CNN.com.* 10 Mar. 2010. Web. 22 June 2012.

2. John Doolittle

Grimaldi, James V., and Susan Schmidt. "FBI Searches Congressman's Home." *Washington Post.* 18 Apr. 2007. Web. 30 May 2012.

Thomson, Gus. "Ex-Congressman John Doolittle Steps Into New Lobbying Role." *Auburn Journal.* 23 Sept. 2010. Web. 30 May 2012.

Weisman, Jonathan. "Congressman Quits Panel After Raid." *Washington Post.* 20 Apr. 2007. Web. 30 May 2012.

"Abramoff: The House That Jack Built." *ThinkProgress.com.* 3 Jan. 2006. Web. 30 May 2012.

"CREW's Most Corrupt Report 2006: Beyond DeLay." *crewsmostcorrupt.org.* N.d. Web. 30 May 2012.

1. Sam Adams

Adams, Sam. "Mayor Sam Adams." *Twitter.com.* N.d. Web. 30 Apr. 2012.

Jaquiss, Nigel, Beth Slovic, and James Pitkin. "The Adams Report." *Willamette Week.* 24 June. 2009. Web. 30 Apr. 2012.

JMartens. "Mayor Adams Recall Effort Comes Up Short, Again." *The Portlander.* 20 Apr. 2010. Web. 30 Apr. 2012.

Sharples, Tiffany. "Can Portland's Gay Mayor Survive a Scandal?" *Time.* 27 Jan. 2009. Web. 30 Apr. 2012.

"City of Portland, Oregon - Office of Mayor Sam Adams." *Kickstarter.com.* N.d. Web. 30 Apr. 2012.

ACKNOWLEDGMENTS

First and foremost, we'd like to thank the American people for making this book possible. Had you not elected (and in some cases, reelected) these *Lyin' Cheatin' Bastards*, we would have never had the chance to write about their profoundly shameless behavior.

We also have to give a shout out to the American political system, which continues to foster corruption and moral depravity, despite the constant head shaking and hand-wringing by the pundits and the people. We may claim to want honest and faithful representation, but we are easily entranced by their well-honed spin and rhetoric. While we're shaking their hands, they're picking our pockets with a wink and a smile.

We want to thank our parents for raising us right—for instilling in us a moral compass that demands we expect better from our elected officials and shine a floodlight on the men and women tarnishing our country with their complete disregard for the sanctity of their office.

Great gratitude also goes to our friends, families and significant others who put up with long hours of us rambling on about bathroom escapades, bra stuffing, and the possibility of Guam tipping over. We could not have written about these asinine antics without your support and encouragement, and understanding of our strange Internet search histories.

This book would not have made it in your hands without the keen eye of copy editor Sarah Roggio. And it would not look as good without the many talents of book designer Patricia Frey and graphic designer Jackie Capozzoli. Last, but not least, we would like to thank Ilyce Glink for her time, knowledge, patience, and never-ending good humor throughout this project.

INDEX